STATUS OF STATE CENTRAL LIBRARIES IN INDIA

D1831714

STATUS OF STATE CENTRAL LIBRARIES IN INDIA

An Analytical Study

by

Dr. R. Ramasamy
M.A., M.L.I.S.B.; Ed. Ph.D.

Edited by
Dr. Krushna C. Panda
DLIS, Sambalpur University
Raja Rammohun Roy Library Foundation

GYAN

GYAN PUBLISHING HOUSE

Delhi–110 002

STATUS OF STATE CENTRAL LIBRARIES IN INDIA

(Library Science)

Rs. 790

© Dr. R. Ramasamy

ISBN: 81-212-0823-8

All rights reserved. No part of this book may be reproduced in any manner without written permission

Published in 2009 in India by
Gyan Publishing House
5, Ansari Road, Daryaganj
New Delhi–110 002
Phones: 23282060, 23261060; Fax-23285914

e-mail: gyanbook@vsnl.com
Vist our website at: http://www.gyanbooks.com

Lasertypesetting at: Varsha Graphics, Delhi
Printed at: G. Print Process, Delhi

Dedicated to

my wife

Mrs. R. Malarvizhi,

the dynamic woman behind

the success of all my endeavours

Contents

List of Tables

List of Charts and Maps

CHARTS

MAPS

List of Abbreviations/Acronyms

AACR	:	Anglo Americans Cataloguing Rules
ALA	:	American Library Association
CALIBNET	:	Calcutta Library Network
CAS	:	Current Awareness Service
CD-ROM	:	Compact Disk - Read Only Memory
CPU	:	Central Processing Unit
DDC	:	Dewey Decimal Classification
DELNET	:	Delhi Library Network
E-mail	:	Electronic Mail
GB	:	Gigabyte
IFLA	:	International Federation of Library Associations
ILL	:	Inter Library Loan
INFLIBNET	:	Library and Information Network
IT	:	Information Technology
Lt. Col.	:	Lieutenant Colonel
MB	:	Megabyte
MHz	:	Megahertz
MS-DOS	:	Microsoft Disk Operating System
MS-WORD	:	Microsoft Word
MALIBNET	:	Madras Library Network
NEFA	:	North East Frontier Agency
NICNET	:	National Informatic Centre Network
OCLC	:	Online Computer Library Centre
OCR	:	Optical Character Recognition
RRRLF	:	Raja Rammohun Roy Library Foundation
SCL	:	State Central Library

SCLs	:	State Central Libraries
SDI	:	Selective Dissemination of Information
Sq. Km	:	Square Kilometres
UGC	:	University Grants Commission
UK	:	United Kingdom
UNESCO	:	United Nations Educational Scientific and Cultural Organisation
USA	:	United States of America
UT	:	Union Territory
WAN	:	Wide Area Network
WWW	:	World Wide Web
WIN-95	:	Windows 95
WIN-98	:	Windows 98

Preface

Books are the records of man's experiences, thoughts, knowledge and wisdom and they speak to millions of fellow beings. Libraries are the temples of learning through books. History has recorded the existence of library at important places all over the world from times immemorial.

Renaissance beginning in Europe in 15th Century A.D. brought a new awakening; and science and scientific outlook emerged, with the result arts and literature also got impetus. It was soon realised that spread and dissemination of knowledge through libraries were the responsibilities of the State. Navigation and industrialisation vigorously aided the growth of science and technology.

The midfifties of this century witnessed the biggest and the most powerful revolution in the shape of information explosion; and ushered in electronics and computers. Almost a new industrial civilisation was born. Our country, India which gained independence in 1947 after a bitter experience of colonial oppression for over 150 years, has been called upon to take up the challenge of overcoming backwardness.

In this background, the present study - vast, wide and comprehensive in several aspects - covering almost all the State Central Libraries functioning in India has been undertaken and presented. In this study, Chapter - 1 aims at presenting the subject matter in proper perspective which necessarily involves an explanation of the methodology and aims at objective study. Chapter - 2 traces the evolution as well as the structure of State Central Libraries in different parts of the country and the role played by the Governments - both Central and State in shaping them. Chapter - 3 deals with the actual functioning and usefulness of the library : Collection, membership, accommodation, administration, finance and other related issues.

Chapter - 4 details the different types of services and assistances rendered by SCLs. Chapter - 5 deals with the problems faced by the State Central Libraries such as enlarging library activities, promotion of reading habits in the context of the library movements and related issues. Chapter - 6 attempts to bring to focus the future prospects of SCLs. And finally, Chapter -7 frames certain hypotheses based on the data and materials collected from almost all SCLs and offers suggestions for a progressive reorientation of the library policy in connection with State Central Libraries.

Computerisation is bound to revolutionise the entire library policy. Library movement and study of library science to accord with it have assumed greater dimensions in recent times. There is an ever growing urge to evolve a new outlook.

This study is, perhaps, the first to notice all the problems with an all India perspective. No doubt that it will encourage and stimulate further study in a vast field awaiting exploitation.

Dr. R. Ramasamy

Acknowledgements

First and foremost, I thank Dr. Krushna C. Panda, Senior Faculty, P.G. Department of Library and Information Science, Sambalpur University for his valuable guidance and during the entire period of my research Project. Right from the initial stage of evolving the concept of the project, leading to the drafting of the aims, scope, limitations, hypotheses, methodology and analysis of the questionnaires, he has played a major role in every aspect of my research. He has brought out the potentialities in me which I am not myself aware. I am ever grateful to him for critically editing the manuscript and guiding me to bring out this report.

I thank Dr. R. Bhattacharjee, Director and Shri K.K. Banerjee, Executive Officer, Raja Rammohun Roy Library Foundation, Kolkata for the kind permission accorded to me in undertaking research project inspite of my pressing official duties. I am specially grateful to Dr. V.K. Thomas, Research Officer, Raja Rammohun Roy Library Foundation, Kolkata for introducing my guide Dr. K.C. Panda to me and for his valuable assistance and suggestions offered to me during the research project.

Thiru N. Avudaiappan, Sr. Lecturer, Directorate of Public Libraries, Tamil Nadu States and formerly Librarian, Connemara Public Library, Chennai has extended his voluntary support to make the study a success. My thanks are due to him. I am also thankful to Dr. T. Anbupalam and Thiru. Ramanujam Ravanan, Lecturers, Department of Statistics, Presidency College, Chennai for their help in statistical computing and analysis of the data for the last chapter of the study.

My daughter Selvi. R. Lavanya, studying B.E. (Computer Science) has typed and entered the initial chapters of the report excellently in my computer. I am therefore grateful to my daughter R. Lavanya for her sincerity and hardwork at this young age. My second daughter Selvi. R. Saranya and my dear wife Mrs. R. Malarvizhi have always been providing constant moral support and understanding in all my efforts. I am indeed grateful to the members of my family for the help and co-operation extended to me during the entire period of this research project.

Publication of a research report is not an easy task. With the introduction of my colleague Shri M.V. Gaikwad of Mumbai Zone. I am indeed grateful to him for reading accepting to Publish the report in book form.

Last, but the most important of all, I am immensely thankful to the following Chief Librarians and Library Authorities of State Central Libraries of various States and Union Territories of India for furnishing the basic data for the Questionnaire on the status of their respective State Central Libraries. Without their co-operation and kind help, this project could not have been possible :

1. **Shri R. Goswami,** Librarian-in-Charge, State Library, Port Blair, Andaman and Nicobar Islands U.T. - 744 101.
2. **Shri Mohd. Naimuddin,** Chief Liberian-in-Charge, State Central Libary, Afzalgunj, Hyderabad, Andhra Pradesh - 500 012.
3. **Shri T. Ratan,** Chief Libarian, State Central Library, Itanagar, Arunachal Pradesh - 791 111.
4. **Mrs. R. Das,** Reference Librarian, State Central Library, Guwahati, Assam - 781 001.
5. **Dr. R.S.P. Singh,** Librarian, Sachidananda Sinha Library, Patna, Bihar - 800 001.
6. **Mrs. Ramola,** State Librarian, T.S. Central State Library, Sector - 17, Chandigarh - 160 017.
7. **Dr.Banwari Lal,** Director, Delhi Public Library, Delhi - 110 006.
8. **Ms. Rodrigues,** Librarian, Central Library, Panaji, Goa - 403 001.
9. **Shri Bakulesh C. Bhuta,** Librarian, State Central Library, Sector - 17, Gandhinagar, Gujarat State - 382 017.
10. **Shri Bhagwat Singh,** State Librarian, State Central Library, Ambala Cantonment, Haryana - 133 001.
11. **Shri Sudesh Kumar Sood,** Chief Librarian, Moti Lal Nehru Central State Library, Solan, Himachal Pradesh - 173 212.
12. **Shri T. Malleshappa,** Director, Dept. of Public Libraries and **Shri S.S. Naga Shetty,** Chief Librarian, State Central Library, Cubbon Park, Bangalore, Karnataka - 560 001.
13. **Mrs. Saramma George,** State Librarian, State Central Library, Trivandrum - 695 033.

14. **Shri P. Attakoya,** Library Development Officer, Central Library, Kavaratti Island, Lakshadweep - 682 555.
15. **Shri A. Nelson,** Librarian, Maulana Azad Central Library, Bhopal, Madhya Pradesh - 462 001.
16. **Shri M.B. Meshram,** Librarian, State Central Library, Townhall, Mumbai, Maharashtra - 400 023.
17. **Shri H. Devendra Singh,** Chief Librarian, State Central Library, Imphal, Manipur - 795 001.
18. **Shri A. Tariang,** Librarian, State Central Library, Shillong, Meghalaya -793 001.
19. **Mrs. Carol. Vlms. Dawngkimi**, State Librarian, State Library, Aizwal, Mizoram - 796 001.
20. **Shri Kevinino P. Meru,** Director, State Library, Kohima, Nagaland - 797 001.
21. **Shri A.K. Tripathy I.A.S.,** Director - Culture and Tourism, Harekrushna Mahtab State Library, Bhubaneswar, Orissa - 751 001.
22. **Shri B. Appalasamy,** Librarian -in - Charge, Romain Rolland Library, Pondicherry - 605 001.
23. **Shri Raghbir Singh,** Chief Librarian, Musafir Memorial Central State Library, Patiala, Punjab - 147 001.
24. State Librarian-in-Charge, Dr.Radhakrishnan State Central Library, Jaipur, Rajathan - 302 015.
25. **Thiru N. Avudaiappan,** Librarian, Connemara (State Central) Public Library, Chennai, Tamil Nadu State - 600 008.
26. **Shri Kamal Yadav,** Librarian, Central State Library, Allahabad, Uttar Pradesh - 211 001.
27. Librarian-in-Charge, State Central Library, Kolkata, West Bengal - 700 054.

Dr. R. Ramasamy

1

Introduction

Introduction

One of the most precious and prestigious possessions of a country is its libraries. The libraries nourish and sustain a society and its culture. Libraries are not only the store-houses of knowledge but they also determine the values and standards of life that the people of a country pursue and achieve. It is one of the noblest duties of a welfare State to provide its citizens free access to these store-houses of knowledge.

The present civilization is an epitome of knowledge and memories accumulated by generations of both the past and the present. Especially in the last decade, man's knowledge has been revolutionalised to a great extent. The information needs of the users are becoming more and more diverse and complex day by day requiring an access to the widest possible range of literature on multifarious subject fields. Under these circumstances, the public libraries in particular of which the State Central Libraries form an integral part, play the role of an acquirer, processor, preserver and disseminator of knowledge.

There is hardly any escape for mankind from the rapidly changing trends and increasing impact of these public libraries on their social, cultural, intellectual, recreational, scientific and technological advancements. Most of the public libraries hardly fulfill even the basic aspirations and requisites of their users owing to spiralling cost of publications coupled with severe curtailments of library grants by the State Governments.

Indian public libraries are generally grouped under two broad categories:

(i) Government Libraries; and

(ii) Non-government libraries.

The Government libraries, though may not be essentially established under the 'mandate of law', are mostly free libraries.

Non-government libraries, on the other hand, are run by various local bodies, voluntary organisations, trusts, charitable institutions, etc. Among them, a few are aided and some are unaided. These libraries normally charge a marginal fee from their members.

Any discussion on State Central Libraries which form an integral part of their respective State public libraries, cannot detach State public libraries from its scope.

Among the myriad types of libraries functioning in a nation, it is the public library that usually serves the educational, informational and recreational needs of its citizens on a wide range of subject areas. The public library, in this context, becomes a recourse of help to fulfill the above needs of its citizens only when a citizen seeks to know and understand something of his own interest by stepping into a local public library available in the near vicinity. The public library is, therefore, an organ of social democracy and an instrument of the personal self-realisation.

The public library can be considered as a university of the people offering a liberal education to all its clientele. J.H. Shera (1970; p.60), in his book *Sociological Foundation of Librarianship*, therefore, rightly prefers to think of the library as a social agency rather than as an institution. Since the concept of a State Central Library is blended with the concept of public library of the concerned State, the image of a public library can be seen from the succeeding paragraphs.

The Public Library

The concept of 'public library' is undergoing radical changes in modern days. It is no longer considered as a mere repository or store-house of books but is expected to perform the functions of an information centre for all categories of people. The focus of a modern public library, therefore, remains on dissemination of information to the common man.

The public library is a democratic institution which has to serve the entire community without any distinction of colour, caste, creed, status, sex, age, educational qualification or any such considerations. The modern public library of to-day is of the people, by the people and for the people. However, the phrase 'Public Library' denotes, differently to different authors, which could be seen from the following definitions:

The Sinha Committee (India; 1959; p. 32) considered public

library as an auxiliary educational institution providing a means of self education. S.R. Ranganathan (1960; p. 27) has codified 'public library' as a library, owned and maintained by the public of its area for the socialisation of its books and kindred materials for free service to the people of the area.

The revised Unesco Public Library Manifesto (Unesco; 1995; p. 10) defines 'public library' as "a living force of education, culture and information and an essential agent for the fostering of peace and spiritual welfare through the minds of men and women; a local gateway of knowledge which provides a basic condition for lifelong learning, independent decision making and cultural development service social groups".

Encyclopaedia of Library and Information Science (Kent and Lancour; 1987; p. 636) states that, "Public library is a public institution, supported by taxation, one that opens its collections, facilities and services without distinction to all citizens". *Librarian's Glossary* (Harrod; 1987; p. 26) describes public library as "a library provided wholly or partly from public funds, and the use of which is not restricted to any class of persons in the community but is freely available to all".

Thomas (1997; p. 3) defines public library as the "one which is authorised by legislation, open to the public without charge and financed out of public fund".

Thus, the true concept and character of a public library can be summed up in the words of William Ewart (Mukherjee and Sengupta; 1972; p. 46-47) who considered public library as that library which is *funded* by the people; *supported* by the people; and *enjoyed* by the people; and is *established* by law and maintained at *public expense* out of local rates and sometimes by state taxes. Hence, a library is a service institution.

Types of Public Libraries

The public libraries can be classified according to their targeted users, their level of operations and types of services offered to the public. The Unesco Public Library Manifesto (Unesco; 1995 p. 10) states that, the public library network must be designed in relation to national, regional, research and special libraries as well as libraries in schools, colleges and universities.

The two distinct groups of public libraries can be seen as follows:

CHART 1.1
Categories of Public Libraries

Public Libraries

Government
↓
National Library
↓
State Central Library
↓
Regional/Divisional Library
↓
District Central Library
↓
Taluk Library
↓
Branch Library
↓
Village/Town Library
↓
Delivery Station/
Book Deposit Centre

Non-Government
↓
Run by Local Bodies
↓
Registered Societies
↓
Social Organisations/Clubs/
Associations
↓
Rental/Circulating
Library
↓
Run by Philanthropists/
Individuals

The public libraries, however, can be geographically divided as follows:

(i) National Library;
(ii) State Central Library;
(iii) Regional/Divisional Library;
(iv) District Central Library;
(v) Taluk Library;
(vi) Branch Library;
(vii) Village/Town Library;
(viii) Delivery Station/Book Deposit Centre;

National Library is the apex public library of a nation. "The national library (of India) serves as the permanent repository of all reading materials and information produced in India, as well as printed materials written by Indians and concerning India written by foreigners wherever published and in whichever language. It receives all published materials in India under Delivery of Books (Newspapers) Act, 1954 as amended in 1956" (Dasgupta; 1998: p.166).

State Central Library (SCL) is the apex library of a State located in the capital of the concerned State. It has to play the role of a leader among the public libraries of the State. It should strive to establish standard procedures and guidelines for the effective functioning of all public libraries in the State. The State Central Library has to be the co-ordinating authority for the public libraries of the State. A State Central Library is a replica of a national library. It performs the same functions and provides the same services for a State as a National Library does for the nation, except being different in its geographical character.

In Model Public Libraries Act, S.R.Ranganathan (1972; p. 57) outlines that, a State Central Library System should consist of:

(a) State Service Library;
(b) State Branch Service Library;
(c) State Copyright Library;
(d) State Library for the Blind;
(e) State Bureau of Inter Library Loan;
(f) State Bibliographic Bureau; and
(g) State Bureau of Technical Services.

D.R. Kalia (1998; p. 27) lists out some of the functions of the State Central Libraries. They are required to perform the following six basic functions:

"(i) Establish linkages with all the libraries forming part of the State Public Library System;
(ii) Share their resources with them, through computerised network;
(iii) Compile State Bibliography of books and journals published out of the State in any languages;
(iv) Provide bibliographic and documentation services in the form of articles on the State and of State official documents;
(v) Act as an exchange centre for the State; and
(vi) Be a depository of less used materials deposited with them by other libraries in the State on trust".

P. Padhi and K.C. Panda (1988; p. 13) have enumerated the following eleven functions for the State Central Library as a part of the State Library System:

"(i) It is a repository of the publication in and about the State both for serials and monographs;

(ii) It brings out a State Bibliography of all such publications in a classified order on the lines of the National Bibliography;

(iii) It provides common technical services, such as centralised selection, acquisition of material, classification, cataloguing and makes available printed catalogue cards or computerized catalogue in book form so that the same publication is not catalogued individually by other libraries in the State. This cuts down the cost of cataloguing and the staff and, the time so saved is utilized in rendering reader's services;

(iv) It stocks less used materials, such as official documents, corporate publications of research and training institutions, conference documents, back files of journals and newspapers and makes them available to other libraries as a part of resource sharing scheme through supply of xerox copies;

(v) It lends support to research programmes undertaken by educational and research institutions so that duplication of material is avoided and isolated functioning of different libraries is put to an end. The resource and services of all libraries in the State are put together and inter-linked through a well organised State Library System in the form of a grid which is cost effective;

(vi) It tries to meet the demand for library and information services in its totality and identifies various interest groups by subject in order to meet specialized need of each group. It organizes a variety of collections in a departmentalized manner, such as: (1) Reference; (2) State; (3) Official documents; (4) Conference documents; (5) Publications of corporate research and training institutions; (6) National collection and international collection for comparative study; (7) Depository; and (8) Subject collections, such as humanities (language and literature), social sciences, science and technology and applied sciences, including medicine, engineering, industrial production and management, fine arts and braille collections;

(vii) It provides technical advice to the government and different library authorities, formulates norms and standards on resources and services of all categories of libraries;

(viii) It builds up an expertise among its staff and makes their services available to other libraries and agencies;

(ix) It provides leadership in professional matters by organizing seminars, workshops and refresher courses for working librarians;

(x) It introduces information technology in the libraries through computerized operations and offers training facilities for their adoption and popularization; and

(xi) It maintains a Research and Development (R & D) Unit for regular conduct of research in technical matters and makes its findings available through a regular programme of publications".

Regional/Divisional Libraries are established to cater to the reading needs of a particular region/revenue division of a State, roughly comprising of an area of three to seven Districts. A regional/divisional Library in some States function as the 'Library of Libraries' by lending books only to the Libraries/Institutions located in the respective region. A few Regional/Divisional Libraries serve as Reference Libraries without providing lending services.

District Central Library is the apex library of the District, usually located in the District capital. Books and other reading materials are purchased, technically processed and distributed to all public libraries in District by the District Central Library Authority. The administration, inspection and monitoring of various public libraries located in the District are carried out by the District Central Library Authority. The District Central Library is the central hub of all the libraries located in the District. In some States where Public Library Acts are in force, Local Library Authorities are constituted to administer the Public Library System in the District.

Similarly, while a **Taluk Library,** situated in a Taluk

headquarter, serves the users living in any part of the Taluk, a **Branch Library** is established in villages/towns which are exceeding a specified population limit, say 5000. In a particular Taluk, there may be many Branch Libraries. A Branch Library caters to the reading needs of several other villages situated around the place in which the library is located.

Village/Town Library is being run for the benefit of the people living in a particular village/town.

The Delivery Station/Book Deposit Centre is an extension library of the nearby Public Library without any permanent stock of books. The libraries of the Delivery Station/Book Deposit Centre borrows a limited number of books (say 500) from the parent public library which are lent to the Members of Delivery Station/Book Deposit Centre. After utilisation by the Members, the borrowed books are returned to the parent public library and other set of books are borrowed for distribution to the Members of the respective Delivery Station. In this manner, the entire stock of the parent public library is made available to the borrowers of different Delivery Stations which are normally located in the interior villages/hamlets.

In the present study, however, I have taken up only one of the ten types of public libraries, namely, the State Central Library with an attempt to cover their status in greater details.

Statement of the Problem

Status of the State Central Libraries in India: An analytical study is a topic of great importance and interest not only to the scholars and professionals connected with public libraries, but also to the policy makers, planners, State Library Authorities and the Central Government. This study is primarily concerned with the apex public library system of different States and Union Territories of India.

Scope and Limitation of the Study

The scope of the present study primarily confines to the State Central Libraries of 24 States and 6 Union Territories of India. However, the present study has set forth the following limitations keeping in view its timely completion and access to information:

The present study aims to identify the status of State Central Libraries of 24 States and 6 Union Territories of India as per the responses received, (i.e., limitation by geography/territory being studied);

This study includes in its ambit only the State Central Libraries as the apex Public Library System of the respective States and Union Territories but does not include in its scope the National Library, Regional Libraries, Divisional Libraries, District Central Libraries, Taluk Libraries, Branch Libraries, Town/Villages Libraries, Delivery Stations/ Book Deposit Centres etc., (i.e., limitation by the category/type of Public Library System being studied);

The present study considers the status aspects of these apex libraries primarily in terms of their collection development, manpower, finance, governance, space and physical facilities, automation, membership pattern, technical scenario and the language imbalance, if any. However, other aspects concerning the status and functioning of these apex libraries are given least attention owing to its vast geographical coverage and limited time frame (i.e., limitation by the type of status aspects being studied);

This study considers only those State Central Libraries which are functioning only in the capital cities of the respective States and Union Territories (as per the response received) and have been recognised by the Authorities of Law for the purpose of receiving grants and other governmental assistances (i.e, limitation by the type of State Central Libraries being studied);

As such in case of States and Union Territories having more than one State Central Libraries such as Gujarat (having 3 State Central Libraries), only the main State Central Library is taken into account. Similarly, the needs, opinions, and attitudes of the individual users and the staff of these State Central Libraries remained out of scope of the present study.

Aims and Objectives

One of the important objectives of the present study, among other things, is to analyse and evaluate the on-going status and functioning of the State Central Libraries of States and Union Territories in India. This study, however, is admirably designed to meet the following objectives:

To ascertain the genesis and growth of the State Central Library System in India;

To find out the role played by the various agencies such as

State Government, Central Government, Raja Rammohun Roy Library Foundation (RRRLF) and other Voluntary Organisations in promotion and development of the State Central Libraries in India;

To find out the present status of State Central Libraries in terms of their collection development, manpower, language divisions, finance, governance, space and physical facilities, automation, membership composition pattern and such other relevant factors which jointly contribute for the overall growth of the apex library system in the States;

To examine the current pattern of governance through which the State Central Libraries are passing through;

To evaluate the various activities and services provided by these apex libraries along with their deficiencies, if any;

To identify the various problems and constraints encountered by these State Central Libraries which ultimately lands a threat to their real growth;

To anticipate the possible hopes and prospects which such apex library bodies would bring to the society under a supportive and compatible environment; and

To suggest appropriate measures or solutions to any or all of these problems faced by the State Central Libraries.

Hypothesis

A hypothesis as a provisional central idea becomes the basis for fruitful investigation in social research of any magnitude. A researcher, therefore, must choose from the complexity of observed events those significant and relevant facts which will most adequately explain the problem under study in order to show the essential relationships which exist between the various elements within the complexity.

In this search for the significant facts he may fall back on previous experience, his own or that of others, and single out those factors that are known to have explained similar situations in the past (Young; 1994; p. 103). On the basis of both observations and experience, the researcher has to build certain assumptions as to the relations of facts. For the purpose of the present study, I have therefore, initially formulated the following hypotheses so as to prevent the possibilities of blind search:

The State Central Libraries being the apex of the Public

Library Systems of the respective States are in a state of sombre owing to the poor allocation of the funds by their authorities;

The State Central Libraries, owing to their undiscriminating and open membership policy, are having a wide range of cross-sectional user population at their credit than any other library system has;

Owing to the repository character of the State Central Libraries under the provisions of the Press and Registration of Books Act 1867, there is an imbalance in their collection development between the books in the respective regional languages and the books of other languages;

The State Central Libraries being the leaders of the Public Library System are having a human force of reasonable size to take care of their technical processing of the acquired documents in order to ensure the scientific and helpful organisation of the documents on the shelves for their effective use;

The State Central Libraries being the non-profit organisations hardly receive any attention of the State authorities in the matter of automation/computerisation of their information retrieval related activities as well as house-keeping operations and, due to their low budget profile, the State Central Libraries seem to be at the threshold of the beginning of automation so as to keep pace with the national trend;

The State Central Libraries are enjoying a better space structure in terms of their building and other physical facilities compared to any other Public Library System; and

Owing to their vast resources and sound infrastructure, the State Central Libraries are rendering almost all modern services to their clientele ranging from layman to intellect and from simple homelending to indexing and highly complex on-line services, but on a limited scale.

Methodology

In order to collect information on the status of State Central Libraries in India and to test the validity of the foregoing hypotheses, a Questionnaire designed for the purpose was mailed to the State Central Libraries of 24 States and 6 Union Territories included in the survey. Owing to the vastness of the geographical area covered in the study, I have met personally the following ten respondents of the State Central Libraries on the dates mentioned below to have a better understanding of the system through interaction in order to discover the place they stand:

TABLE 1.1
Researcher - Respondent Interaction

Sl. No.	*Name of the Library*	*State/Union Territory*	*Place*	*Date of Visit*
1.	State Central Library	Maharashtra	Mumbai	15.12.97
2.	State Central Library	Pondicherry	Pondicherry	10.02.98
3.	State Central Library	Kerala	Thiruvananthapuram	11.03.98
4.	State Central Library	Assam	Guwahati	22.04.98
5.	State Central Library	Meghalaya	Shillong	25.04.98
6.	State Central Library	West Bengal	Calcutta	27.04.98
7.	State Central Library	Tamil Nadu	Chennai	03.05.98
8.	Delhi Public Library	Delhi	Delhi	23.05.98
9.	State Central Library	Karnataka	Bangalore	22.07.98
10.	State Central Library	Andhra Pradesh	Hyderabad	17.08.98

Thus, I have administered the structured Questionnaire followed with an interview as and when the opportunity came. The filled-in Questionnaires, however, were collected by prolonged correspondence from the remaining State Central Libraries.

Literature Reviewed

Review of literature is an essential requirement for any field of research as it is necessary for a scholar to know well in advance the quantum of literature unfolded on a particular subject in length and breadth. This helps the scholar to be aware of the ground already covered, so that he may proceed further in the right direction. Though a few studies on State Central Libraries in India have been undertaken, most of these studies seem to have been done only on a particular State Central Library. Some of such studies that deserve mention are as under:

Seethapathy (1978) has surveyed the extent of changes occurred in the environment of Connemara (State Central) Public Library for two and half decades and assessed the extent to which the library has responded to the changes occurred in its environment.

Govinda Krishnan (1980) observes by analysis that, the

Connemara (State Central) Public Library has more regular users compared to District Central Library, Madras.

Apprising the origin and development of Harekrushna Mahtab State Central Library of Orissa, P. Padhi and K.C. Panda (1988; p. 24) have informed that "the incidence of use of the library is unprecedented in the annals of public library development since perhaps no other library in the country can claim to have attracted 4 to 5 hundred readers per day within a few days of its opening".

Inamdar (1990; p.40-54) formulates certain guidelines for selection and acquisition of materials for State Central Libraries with special reference to the State Central Library of Andhra Pradesh. He believes that, by following these guidelines in its future work, the State Central Library would be able to provide a leadership to all libraries in the system and can satisfactorily meet all obligations imposed by the Andhra Pradesh Public Libraries Act, 1960.

Kalia et.al., (1991; p. 41) have expressed that, the State Central Library is supposed to provide leadership in the development of Public Library System in the State besides being a coordinating and common service centre. They have also recommended that, the State Central Libraries may be renamed as State Reference Libraries.

Ghosh (1991; p. 361) is of the opinion that "the State Central Library collection is very important and valuable property which can't be separated from our heritage. It must be preserved for future".

The scholar, therefore, recommends that each State Central Library must have a separate Conservation Division to take care of all preservative and conservative activities of the Public Library System (PLS) of the State.

Avudaiappan (1991; p. 108-21) has analysed the possible areas of cooperation between the State Central Library and District Central Libraries and also between the State Central Libraries and National Depository Libraries. The said study has asserted that, the State Central Libraries can play a major role between District Central Libraries and National Depositary Libraries through resource sharing and also by library co-operation.

By making a detailed analysis of the various systems of public libraries at the State level, Rath (1991) has observed that, the State Central Library should be an apex library and act as research and reference library of the respective State.

Basker (1993) in his comparative study on the use of English fiction in the Connemara (State Central) Public Library and the British Council Library has asserted that, the use of English fiction both in the Connemara (State Central) Public Library and in the British Council Library, Madras are more or less identical.

Ramola and Arora (1994; p. 420-5) in their study, have outlined the measures taken by the Central State Library at the Union Territory of Chandigarh to computerise some of the functions of the State Central Library so as to make the library a *'Reader-friendly library'*.

A.K. Ohdedar (1996; p. 331) has made a critical analysis of the establishment and functioning of the State Central Library of West Bengal at Kolkata and laments that "Obviously, from the very start, the State Central Library has deviated from its intended function and carried on only as reference library without any connection with the State Library System".

While presenting the status report of the State Central Library, Haryana, Janakraj (1996; p. 286-95) hopes that, the State Central Library would start moving in the right direction after the formation of the Directorate of Public Libraries in Haryana.

After analysing the various functions of the State Central Library of Hyderabad, Mohamed Taher (1996; p. 36-49) recommends that, the State Central Library of Hyderabad should be immediately changed as State Central Reference Library and the entire system of the library such as, staff, resources, attitudes, motivation and finance-should be overhauled.

Pia de Menezes Rodriques (1996; p. 271-85) sums up the activities of the State Central Library, Goa while informing that the status of the library was raised to that of a National Library during the year 1897 under the Portuguese rule.

M.A.C. Esperanza (1996) reviews the functions of the State Central Library, Patna and laments that, the amount alloted to the library was inadequate and sufficient staff members are not available to render efficient services so as to satisfy the growing needs of the modern readers of the library.

S.N. Khanna (1996; p. 236-49) in his study summarises the past and present of the Delhi Public Library and argues that since no public library in India has as many multifarious activities as Delhi Public Library has in its ambit which certainly entitles Delhi

Public Library to be the National Public Library of India.

S.R. Ijari and H.A. Khan (1996; 293-301) have informed that though the State Central Library of Karnataka State at Bangalore was providing lending facilities in the beginning as per the provisions of the Karnataka Public Library Act, 1965, the State Central Library was designated as State Central Reference Library by the State Government in 1986 and the lending facilities were discontinued.

Sounderrajan (1996; p. 302-6) lists out the various activities of Romain Rolland Library, the State Central Library of the Union Territory of Pondicherry and informs that the library established in the year 1827, was named after the great French scholar Romain Rolland who was a close friend of Mahatma Gandhi, when his birth centenary was celebrated in the year 1966.

Velaga Venkatappaiah (1996; p. 326) traces the history and olution of the Connemara (State Central) Public Library of Tamil du and concludes that "this library is supposed to be the best rary in South India in having high quality reading materials d in serving the public for over one hundred years".

Analysis of all these literature reviewed above shows that, ost of these studies concentrate on a particular area of interest their respective State Central Libraries such as environment, ollection, leadership, co-operation, and the use of materials by heir users in a very limited way. Thus, none of these studies seem to be comprehensive in their approach to the myriad status of their respective State Central Libraries.

Study Sample

The ever-recurring question that often crops up in the mind of a researcher. How many cases does he need? Some proposed *"at least one hundred"*. But, if they weigh their desire against available time and energy, they would certainly use to revise the number downward to 15 to 20 or at the most 25. These are some of the practical limitations which cannot be overlooked (Young; 1994; p. 16).

Well known Statistician Margaret Hagood (Young; 1994; p. 16-7), however, rightly describes this situation as a *'risky assumption'*. She, therefore, suggests three basic criterions as a guide in the choice of a sample.

They include:

the sample must represent the universe (i.e., it must be unbiased);

it must be of adequate size to produce reliable results (i.e., as measured in terms of specific range of error); and

the sample must be efficient (i.e., in comparison with alternate designs).

The study was undertaken prior to the year 2000. Hence, the newly formly States of Chhattisgarh, Uttaranchal and Jharkhand have not been covered in this research project. However, the data on the new states from part and parcel of their respective parent State. In India, there are 25 States and 7 Union Territories. However, D.R. Kalia informs that "all States except Sikkim have State Central Libraries. Out of 7 Union Territories, all have State (Central) Libraries except Daman and Diu" (Kalia; 1998; p. 32).

Hence, for the present study, a total of 30 units of State Central Libraries (functioning in 24 States and 6 Union Territories) required investigation. The list of 30 SCLs taken up for the study is furnished in Table 1.2 mentioning the proper names of the SCLs, their location, address and the State/Union Terriotory in which they are located.

Instead of taking a sample survey of minimum units as required in statistical and research methods, I have preferred to study all the units for investigation thereby making a 100 per cent survey of the project being undertaken in order to produce reliable results.

However, owing to the vast geographical area and in spite of the honest efforts, persistent and prolonged correspondences as well as vigorous persuasion undertaken by the Investigator to achieve a 100 per cent survey, only 27 out of 30 units have responded with their filled-in Questionnaires, thus achieving the sample response of 90 per cent which is quite encouraging and reliable.

TABLE 1.2
List of State Central Libraries

Sl. No.	*Name of SCL*	*Place*	*State/U.T.*	*Address*
1.	State Library	Port Blair	Andaman & Nicobar Islands	744 101
2.	State Central Libary	Hyderabad	Andhra Pradesh	500 012
3.	State Central Library	Itanagar	Arunachal Pradesh	791 111
4.	State Central Library	Guwahati	Assam	781 001
5.	Sachidanada Sinha Library	Patna	Bihar	800 001
6.	T.S. Central State Library	Chandigarh	Chandigarh	160 017
7.	Central Library	Silvasa	Dadra and Nagar Haveli	—
8.	Delhi Public Library	Delhi	Delhi	110 006
9.	Central Library	Panaji	Goa	403 001
10.	State Central Library	Gandhinagar	Gujarat	382 017
11.	State Central Library	Ambala Cantonment	Haryana	133 001
12.	Moti Lal Nehru Central State Library	Solan	Himachal Pradesh	173 212
13.	SPS Central Public Library	Srinagar	Jammu and Kashmir	190 001
14.	State Central Library	Bangalore	Karnataka	560 001
15.	State Central Library	Trivandrum	Kerala	695 033
16.	Central Library	Kavaratti	Lakshadweep	682 555
17.	Maulana Azad Central Library	Bhopal	Madhya Pradesh	462 001
18.	State Central Library	Mumbai	Maharashtra	400 023
19.	State Central Library	Imphal	Manipur	795 001
20.	State Central Library	Shillong	Meghalaya	793 001
21.	State Library	Aizwal	Mizoram	796 001
22.	State Library	Kohima	Nagaland	797 001
23.	Harekrushna Mahtab State Library	Bhubaneswar	Orissa	751 001
24.	Romain Rolland Library	Pondicherry	Pondicherry	605 001
25.	Musafir Memorial Central State Library	Patiala	Punjab	147 001
26.	Dr. Radhakrishnan State Central Library	Jaipur	Rajasthan	302 015
27.	Connemara (State Central) Public Library	Chennai	Tamil Nadu	600 008
28.	Birchandra State Central Library	Agartala	Tripura	799 120
29.	Central State Library	Allahabad	Uttar Pradesh	211 001
30.	State Central Library	Calcutta	West Bengal	700 054

Significance of the Study

The State Central Library provides leadership to the entire Public Library System of the State. The State Central Library is on the top of the pyramidal structure of the public libraries functioning in a State like the National Library of a country that serves the entire nation. The only difference between these two categories of libraries, however, is the geographical domain being covered by them. Thus, the State Central Library performs the same functions and provides the same services for a particular State while a National Library is performing for the whole country.

Recognising the significance of the State Central Library, the National Policy on Library and Information System (1990), emphasises that:

"the role of State Central Library is crucial in networking and the establishment of uniform library procedures within the State. The State Central Library ... has to perform as the co-ordinating agency for Public Libraries in the State" (India; 1990; p. 62).

Ranganathan (1962; p. 40) has spelt out clearly the functions of State Central Library as:

"(a) a reservior of information and knowledge for the entire State;

(b) a centre to prepare and implement the District and State Library Plans; and

(c) generally to do all that is necessary to function as the main contact house within the entire National Library network at the State level".

The significance of the present study, therefore, can hardly be ignored in the light of the crucial role a State Central Library plays in terms of its leadership quality, being a centre for preserving the cultural posterity, a true disseminator of knowledge and an effective clearing centre for public request on their educational, social, cultural, informational, and recreational needs on a wide spectrum of subject interests.

Originality of the Study

Several studies have been conducted on each State Central Library in isolation. These studies are mostly done by the librarians who are serving in different State Central Libraries.

The Library and Information Science researcher hardly comes across any such comprehensive study comparing the status and activities of State Central Libraries functioning in different States and Union Territories of the country.

A literature survey published in CLIS Observer (Vol. 5. No. 3-4; 1988) as *"Public Library Development in India : A Bibliography"* compiled by P.K. Rath lists 91 studies done at various universities in India at Ph.D and M.L.I.Sc. Level (Rath; 1988; p. 25-30).

From among these 91 studies, I could find only 7 studies pertaining to the individual State Central Libraries in India but none comparing the status of State Central Libraries of various States and Union Territories. Therefore, a comprehensive study on the status of different State Central Libraries in India, covering the myriad aspects has become imminent.

Scheme of the Work

The whole area of the present study, for the sake of convenience, has been grouped under seven major chapters.

Chapter -1 of the present study is introductory that primarily throws light on introduction proper, statement of the problem, scope, limitations, aims and objectives of the study, hypotheses and methodology adopted, literature reviewed, study sample, significance and originality of the work, scheme of the work and the physiography of different States/Union Territories being studied so as to provide background information on the subject.

Chapter - 2 of this study depicts the genesis of public libraries in India, growth of State Central Libraries in India, role of State Central Libraries in promoting literacy, inculcating reading habits and in preserving the State's cultural heritage along with the role of various agencies such as State Governments, Raja Rammohun Roy Library Foundation (RRRLF) and Voluntary Organisations in promotion of State Central Libraries in India and the organisational structure of these State Central Libraries.

Chapter - 3 provides an insight into the existing status of State Central Libraries in India in terms of their collection development, manpower, finance, governance, space and physical facilities, areas of automation, membership composition pattern and its domination, degree of their dependability upon the district and other branch libraries, repository function, technical status, various language divisions, impact of library legislation on the life styles of State Central Libraries and their future trends.

Chapter - 4 deals with the various activities of/and services provided in the State Central Libraries in India such as lending documents for home reading, Current Awareness Services, Selective Dissemination of Information Service, Bibliographic Service, Reference Service, Referral Service, Inter Library Loan, Online Searching through Computerised Networks, Indexing Service, Abstracting Service and different extension activities.

Chapter - 5 analyses various problems such as social, economic, environmental, technical, manpower and financial problems encountered by the State Central Libraries, included in the survey.

Chapter - 6 on the other hand, enumerates the different prospects of State Central Libraries including the increased productivity, extension of library services and activities, participation in networking, promotion of reading habits and restoring the social order and peace.

Chapter - 7 analyses and interprets the data collected including testing the hypotheses and explains the various constraints encountered. This chapter being the last, offers suggestions for improving the State Central Library System and reflects a concluding view of the whole gamut of the study. Areas for further study have also been enumerated at the end to guide future researchers.

A Brief Physiography of the States and Union Territories of India

To have an idea about the vastness of various States and Union Territories included in this study, a brief physiographical note on each of the State and Union Territory is furnished below in their alphabetical order as it would help to check irrational attempts to undermine the services of a particular State Central Library compared to another, without verifying and comparing their vast geographical, infrastructural, social, economical and demographical conditions.

Further, though the physiographical conditions of different States and Union Territories have a little bearing on the size, quality and resources of their respective State Central Libraries, a consolidated table showing these conditions would help easing a comparative analysis of the status of the State Central Libraries without undermining their differences in library services, as reflected in Table 1.3.

TABLE 1.3
Physiography of States and Union Territories of India

Name of State/ UT	Date of Formation of the Territory	Date on which Statehood is Accorded	Population	Area (sq. kms.)	State Capital	Literacy Rate	Spoken Languages	Boundary
(1)	(2)	(3)	(4)	(5)	(6)	(7)	(8)	(9)
Andhra Pradesh	01.11.1956	—	6,65,08,008	2,75,068	Hyderabad	45.11%	Telugu & Urdu	N—Orissa and M.P. S—Tamil Nadu E—Bay of Bengal W—Maharashtra and Karnataka
Arunachal Pradesh	—	20.02.1987	8,64,558	83,743	Itanagar	41.22%	17 Tribal Languages	N—China S—Assam E—Myanmar W—Bhutan
Assam	—	—	2,22,94,562	78,438	Guwahati	53.42%	Assamese	N—Bhutan & A.P. S—Meghalaya and Mizoram E—Nagaland and Manipur W—Bangladesh, Tripura and W.B.
Bihar	—	—	8,63,74,465	1,73,877	Patna	38.54%	Hindi	N—Nepal S—Orissa E—West Bengal W—U.P. and M.P.

(Contd.)

(1)	(2)	(3)	(4)	(5)	(6)	(7)	(8)	(9)
Goa	19.12.1962	30.05.1987	11,69,793	3,702	Panaji	76.96%	Konkani and Marathi ,	N—Maharashtra S—Karnataka E—Karnataka W—Arabian Sea
Gujarat	—	01.05.1960	4,13,09,582	1,96,024	Gandhinagar	60.91%	Gujarati	N—Pakistan and Raj. S—M.P. and Mahara. E—M.P. W—Arabian Sea
Haryana	—	01.11.1966	1,64,63,648	44,212	Chandigarh	55.33%	Hindi	N—H.P. and Punjab S—Rajasthan E—Uttar Pradesh W—Punjab and Raj.
Himachal Pradesh	15.04.1948	25.01.1971	51,70,877	55,763	Shimla	63.54%	Hindi and Pahar	N—Jammu and Kash. S—U.P. and Haryana E—U.P. and Tibet W—Punjab and Hary.
Jammu and Kashmir	—	26.01.1957	77,18,700	2,22,236	Srinagar (Summer) Jammu (Winter)	26.17%	Kashmiri, Urdu, etc.	N—China S—H.P., Punjab and Pak. E—Tibet W—Pakistan
Karnataka	—	01.11.1956	4,48,17,397	1,91,791	Bangalore	55.98%	Kannada	N—Goa and Maha. S—Tamil Nadu and Kerala E—Andhra Pradesh W—Arabian Sea

(1)	(2)	(3)	(4)	(5)	(6)	(7)	(8)	(9)
Kerala	—	01.11.1956	2,90,98,518	38,863	**Thiruvanthapuram**	90.5%	**Malayalam**	N—Karnataka S—Tamil Nadu E—Tamil Nadu W—Arabian Sea
Madhya Pradesh	—	—	6,61,81,000	4,43,446	Bhopal	43.45%	Hindi	N—Rajasthan, U.P. and Bihar S—Andhra and Mahar. E—Bihar and Orissa W—Gujarat and Raj.
Maharashtra	—	01.05.1960	7,89,37,187	3,07,713	Mumbai	63.10%	Marathi	N—Guj. and M.P. S—Andhra, Goa & Karnataka E—M.P. and Andhra W—Arabian Sea
Manipur	1956	1972	18,37,149	22,237	Imphal	60.96%	Manipuri and English	N—Nagaland S—Mizoram E—Myanmar W—Assam
Meghalaya	—	21.01.1972	17,74,778	22,429	Shillong	48.26%	Khafi, Garo and English	N—Assam S—Bangladesh E—Assam W—Bangladesh
Mizoram	—	20.02.1987	6,89,756	21,081	Aizwal	82.27%	Mizo and English	N—Assam and Mani. S—Myanmar E—Myanmar W—Bangladesh and Tripura

(*Contd.*)

(1)	(2)	(3)	(4)	(5)	(6)	(7)	(8)	(9)
Nagaland	—	01.12.1963	12,09,546	16,579	Kohima	61.30%	English etc.	N—Arunachal & Assam S—Manipur E—Myanmar W—Assam
Orissa	—	19.08.1949	3,16,59,729	1,55,707	Bhubaneswar	48.65%	Oriya	N—Bihar & W.B. S—Andhra E—Bay of Bengal W—M.P.
Punjab	01.11.1960	—	2,02,81,969	50,362	Chandigarh	57.14%	Punjabi	N—J. & K. S—Hary. & Raj. E—H.P. W—Pakistan
Rajasthan	01.11.1956	—	4,40,05,990	3,42,239	Jaipur	38.81%	Hindi & Rajasthani	N—Punjab & Pak. S—M.P. & Gujarat E—U.P. & Haryana W—Gujarat & Pak.
Tamil Nadu	01.11.1952	—	5,58,58,946	1,30,058	Chennai	63.72%	Tamil	N—Andhra & Karn. S—Indian Ocean E—Bay of Bengal W—Assam
Tripura	—	21.01.1972	27,57,205	10,492	Agartala	60.39%	Bengali, Kakbark & Manipuri	N—Assam S—Bangladesh & Miz. E—Bay of Bengal W—Kerala & Karnat.

(Contd.)

(1)	(2)	(3)	(4)	(5)	(6)	(7)	(8)	(9)
Uttar Pradesh	—	—	13,91,12,287	2,94,411	Lucknow	41.71%	Hindi	N—Tibet & Nepal S—Rajasthan & M.P. E—Bihar W—Haryana & Raj.
West Bengal	—	—	6,79,82,732	88,572	Calcutta	57.70%	Bengali	N—Sikkim & Bhutan S—Bay of Bengal E—Assam & Bangla. W—Orissa, Bihar & Nepal
Andaman & Nicobar Islands	—	—	2,80,661	8,249	Port Blair	73.74%	Bengali, Hindi, Nicobarese etc.	N—Bay of Bengal S—Bay of Bengal E—Bay of Bengal W—Bay of Bengal
Chandigarh	1966	—	6,42,045	114	Chandigarh	78.73%	Punjabi & Hindi	N—Punjab S—Haryana E—Punjab & Hary. W—Haryana
Dadra and Nagar Haveli	11.08.1961	—	1,38,477	491	Silvasa	39.49%	Bhilli, Bhilad, Gujarati & Urdu	N—Gujarat S—Maharashtra E—Gujarat W—Arabian Sea

(Contd.)

(1)	(2)	(3)	(4)	(5)	(6)	(7)	(8)	(9)
Delhi	1959	—	93,70,475	1,483	Delhi	76.09%	Hindi, Punjabi & Urdu	N—Haryana S—Haryana E—U.P. W—Haryana
Lakshdaweep	1956	—	51,707	32	Kavaratti	79.23%	Malayalam	N—Arabian Sea S—Arabian Sea E—Arabian Sea W—Arabian Sea
Pondicherry	—	—	8,07,785	492	Pondicherry	74.91%	Tamil, Malayalam, Telugu & French	N—Tamil Nadu S—Tamil Nadu E—Bay of Bengal W—Tamil Nadu

N = North; S = South; E = East, and W = West.

The States

Andhra Pradesh

Andhra Pradesh State, earlier known as 'Andhra Desa', attained its present statehood on 1st November 1956, on being separated from the composite Madras State based on linguistic division during 1953 and by the merger of Hyderabad State due to the passing of the States Reorganisation Act, 1956. The State is having a population of 7, 57, 27, 541 and an area of 2,75,068 sq. km. Having Hyderabad as its capital, the State is bounded on north by Orissa and Madhya Pradesh, on west by Maharashtra and Karnataka, on south by Tamil Nadu and east by the Bay of Bengal. The literacy rate is 61.11 per cent and the climate is normally hot and humid (India; 2002; p. 681).

Arunachal Pradesh

The State of Arunachal Pradesh has become a full-fledged State only on 20 February 1987. It was known as North East Frontier Agency (NEFA) since 1948 before it became Union Territory during 1972 and a separate State in 1987. With an area of 83,743 sq. km., the State has a population of 10,91,117 and a literacy rate of 54.74 per cent. Having Itanagar as the capital, the State is surrounded on three sides by the international borders with Bhutan to the west, China to the north, Myanmar to the east and Assam in south respectively (India; 2002; p. 684).

Assam

Known in ancient history as Kamrupa, the State of Assam is situated in the north-east corner of India and surrounded by Bhutan and Arunachal Pradesh on the north, Nagaland and Manipur on the east, Meghalaya and Mizoram on the south and Bangladesh, Tripura and West Bengal on the west. Having an area of 78,438 sq. km, the State has a population of 2,66,38,407 Guwahati is the capital of the State. The State has a literacy rate of 64.28 per cent. The State's climate is of humid tropical type in the plains and sub-alpine in the hills (India; 2002; p. 686).

Bihar including Jharkhand

The capital of the State is Patna better known as Pataliputra in ancient history. With an area of 1,73,877 sq.km. the State has a population of 10,97,88,224 and a literacy rate of 50.83 per cent Being one of the major States of the Indian Union, Bihar is bounded on north by Nepal, on east by West Bengal, on west by Uttar Pradesh and Madhya Pradesh and on south by Orissa (India; 2002; p. 690 and 710).

Goa

Goa was liberated from the Portuguese colonial rule on December 19, 1961 and was given the status of Union Territory until 1987 and subsequently became a separate State on 30 May 1987 as the twenty-fifth State in the Indian Union. Being the smallest State-areawise-in India, Goa is bounded on the north by Maharashtra, south and east by Karnataka while the west is the Arabian sea. Panaji is the capital of the State. The State has an area of 3,702 sq. km. with a population of 13,43,998 and a literacy rate of 82.32%. Goa's climate is warm and humid (India; 2002; p. 695).

Gujarat

The present State of Gujarat came into being on 1 May 1960 after having separated from the erstwhile bilingual State of Bombay. The State has an area of 1,96,024 sq. km. and a population of 5,05,96,992. The capital of the State is the newly developed Gandhinagar and the literacy rate is 69.97 per cent. The State is bounded by the Arabian sea on west, Pakistan and Rajasthan in north and north-east respectively, Madhya Pradesh in south-east and Maharashtra in south. As the tropic of cancer passes through the northern border of Gujarat, the State has an intensely hot or cold climate (India; 2002; p. 697).

Haryana

Haryana was made into a full-fledged State from 1 November 1966. With an area of 44,212 sq. km., the State is bounded by Uttar Pradesh in east, Punjab in west, Himachal Pradesh in north and Rajasthan in south. Union Territory of Delhi juts into Haryana. The State's capital of Chandigarh is also serving as the capital of Punjab State. The population of the State is 2,10,82,989 with a literacy rate of 68.59 per cent. The climate of Haryana is very hot in summer and biting cold in winter (India; 2002; p. 700).

Himachal Pradesh

The territory of Himachal Pradesh was formed on 15 April 1948 and on 25 January 1971, it was made a full-fledged State.

The State is bordered by Jammu and Kashmir on its north, Punjab on west and south-west, Haryana on west, Uttar Pradesh on south-east and by Tibet on east. The State has an area of 55,763 sq. km, a population of 60,77,248 with literacy rate of 77.13 per cent. Shimla is the capital of the State. The southern part of Himachal Pradesh is as hot as plains, while the northern region has a temperate summer and a winter with extreme cold and heavy snowfall (India; 2002; p. 703).

Jammu and Kashmir

The only State in India having a separate constitution which came into being from 26 January, 1957. The area of the State is 2,22,236 sq. km. which includes some part of the illegal occupation by Pakistan and China. The State also has another distinction of having two capitals - Srinagar during summer and Jammu during winter. The State has a population of 1,00,69,917 and a literacy rate of 54.46 per cent. The State lies in the extreme north of the nation and is bounded on the north by China, on the east by Tibet and on the south by Himachal Pradesh, Punjab and Pakistan. Jammu Kashmir is called as *Paradise on Earth* (India; 2002; p. 707).

Karnataka

Formerly known as Mysore State, the State of Karnataka attained its present name on 1 November 1973. The State has an area of 1,91,791 sq. km. with a population of 5,27,33,958. The capital of the State is Bangalore which is popularly known as City of Gardens, Silicons and Sports. 67.04 per cent of the population of the State are literates.

Karnataka lies to the south of Goa and Maharashtra, to the east and west of Andhra Pradesh, to the north-west of Tamil Nadu and to the north of Kerala respectively (India; 2002; p. 711).

Kerala

Kerala has an area of 38,863 sq. km. which is only 1.18 per cent of the total area of the country wheras it has a population of 3,18,38,619 forming 3.43 per cent of the total population of the country. Having Thiruvananthapuram as the capital of the State, it is bounded by Tamil Nadu on the east and south, Karnataka on the north and north-east with Arabian sea on the west. The State of Kerala came into being in the present form only on 1 November 1956. Kerala is the first fully literate State in India with its literacy rate standing at 90.92 per cent (India; 2002 p. 715).

Madhya Pradesh (including Chhattisgarh)

Madhya Pradesh is the largest State in India (until 2000) with an area of 4,43,446 sq. km. and a population of 8,11,81,074. The State is surrounded by seven States—Rajasthan on the north-west, Uttar Pradesh on the north, Bihar on the north-east, Orissa on the east, Andhra Pradesh and Maharashtra on the south and Gujarat on the west. Bhopal is the capital of the State. The climate is extremely hot and cold in the north, temperate and breezy in the central plateau and hot and humid in the eastern and southern plains owing to its vastness (India; 2002; p. 693, 719).

Maharashtra

With an area of 3,07,713 sq. km. and a population of 9,97,52,247, Maharashtra State is bounded by the Arabian sea in the west, Gujarat in the north-west, Madhya Pradesh in the north, Andhra Pradesh in the south-east and Karnataka and Goa in the south respectively.

The administrative evolution of the State of Maharastra was effected on 1 May 1960 after bifurcation of the erstwhile Bombay State into Maharashtra and Gujarat. The State has a literacy rate of 77.27 per cent to its credit (India; 2002; p. 723).

Manipur

Manipur had been a Union Territory from 1956 and became a full-fledged State from 1972. With Imphal as the capital, the State is bounded by Nagaland in the north, Mizoram in the south, Myanmar in the east and Assam in the west. Having an area of 22,237 sq. km., Manipur has a population of 23,88,634 with 68.87 per cent literacy rate (India; 2002; p. 727).

Meghalaya

Meghalaya became a full-fledged State on 21 January 1972 after bifurcation from Assam. It is bounded on the north and east by Assam and on the south and west by Bangladesh. The State has an area of 22, 429 sq. km. with a population of 23,06,069. The literacy rate of the State is 63.31 per cent. Shillong is the capital of

Meghalaya. Cherrapunji, situated in Meghalaya, receives the maximum rainfall in the whole world with a rate of 11,873 mm annual rainfall (India; 2002; p. 730).

Mizoram

Mizoram is a mountainous region which attained statehood on 20 February 1987. The State occupies the north-east corner land of India bounded on the north by Assam and Manipur, on the east and south by Myanmar, on the west by Bangladesh and Tripura. Mizoram has an area 21,081 sq. km. where 8,91,058 people are living. 88.49 per cent of the people are literates in the State. Aizawl is the capital town of Mizoram (India; 2002; p. 732).

Nagaland

Having attained the statehood on 1 December 1963, Nagaland has a population of 19,88,636 people living in an area of 16,579 sq. km. with 67.11 per cent literacy rate. Kohima is the capital of Nagaland. The State is bounded by Arunachal Pradesh in the north, Assam in west, Manipur in south and Myanmar in the east respectively (india; 2002; p. 735).

Orissa

Orissa, formerly known as Kalinga, attained its independent statehood on 19 August, 1949. The State is having a population of 3,67,06,920 with 63.61 per cent literates living in an area of 1,55,707 sq. km. With temple city Bhubaneswar as its capital, the State is bounded by Bay of Bengal on the east, West Bengal on the north-east, Bihar on the north, Madhya Pradesh on the west and Andhra Pradesh on the south. Orissa has an equable climate-neither too hot, nor too cold. However, in the western districts like, Bolangir, Sambalpur and Sundargarh extreme climates prevail where the temperature touches 50°C in summer (India; 2002; p. 736).

Punjab

Punjab is bounded on the west by Pakistan, on the north by Jammu and Kashmir, on the north-east by Himachal Pradesh and on the south by Haryana and Rajasthan spreading to an area of 50,362 sq. km. The reorganised Punjab State came into being from November 1,1960. The State has a population of 2,42,89,296 people with a literacy rate of 69.95 per cent. Chandigarh is the joint capital for Punjab and Haryana (India; 2002; p. 740).

Rajasthan

With an area of 3,42,239 sq. km. Rajasthan is the largest State in India in 2001. The State was known as 'Rajputana' before independence. Rajasthan is bounded by Pakistan on the west and north-west, Punjab on the north, Haryana and Uttar Pradesh on the north-east and east, Madhya Pradesh on the south and south-east and Gujarat on the south-west. The present State of Rajasthan came into being on November 1, 1956 after the merger of several princely States after independence. The *'Pink City'* Jaipur is the capital of Rajasthan. The State has a population of 5,64,73,122 and a literacy rate of 61.03 per cent (India; 2002; p. 743).

Tamil Nadu

The State of Tamil Nadu, situated on the south-east side of the Indian Peninsula, is bounded on the east by the Bay of Bengal, in the south by Indian Ocean, in the west by the Arabian Sea and the States of Kerala and Karnataka, and in the north by Andhra Pradesh and Karnataka. The present State of Tamil Nadu came into being on November 1, 1956 from the composite Madras State owing to the linguistic reorganisation of States. Having an area of 1,30,058 sq. km. the State has a literacy rate of 73.47 per cent among the population of 6,21,10,839 people. Chennai is the capital of the State (India; 2002; p. 749).

Tripura

Tripura has an area of 10,492 sq. km. where 31,91,168 people are living with a literacy rate of 73.66 per cent. Agartala is the capital of the State. Tripura is surrounded by Bangladesh on three sides with Assam and Mizoram bordering on the north-east. It became a full-fledged State on January 21,1972 (India; 2002; p. 754).

Uttar Pradesh (Including Uttaranchal)

Uttar Pradesh is the largest State in India in terms of population with 17,45,32,421 people living in the State having a literacy rate of 64.82 per cent. Lucknow is the capital of the State. The State has an area of 2,94,411 sq. km. which is bounded by Tibet and Nepal in north, Himachal Pradesh in north-west, Haryana in west, Rajasthan in south-west, Madhya Pradesh in south and Bihar in east. The State of Uttar Pradesh got its present name in January 1950, which was previously called as United Province (India; 2002; p. 755, 758).

West Bengal

The State of West Bengal, spread over to an area of 88,752 sq.km. is bounded on the north by Sikkim and Bhutan, on the east by Assam and Bangladesh, on the south by the Bay of Bengal and on the west by Orissa, Bihar and Nepal. The entire State belongs to the high rainfall region-varying from 1,006 mm to 2,933 mm. The State has a population of 8,02,21,171 with a literacy rate of 69.22 per cent. Kolkata is the capital of the State. (India, 2002; p. 762).

Union Territories

Andaman and Nicobar Islands

The Union Territory of Andaman and Nicobar Islands is a group of 572 Islands situated in the Bay of Bengal spreading to a land area of 8,249 sq. km. There are 3,56,265 people living in this Union Territory with a literacy rate of 81.18 per cent. The capital of this Union Territory is Port Blair (India ; 2002; p. 765).

Chandigarh

Chandigarh city with an area of 114 sq. km. has been a Union Territory since 1966. It is the capital of both Punjab and Haryana States and is bounded by both the States.

The Union Territory has a population of 8,76,000 with 81.76 per cent literacy rate. The capital of the Union Territory is Chandigarh itself (India; 2002; p. 767).

Dadra and Nagar Haveli

The Union Territory of Dadra and Nagar Haveli was integrated into the Indian Union on 11 August, 1961. With Silvasa as its capital, this Union Territory lies near the west coast surrounded by the States of Gujarat and Maharashtra spread over to an area of 491 sq.km. The Union Territory has a population of 2,20,451 with a literacy rate of 60.03 per cent (India; 2002; p. 769).

Delhi

After independence, Delhi became the capital of India and was made a Union Territory in 1959. Delhi is surrounded by Haryana on all sides except east where Uttar Pradesh touches it. Delhi has an area of 1,483 sq. km. where 1,37,82,976 people are living. The literacy rate is 81.82 per cent. The weather condition is extreme hot in summer and chilling cold in winter. The capital of this Union Territory is Delhi itself. However, the Government of India is planning to provide full fledged statehood to Delhi soon (India; 2002; p. 772).

Lakshadweep

The smallest Union Territory of India, Lakshadweep has a total land area of only 32 sq.km. There are 36 islands in this Union Territory out of which only 10 are inhabited. Lakhsadweep is surrounded on all sides by Arabian Sea. The Union Territory has a population of 60,595 with a literacy rate of 87.52 per cent. Kavaratti Island is the capital of Lakshadweep. The Union Territory was formed in 1956 (India; 2002; p. 774).

Pondicherry

The Union Territory of Pondicherry encompasses an area of 492 sq.km. This Union Territory comprises of four former French territories - Pondicherry, Karaikal, Mahe and Yanam. Pondicherry and Karaikal are surrounded by Tamil Nadu on three sides and Bay of Bengal on the east. Mahe is situated in Kerala with Arabian Sea on the west and surrounded by Kerala State on three sides. Yanam is situated in Andhra Pradesh which surrounds it on three sides while Bay of Bengal lies in the east. Pondicherry is the capital of this Union Territory. The Union Territory has a population of 8,07,785 people with 74.91 per cent literacy rate (India; 1998; p. 666).

Conclusion

The concept and the name of *State Central Library* has long been familiar since these libraries have been catering for a public, ranging from the Head of the State at the capital down to the students and the lay public at the rural-folk, thus effectively open to all classes of community who would wish to, and are capable of availing their services on almost all subject interests without any bias or discrimination. These State Central Libraries may, therefore, be perceived as those libraries which are supported by State funds and which meet State's-rather than national, local, or sectional-needs within their respective geographical characters.

However, a brief genesis of public libraries in India of which these State Central Libraries form an integral part, along with their role and organisational structure are depicted in the succeeding chapter as a part of their background study.

Bibliography

1. Auvdaiappan, N. Role of State Central Library: Its relation with District Central libraries and National Depository Libraries. In *Proceedings of the National Seminar on Public Library Movement*, Chennai. 1991. Tamil Nadu, Directorate of Public Libraries, Chennai, 1991, pp. 108-121.

2. Baskar, P. Use of fiction (English) in the Connemara (State Central) Public Library and the British Council, Madras: A Comparative Analysis MLIS Dissertation. (unpublished). May 1993. Dept. of Library Science; University of Madras; Chennai.

3. Dasgupta, Kalpana. National Library : Programmes, Problems and Prospects. In JAIN, M.K., ed. 50 years Library and Information Services in India, 1998, Shipra Publication; Delhi, p. 166.

4. Esperanza, M.A.C. The State Central Library, Patna. In Gupta, B.M. ed. Handbook of Libraries, Archives and Information Centres in India. Vol. 16: Library Development in India. 1996. Segment Books; New Delhi, pp. 236-49.

5. Ghosh, Malabika. Need for the Conservation Activities in State Central Library. In Proceedings of the National Seminar on Public Library Movement, Chennai. 1991. Tamil Nadu, Directorate of Public Libraries, Chennai, 1991, pp. 361-64.

6. Govinda Krishnan, U.B. Reading Pattern: Connemara (State Central) Public Library and District Central Library, Madras. MLIS. Dissertation. (unpublished). May 1980. Dept. of Library Science; University of Madras; Madras.

7. Harrod, L.M. Librarian's Glossary and Reference Book. 1987. Gower Publishing; London, p. 636.

8. Inamdar, N.B. Guidelines for Selection and Acquisition of Materials for State Central Libraries—A case study of Andhra Pradesh. *Granthana:Indian Journal of Library Studies.* 1, 1; January 1990, pp. 40-54.

9. India. Committee of National Policy on Library and Information System. National Policy on Library and Information System—A Presentation. *Granthana: Indian Journal of Library Studies.* 1, 1; January 1990, pp. 62-72.

10. India. Ministry of Education and Youth Services. Report of the Advisory Committee for Libraries. 1959. Ministry of Education; New Delhi, p. 32.

11. India. Research, Reference and Training Division. India 2002; A Reference Annual. 2002. Ministry of Education; New Delhi, p. 868.

12. Ijari, S.R. and Khan, H.A. State Central Reference Library, In Gupta, B.M. ed. Handbook of Libraries, Archives and Information Centres in India. Vol. 16; Library Development in India. 1996. Segment Books; New Delhi, pp. 293-301.

13. Janakraj. State Central Library, Haryana. In Gupta, B.M. ed. Handbook of Libraries, Archives and Information Centres in India. Vol. 16: Library Development in India. 1996, Segment Books; New Delhi, pp. 286-95.

14. Kalia, D.R. Libraries in Fourth Five Year Plan. Proceedings of the All India Library Conference of the Indian Library Association, 15th, Mysore, 1965. Indian Library Associatio; Delhi, 1966, pp.13-37.

15. Kalia, D.R. Public Libraries. In Jain, M.K. ed. 50 years Library and Information Services in India. 1998, Shipra Publication; Delhi, pp. 27-32.

16. Kalia, D.R., *et.al.*, Guidelines for Public Library Systems and Services. *Granthana:India Journal of Library Studies*. 2(1); 1991, pp. 31-84.

17. Kent, Allen and Lancour, Harold ed. Encyclopaedia of Library and Information Science. Vol. 24. 1978. Marcel Dekker; Newyork, p. 267.

18. Khanna, S.N. Delhi Public Library: Past, Present and Future. In Gupta, B.M. ed. Handbook of Libraries, Archives and Information Centres in India. Vol. 16: Library Development in India. 1996. Segment Books; Delhi, pp. 236-49.

19. Mukherjee, Subodh Kumar and Sengupta, B. Library Organisation and Administration. 1972. World Press; Calcutta, pp. 46-47.

20. Ohdedar, A.K. State Central Library, West Bengal. In Gupta, B.M. ed. Handbook of Libraries, Archives and Information Centres in India. Vol. 16 : Library Development in India. 1996. Segment Books; New Delhi, p. 331.

21. Padhi, P. and Panda, K.C. Harekrushna Mahtab State Library, Orissa: An appraisal. *CLIS Observer*. 5(3-4); July/Dec. 1988, pp. 13-24

22. Ramola, K.C. and Arora, S. Computerisation of Central State Library at Chandigarh. In Proceedings of the All India

Conference of the Indian Library Association, 39th, Bangalore, 1994. Indian Library Association; New Delhi, 1994, pp. 420-25.

23. Ranganathan, S.R. Andhra Pradesh Seminar on the Organisation and Administration of Public Libraries. 1962. Department of Public Libraries; Andhra Pradesh; Hyderabad, pp. 40-43.

24. Ranganathan, S.R. Library Development Plan. Thirty years programme for India with drafts of Library Bill for Union and constituent States. Delhi; University of 1960; Delhi, p. 274.

25. Ranganathan, S.R. Model Public Libraries Act. In Ranganathan, S.R and Neelameghan, A. Public Library System. 1972. Sarada Ranganathan Endowment for Library Science; Bangalore, p. 57.

26. Rath, P.K. Public Library Development in India : A bibliography. *CLIS Observer.* 5 (3&4); July/Dec. 1988, pp. 25-30.

27. Rath, P.K. Role of State Central Library and its Relation with District Central Library under the Public Library System. In *Proceedings of the national seminar on public library movement,* Chennai. 1991. Tamil Nadu, Directorate of Public Libraries, Chennai, 1991, pp. 122-30.

28. Rodriques, Pia De Menezes. Goa State Central Library : Past, Present and Future Plans. In Gupta, B.M., *ed.* Handbook of Libraries, Archives and Information Centres in India. Vol. 16: Library Development in India. 1996. Segment Books; New Delhi, pp. 271-85.

29. Seethapathy, R.K. Connemara (State Central) Public Library : Its Response to Social Changes. MLIS. Dissertation. (unpublished). May 1978. Dept. of Library Science; University of Madras; Madras.

30. Shera, J.H. Sociological Foundation of Librarianship, 1970. Asia Publishing House; Bombay, p. 60.

31. Sounderrajan, K. Romain Rolland Library, Pondichery. In Gupta, B.M. ed. Handbook of Libraries, Archives and Information Centres in Inda. Vol. 16: Library Development in India, 1996, Segment Books; New Delhi, p. 302-6.

32. Taher, Mohamed. Functions of the State Libraries : A Case Study of A.P. State Central Library, Hyderabad. In Gupta, B.M., *ed.* Handbook of Libraries, Archives and Information Centres in India. Vol. 16: Library Development in India, 1996, Segment Books; New Delhi, pp. 236-249.

33. Thomas, V.K. Public Libraries in India: Development and Finance, 1997. Vikas Publishing House; New Delhi, p. 3.

34. UNESCO Public Library Manifesto, 1994. UNESCO. UNISIST Newsletter. 23(1), 1995; Paris, p. 10.

35. Venkatappaiah, Velaga. Connemara (State Central) Public Library, Madras. In Gupta, B.M., *ed.* Handbook of Libraries, Archives and Information Centres in India. Vol. 16: Library Development in India, 1996. Segment Books; New Delhi, p. 326.

36. Young, P.V. and Schmid, C.F. Scientific Social Surveys and Research, 1994. Prentice Hall Publishing House; New Delhi, pp. 16, 103.

2

Genesis of Public Libraries and Growth of State Central Libraries in India

Introduction

The study of any subject should begin with probing the evolution or the genesis of the particular field of knowledge. Unless one learns the past, the present cannot be understood properly and it will not be possible to predict the future.

Hence, this chapter aims to study the genesis of public libraries in India which ultimately led to the growth of the State Central Libraries in various States and Union Territories in India. The role of State Central Libraries in promoting literacy, inculcating the reading habits among the people and in preserving the State's cultural heritage has been analysed. The role and contribution of various agencies such as State Governments, Central Government, Raja Rammohun Roy Library Foundation and voluntary organisations in promotion of State Central Libraries in India has also been traced. The existing organisational structure of the State Central Libraries has been discussed.

Genesis of Public Libraries in India

The study of the genesis of public libraries in India has to be proceeded along the chronological order so that the evolution can be properly understood in the historical perspective.

The evolution of public libraries may be seen under the following headings:

(1) Ancient and Medieval Period.
(2) Role of the Princely Rulers.
(3) Role of Colonial Rulers upto 19th Century.
(4) Baroda Library Movement.

(5) Before Independence-Freedom Struggle.
(6) After Independence-Public Library Acts.

Ancient and Medieval Period

India has a long history of public libraries spread over to several centuries of the past. The libraries have always been a vital part of the glorious ancient institutions of learning. P.N. Kaula traces the origin of the libraries in Indian soil as follows: "Much is not known about the libraries of those days although we find evidence of sòme kind of libraries in the Indus Valley Civilization stocking a large number of cylinder seals and tablets with inscriptions. During the Buddhist period of Indian history, there are evidences of foreign travellers like, Fa-Hien, Huien-Tsang and I-tsing about great libraries at Nalanda, Taxila, Pataliputra, Vikramasila and Tamralipti" (Kaula: 1997: p. 165).

O.P. Sharma lists out some of the earliest libraries which existed in India during the ancient, medieval and modern periods of history. "In India, libraries in one form or other have existed since pre-historic days is beyond any shadow of doubt. The large collection of early Hindu manuscripts at Nalanda, Taxila, Pataliputra, Visali; of the medieval Hindu period at Ujjain, Banaras, Navadipa and Karachi; and of the modern date at Bikaner, Tanjore, Kashmir bear testimony to the assiduous care with which the libraries were formed and preserved in the country" (Sharma; 1968; p. 9).

If there is any dilemma on whether the libraries of ancient institutions of learning can be counted as public libraries, Raman Nair ascertains that, "the great libraries at Nalanda, Taxila and Pataliputra, even though attached to academic institutions, had more free public library character than any of the present day libraries of their size" (Raman Nair; 1996; p. 131).

There are a few reports about the existence of some ancient libraries in India. "The world's first seat of learning, Taxila University set up in the Post-Vedic period, had a beautiful library attached to it" (Trehan; 1973; p. 170).

A brief account of the library of Nalanda University which had the dual character of both academic and public library is given as follows: "The libraries attached to Nalanda University (Circa 450 A.D.) centered round Dharmaganja or the Mart of Religion, comprising of three large buildings with three different names viz., Ratnasagara, Ratnodadhi and Ratnaranjaka. The Ratnasagara was a nine storied building which housed the rare and sacred works like the Prajnaparamitra Sutra and other tantric works as `Samajaguhya'. It was from these rich stocks of manuscripts that I-sing, the famous traveller from China, was able to copy out whatever he needed to carry home". (Mookerjee and Sengupta; 1977; p. 32). However, by the end of 12th century, both the University and Library at Nalanda were destroyed by the Muslim invaders. There are ample evidences of the existence of libraries in Buddhist monasteries, Jain temples, Hindu mutts and Muslim Madrassas as well as in several other palaces and temples.

Role of Princely Rulers

The ancient and medieval rulers of various Princely States of India have evinced keen interest in establishing public libraries in their respective kingdoms. These libraries were called, 'Saraswathi Bhandars' or 'Granth Bhandars'. However, a brief Statewise analysis of the growth of few vital public libraries made in the succeeding paragraphs, will make the evolutionary scenario of the ancient public libraries more clear.

Andhra Pradesh

The Nizam Government of the erstwhile Hyderabad State established Asafia Library (Dairatul-Marif) in 1888 (presently the State Central Library) under the patronage of Nawab Imadul Mulk and Dafter-e-Diwani Mulki-w-Mal (presently State Archives) (Inamdar and Shakira; 1996; p. 89). The first public library to offer free book service to the people was started in Vishakapatnam in 1886. The name of the library was Shri Saraswati Nilayam established by Manthana Adinarayanamoorthy, a school teacher. As per the Resolution of Government of India dated 3 November 1868, Gustav Oppert made a library tour to South India and observed that there were 30 libraries in Vishakapatnam at that time. Most of these libraries are now defunct (Venkatappaiah; 1968. p. 52).

Delhi

"Mohammed Ghazni is said to have maintained a large library at the capital of his kingdom which had more than 30,000 volumes. Akbar, the great had a splendid library of his own. Humayun Badshah was a lover of books and is said to have lost his life from a fall from his library stair". (Mookerjee and Sengupta; 1977; p. 34). Madhusudana (10th Century), a famous General of Chalukya King, Raja Narayana, founded a residential college called Ghatikhasala, where he appointed six librarians called Saraswati Bhandarikas. Similar instances are there during the time of Eastern Chalukyas of 11th century, Vijayanagara kings of 15th century and the Mathura Nayaka kings of the 16th century (Venkatappaiah; 1996; p. 138).

Gujarat

The Central Library at Baroda and the network of public libraries established by Maharaja Sayajirao Gaekward III in 1910 deserves special treatment. Hence, a separate section 'Baroda Library Movement' is provided in this chapter under section 2.1.4.

Jammu and Kashmir

Maharaja Ranbir Singh and Maharaja Pratap Singh have established two major public libraries in 1879 and 1898 at Jammu and Srinagar respectively. These two public libraries, still functioning at Jammu and Srinagar, are named after these two rulers—Sri Ranbir Singh (SRS) Public Library and Sri Pratap Singh (SPS) Public Library (Baba; 1994; p.146).

Karnataka

In Karnataka State, Mahmud Ghawan, the Prime Minister under the Bahamani Sultan was responsible for the creation of number of libraries during 1766-77, the foremost among them is still functioning as Bidar College Library. The library contained 3,000 palm leaf manuscripts. "The Descriptive Catalogue compiled by Charles Stewart endorses the vast possession of Tippu's Library of Oriental Books... In 1808, Major Stewart Published in Cambridge Lists of books in which he listed large number of books Persian, Arabic and Urdu languages found in Sultan's library. After the defeat of Tippu Sultan, his library of manuscripts was presented to East India Company" (Ijari; 1996; p. 25). In Bijapur, when Adilshahi's dynasty came to power, Sultan Adilshahi founded the 'Adilshahi Library'.

"A glance at the history gives the beautiful account of the foresightedness of Vijayanagara Kings, who lavishly sponsored the promotion of public libraries. It is stated that King Bukka donated the land in 1329 A.D. to Puranika Kavikrishna Bhat for the renovation, upkeep..etc of libraries attached to a Math at Sringeri" (Karisiddappa and Kumbar; 1996; p. 203).

Kerala

The Maharaja of erstwhile Travancore State His Highness Swathi Thirunal took the initiative in establishing Trivandrum Public Library in 1829. The task was assigned to Lt.Col. Cadogan, the then British Resident in Travancore State. Incidentally, Cadogan was the grandson of Sri Han Sloan, the founder of British Museum. Trivandrum Public Library served as a palace library in which those persons who were invited to attend the Durbar of Maharaja alone were admitted. However, the doors of the library were thrown open to the public from 1899. *(I have personally visited this library and gathered information from the Library Authorities.)*

Manipur

The Kings of Manipur maintained a Royal Library under the responsible 'Pandit Loisang' (Council of Learneds) since 427 A.D. and produced books. King Khagemba who ruled from 1596 developed special interest in literature and the Royal Library. The Royal Library and other manuscript libraries were destroyed due to the opposition of local people to accept 'Vaishnavism' as a State religion during the reign of King Garibniwaz Pamheiba [1707-1748] and during the seven year long devastation of Manipur during 1819-1826 due to the occupation of the whole territory of Manipur by the Burmese (Giridhari Singh; 1989; p. 95).

Madhya Pradesh

King Bhoja of Dhar set up an Imperial Library in 12th Century which was known as Bhoja's Imperial Library. In 19th century, the Indore General Library, the oldest surviving public library was founded by Maharaja Tukoji Rao Holkar II in 1854 (Tomar; 1992; p. 46). "The three main princely States, viz., the Holkar State of Indore, the Gwalior State and the Bhopal State had some kind of public library service. Bhopal had 'Hamid's State Library' and Gwalior had 'Madhav Pusthagalaya' as State Libraries" (Wadikar; 1989; p. 84).

Punjab

During the Mughal period, the princes, princesses, nobles and higher-ups in the Darbar had their own libraries. The library of Khan-i-Khanan Abdul Rahim is one such Imperial library. He employed 95 staff members comprising Librarian, Book Binder, Scribe, Translator, etc., and Maulana Ibrahim was the librarian. Maharaja Ranjit Singh, though was totally illiterate, established a library in the Diwan-Khana near Moti Mandir at Lahore and took special interest in developing the library in public interest (Sukhdev Sing; 1996; p. 208).

Rajasthan

'Establishment of libraries in the former States of Rajaputana can be traced back to 14th century. (Maharaja) Rana Kumbha had developed a good collection of manuscripts... Likewise, the rulers of other States in Rajaputana also took interest in developing their palace libraries. Some of the important libraries that deserve mention are:

(1) Raja Grandhalaya of Maharaja Jagat Singh I, Udaipur;
(2) Anood Sanskrit Library, Bikaner,
(3) Palace Library, Jodhpur;
(4) Palace Library, Jhalawar; and
(5) Palace Library, Bharatpur (Sharma; 1996; pp. 206-7).

Tamil Nadu

Thanjavur Maharaja Serfoji III (1798-1832) was responsible for developing Saraswathi Mahal library, one of the very few ancient libraries of India surviving till date.

The library was established during 16th century at Thanjavur by the Chola kings. It was patronised by three dynasties of kings—Cholas, Nayaks and Marathas—who have ruled over the State. The library has a collection of 43,740 palm leaf manuscripts and 52,000 printed books in several Indian and European languages. (I have personally visited this library and collected data through discussion).

Tripura

The Maharaja Birchandra Manikya established a public library in the royal palace at Tripura during 1896. 'Vijayanta Palace Library' functioning in the Royal Palace for several generations formed the nucleus of this library. This library was named as 'Birchandra Library' and declared open to public. Birchandra Library was later moved out of the palace and taken over by the Government of Tripura in 1953.

West Bengal

Tibetan monk Nag-Itno who toured the east India during the twelfth century refers to a big manuscript library attached to the Vihara at Vikramashila for the use of about 8,000 scholars residing there. This Vihara was established by King Dharamapala in the 8th century A.D. (Bhattacharya; 1968; p.172).

It stems from the above descriptions that, most of the first public libraries in Indian States evolved primarily under the initiatives and solicitude of the ancient rulers and kings of princely States (10); followed by Public (4); Overseas Government (3); Indian Government (1); and (1) each by the learned societies and political prisoners spreading their evolution history from 5th century to 20th century as reflected under Table 2.1.

The Role of Colonial Rulers - 19th Century

The Britishers came to India with the objective of widening their commercial markets that ultimately led to the establishment of the British empire in India which became a prestigious unit of global empire where 'the sun shall never set'. India was considered as a jewel in the crown of the global British empire. The historical evidences ascertain that the colonial rulers of India, played a definite role in heralding the public library movement in India. Regarding the contribution of the British rulers in library development in the country, there are two schools of thought. The first school of thought attributes motives behind the actions of the colonial rulers of India. This point of view is better articulated by Prof. S.R. Ijari who says that the objective of establishing the libraries was not mainly to disseminate knowledge or to speed up literacy, but to preserve and concentrate power (Ijari; 1996; p. 125). The other school of thought is of the opinion that the Britishers were really serious in enlightening Indians. B.P. Barua says, "The English were the first to take the initiative in setting public libraries or subscription libraries in the presidency towns of Calcutta, Bombay and Madras in the first half of the 19th century" (Barua; 1985; p. 166). Surya Rao and Babu Rao further substantiate that "The East India Company in India had its libraries in its factories at Hoogly (Calcutta) and in Bombay towards the end of 17th century. In course of time, the English officers established small libraries in the localities where they were residing" (Surya Rao and Babu Rao; 1974, p. 24).

TABLE 2.1
First Public Libraries in Various States of India

Sl. No.	State	Founders	Year	Place	Name of Library
1.	Andaman & Nicobar Islands	Political Prisoners	1911	Port Blair	Cellular Jail Library
2.	Andhra Pradesh	Public	1839	Rajahmundry	Public Library
3.	Bihar	Public	1855	Gaya	Public Library
4.	Delhi	Md. Ghazini	Mughal Period	Delhi	Royal Library
5.	Goa	Portugese Govt.	1832	Panaji	Publica Livaria
6.	Gujarat	Public	1850	Surat	Andrews Library
7.	Haryana	Indian Govt.	1957	Ambala	District Library
8.	Jammu & Kashmir	Maharaja Ranbir Singh	1879	Jammu	Public Library
9.	Karnataka	Md. Ghawan	1766	Bidar	Public Library
10.	Kerala	Lt. Col. Cadogan	1829	Trivandrum	Trivandrum Public Library
11.	Madhya Pradesh	King Bhoja	12th	Dhar	Imperial Library

Contd.

(Contd.)

Sl. No.	*State*	*Founders*	*Year*	*Place*	*Name of Library*
12.	Maharashtra	Asiatic Society of Bombay	1804	Mumbai	Asiatic Society Library
13.	Manipur	King of Manipur	427 A.D.	Manipur	Royal Library
14.	Meghalaya	British Govt.	1903	Shillong	Govt. Public Library
15.	Pondicherry	French Govt.	1827	Pondicherry	Bibliotheque Publique
16.	Punjab	Khan-i-khan Abdul Rahman	Mughal Period	Lahore	Imperial Library
17.	Rajasthan	Rana Kumbha	14th	Rajaputana	Imperial Library
18.	Tamil Nadu	Chola Kings	16th	Thanjavur	Saratwati Mahal Library
19.	Uttar Pradesh	Public	1864	Allahabad	Public Library
20.	West Bengal	King Dharmapala	8th Century	Vikramashila	Vihara Library

While listing out the role of a few reputed Englishmen who established educational institutions in British India, Mookerjee and Sengupta elaborate that, "Warren Hastings, the then Governor General of India, founded the Calcutta Madrassah in 1781. Mr. Jonathan Duncan, the then British Agent, also founded the Banaras Sanskrit College in 1792. Prior to this, in 1784 Sir William Jones founded the Asiatic Society at Calcutta, where along with the collection of curios for the society, the collection of allied literature, both handwritten and in print, automatically followed."

They are of the opinion that, an Englishman was behind the milestone of the beginning of the public library movement in India. "At Calcutta, Mr. J.H. Stocquies, the editor of the local daily "Englishman" drafted a scheme for the establishment of a public library at Calcutta in 1835. This was the start of the public library movement in the country" (Mookerjee and Sengupta; 1977; pp. 37-39). There are other instances of Englishmen playing a dominant role in providing library services for the Indians while primarily taking care of the reading needs of the Britishers serving in India.

Native General Libraries

Bengal Experience. The east and west led the rest of India in the establishment of a new breed of libraries called 'Native General Libraries'. In this category, both the Englishmen and Indians played an equal and complementing role. Choudhury vividly recollects the situation behind the establishment of Calcutta Public Library which he considers as 'the beginning of public library movement in Bengal'.

"In the third decade of the nineteenth century, necessity was felt for the establishment of a public library under the joint efforts of the European and Indian Communities. The first attempt to establish a Public Library for both Indian and European communities was made in 1835. Eminent and distinguished personalities of the then Calcutta met in a public meeting on 20th August, 1835 under Sir Charles Metcalfe. The meeting adapted the following resolution: That it is expedient and necessary to establish in Calcutta a public library of reference and circulation that shall be opened to all ranks and classes without distinction and sufficiently extensive to supply the wants of the entire community in every department of literature".

As a result of this effort, the Calcutta Public Library came into existence on 21st March 1836 (Choudhry; 1989; p.136).

Calcutta Public Library was subsequently followed by 53 native general libraries in Calcutta and other Districts of Bengal region during the second half of the 19th century.

TABLE 2.2
19th Century Native General Libraries in Bengal

Sl. No.	*Name of the Library*	*District*	*Year*
1.	Bayle Hall Library	Midnapore	1851
2.	Hoogly Public Library	Hoogly	1854
3.	Krishnanagar Public Library	Nadia	1856
4.	Konnagar Public Library	Hoogly	1858
5.	Uttarpara Public Library	Hoogly	1859
6.	Bandhad Library - Jayanagar	Majlipur	1869
7.	Ariadaha Association Library	North 24 Parganas	1870
8.	Serampore Public Library	Hoogly	1871
9.	Bensat Association Library	North 24 Parganas	1871
10.	Boral Priyanth Library	South 24 Parganas	1871
11.	United Reading Room	Calcutta	1872
12.	Ambica Sadharan Pathagar	Burdwan	1872
13.	Chandannagar Pusthagar	Hoogly	1873
14.	Shibpur Public Library	Howrah	1874
15.	Sashipada Institute	Calcutta	1876
16.	Barannagar People's Library	Calcutta	1876
18.	Mudially Public Library	Calcutta	1876
19.	Rajpur Public Library	South 24 Parganas	1877
20.	Sadharan Brahmo Samaj Library	Calcutta	1879
21.	Dakshineswara Ramakrishna Library	Calcutta	1879
22.	Taltala Public Library	Calcutta	1882
23.	Bagbazar Reading Library	Calcutta	1883
24.	Rashpur People's Library	Howrah	1883
25.	Pragati Pathagar	Ghatal-Midnapore	1883
26.	Bantra Public Library	Howrah	1884
27.	Ranaghat Public Library	Nadia	1884
28.	Kumartuli Institute Library	Calcutta	1884
29.	Bally Public Library	Howrah	1885
30.	Andul-Mohiary Public Library	Howrah	1886
31.	Mugkalyan Pally Bharat Granthagar	Howrah	1888
32.	Suburban Reading Club	Calcutta	1888
33.	Chaitanya Library	Calcutta	1889
34.	Sporting Club	Calcutta	1889

(Contd.)

Sl. No.	Name of the Library	District	Year
35.	Kalighat Library and Free Reading Room	Calcutta	1889
36.	Bharati Parishad Library	Calcutta	1890
37.	Bansberia Public Library	Hoogly	1891
38.	Agarpara Pathagar	North 24 Parganas	1891
39.	University Institute Library	Calcutta	1891
40.	Suhrid Library	Calcutta	1891
41.	Mahabodhi Society Library	Calcutta	1982
42.	Bangiya Sahitya Parishad Library	Calcutta	1893
43.	Sripur Kalyan Samiti Library	Hoogly	1894
44.	Jamgram Nandhi Sadharan Pathagar	Hoogly	1894
45.	Mondlai Public Library	Hoogly	1894
46.	Belur Public Library	Howrah	1895
47.	Y.M.C.A. Library	Calcutta	1895
48.	Baniapur Library and Reading Club	Calcutta	1897
49.	Saragachi Ramakrishna Mission Library	Murshidabad	1897
50.	Saraswathi Institute	Calcutta	1898
51.	Friend's Union Library	Howrah	1898
52.	Baruipur Kamala Library	South 24 Parganas	1898
53.	Kakatiya Public Library	—	1899

Many leading literary and social personalities such as Surendranath Banerjee, Bankim Chandra Chatterjee and Gurudev Rabindranath Tagore were actively associated with the development of libraries in Bengal. All the above mentioned libraries were primarily the subscription libraries and the formation was brought about mostly by local charities and donations.

Assam. The first library in eastern India named as Assam Government Public Library was established by the British Administration in Shillong during 1903. Although its services were extended to the reading public of Shillong, it generally served the officials of the State Government of Assam (Buragohain; 1989; p. 39).

Maharashtra and Gujarat. The western part of India played a significant role in the history of public library development of India. Being the gateway of India for the Britishers, the Britishers settled in large numbers in and around Mumbai. The erstwhile Bombay State consisted of present Maharashtra, Gujarat and the northern part of Karnataka State.

In the opinion of B.P. Barua, "The genesis of library development can be traced back to the year 1808 when the Bombay Government proposed to register libraries which would receive free copies of books published from the Funds for the Encouragement of literature" (Barua; 1985; p.166). The Asiatic Society of Bombay (1804), and Bombay General Library (1830) are some of the earliest libraries in Maharashtra State. Apart from them, a number of libraries were established in Western India by the enthusiastic and dedicated general public with the support of colonial rulers and the Britishers settled in India during 19th century. (Being a field official connected with a funding agency of the Government of India for public libraries in the country, I have personally visited the following public libraries in western India, as reflected in Table 2.3 and 2.4, consisting of the present Maharashtra and Gujarat States which were established during the nineteenth century):

TABLE 2.3
19th Century Native General Libraries in Maharashtra

Sl. No.	*Name of the Library*	*Address*	*Year*
1.	Asiatic Society Library	Mumbai-400 023	1804
2.	Nagar Wachnalaya	Ratnagiri-415 612	1828
3.	Ahmednagar Zilla Wachnalaya	Ahmednagar-414 503	1838
4.	Sarvajanik Wachnalaya	Nashik-422 001	1840
5.	Nagar Wachnalaya	Satara-415 002	1849
6.	Karveer Nagar Wachnalaya	Kolhapur-416 002	1850
7.	Thane Nagar Wachnalaya	Thane-400 607	1850
8.	Nagar Wachnalaya	Vengrula	1851
9.	Shriram Wachnalaya	Sawantawadi	1852
10.	Shri Hirachand Nemchand Wachnalaya	Solapur-413 001	1854
11.	Dhondo Shamrao Garud Library	Dhule-424 001	1854
12.	Nagarpalika Nagar Wachnalaya	Karad-415 110	1857
13.	R.B.Anant Shivaji Desai Wachnalaya	Kudal-416 520	1860
14.	Babuji Deshmukh Wachnalaya	Akola-444 001	1863

(Contd.)

(Contd.)

Sl. No.	*Name of the Library*	*Address*	*Year*
15.	Sarvajanik Wachnalaya	Bandra-441 904	1863
16.	Wachan Mandir	Thane-420 202	1864
17.	Kakani Nagar Wachnalaya	Malegaon-423 202	1865
18.	Lokmanya Wachnalaya	Arvi-442 201	1867
19.	Amravati Nagar Wachnalaya	Amravati-444 201	1869
20.	Rajaram Sitaram Dixit Library	Nagpur-440 012	1870
21.	Apte Wachan Mandir	Kolhapur-416 115	1870
22.	Sarvajanik Wachnalaya	Bhusaval	1870
23.	Pujya Sane Guui Granthalaya	Amalneer	1872
24.	Sarvajanik Wachnalaya	Wardha-442 001	1872
25.	Nagar Wachan Mandir	Pandharpur	1874
26.	Vallabdas Valji District Library	Jalgon-425 202	1876
27.	Nagar Wachnalaya	Darwha-445 001	1882
28.	Lokmanya Tilak Wachnalaya	Nandurbar-425 412	1883
29.	Mahatma Sarvajanik Wachnalaya	Shevagon-414 001	1885
30.	Nagar Wachan Mandir	Chopda	1885
31.	Sarvajanik Wachnalaya	Pusad-445 204	1886
32.	Nagar Wachnalaya	Yeotmal-445 001	1887
33.	Marathi Grantha Sanghralaya	Thane-400 601	1893
34.	Mumbai Marathi Grantha Sanghralaya	Mumbai-400 014	1898

TABLE 2.4
19th Century Native General Libraries in Gujarat

Sl. No.	*Name of the Library*	*Address*	*Year*
1.	Andrews Library	Surat-395 001	1850
2.	Raichand Dipchand Library	Bharuch-391 001	1858
3.	Government Library	Junagadh-362 001	1865
4.	Stuart Library	Godhara-380 001	1866
5.	Maharao Shri Vijayaraj Sarvajanik Library	Bhuj	1868

(Contd.)

(Contd.)

Sl. No.	*Name of the Library*	*Address*	*Year*
6.	Apparao Bholanath Library	Ahmedabad-380 017	1870
7.	Shri Dwaraka Sarvajanik Pustagalaya	Dwaraka-361 335	1871
8.	Victoria Jubilee Hemchand General Library	Palanpur-384 315	1872
9.	Parekh Vallbram Hemchand General Library	Visnagar-384 315	1878
10.	District Library	Amreli-364 601	1880
11.	Shri G.T.M. Sarvajanik Pustagalaya	Bet Dwaraka-361 350	1883
12.	Desai and Sheth Library	Porbandar-360 575	1886
13.	Sri Fetesinrao Sarvajanik Pustagalaya	Patan-384 265	1890
14.	Shri Manibhai Sarvajanik Pustagalaya	Damnagar-364 260	1890
15.	Sayaji Vaibhav Sarvajanik Pustagalaya	Nasari-396 445	1898
16.	Shri A.S.Dahilaxmi Library	Nadial-387 002	1898

Goa

A central public library known as Publica Livaria was established by Portugese Government in 1832 at Panaji (Goa).

South India

The south and north India were also not lagging behind in the development of public libraries during the nineteenth century.

Connemara Public Library functioning from 1896, Adyar Library and Research Centre founded by Theosophical Society in 1886 and the library of Madras Literary Society established in 1812 as an auxiliary of Royal Asiatic Society are some of the well known public libraries functioning from 19th century till date in Tamil Nadu State.

In Andhra Pradesh State the following Public Libraries were founded in 19th century as mentioned in Table 2.5.

TABLE 2.5
19th Century Native General Libraries in Andhra Pradesh

Sl. No.	Name of the Library	Place	Year
1.	Public Library	Rajahmundry	1839
2.	Theosophical Society Library	Guntur	1850
3.	Sankarananda Library	Secunderabad	1872
4.	Youngmen's Improvement Society Library	Hyderabad	1879
5.	Saraswati Nilayam	Vishakapatnam	1886
6.	Bharat Gunwardhak Samstha	Hyderabad	1887
7.	Gauthami Grandhalayam	Rajahmundry	1898

(lnamdar; 1992; p. 128).

A public library named as 'Bibliotheque Publique' was established as early as 1827 at Pondicherry. In Kerala State, a few public libraries were started during the 19th century in towns such as Ernakulam (1870), Trichur (1873) and Kottayam (1882) with the active participation of the local public.

Karnataka State witnessed the heralding of public library movement through the establishment of a large number of native general libraries. The 'Sarvajanik Vachanalayas' established in Belgaum (1848), L.S. Nagarpur (1854), and Hubli (1865) are some of the good examples of the native general libraries. A number of Taluka libraries were started in Ranebennur (1873), Shirahatti (1881), Gadag (1870), Naragunda (1873), Navalagunda (1820), Kundagol (1893), Chikkodi (1866), Nippani (1875), Gikak (1865), Athani (1865), Sampageon (1866), Khanapur (1868), Soundatti (1870), Bagalkot, Basawan, Bagawadi, Bilagi, Inde, Mulebahal and Karwar (1867). In addition, Coronation Reading Rooms and Libraries were established in a number of places in Karnataka during the 19th century to commemorate the 60 years of the rule of Queen Victoria who assumed the title of Empress of Indian Empire. The public libraries still functioning at Sakleshpur and Hassan are some of the standing examples for such libraries (Asyndi; 1996, p. 126).

North India

During nineteenth century, a few public libraries were

established in different States of North India. In 1855, the first Public Library was established in Gaya by public subscription and donation. The establishment of this library commemorated the visit of Sir Frederic James Halliday, Lieutenant Governor of Bengal (Venketachalappa; 1968; p. 69). The Khuda Baksh Oriental Public Library was started in 1876 at Patna. It has a rich collection of Arabic and Persian manuscripts in addition to a large number of printed books. Presently, the management of the library has been taken over by the Government of India (Surya Rao and Babu Rao; 1994; p. 23).

Maharaja Sawai Ram Singh II took initiative in starting Maharaja's Public Library at Jaipur in 1866 by soliciting the service of Sir Frank Alexander Francis, an Assistant Librarian of the British Museum. The Bihar Hitaishi Public Library, Patna (1882), Gaya Public Library and the Government Urdu Public Library, Patna (1889) have been established in Bihar State during 19th century (Esperanza; 1996; p.148). The Punjab Public Library was established in undivided Punjab in 1884 at Lahore.

In Madhya Pradesh State, Victoria Library was established in 1887. The British Government supported the initiatives of the voluntary organisations in establishing a number of public libraries in the State. Notable among them are Prince Yashwant Library, Khargore (1858), followed by Khandwa Native Library, Khandwa (1868), Burhanpur Library (1868), Municipal District Library, Jabalpur (1885), Madhav Pusthagalaya at Gwalior (1899), Yuvaraj Public Library, Ujjain (1902), Public Library, Sagar (1909), Hamidia State Library, Bhopal (1911) and Kendriya Granthalaya, Gwalior (1928) (Tomar; 1992; pp. 46-47).

The interest of the British rulers in providing library services in Uttar Pradesh State is evident from the paragraphs as reproduced hereunder:

"In the United Provinces, the libraries for teachers were started in 1869 as per Government circular No.13-160 dated 19-04-1869 which reads as follows: With a view to encourage village and other teachers to improve themselves by private reading out of school hours, the Director of Public Instruction wishes that each Deputy Inspector should have a library of useful and interesting vernacular books to be lent to teachers to read. With the sanction of the Chief Commissioner, he, therefore, proposes to grant Rs. 50 per annum to each Deputy Inspector to purchase books and in addition authorises them to collect Re.1 per annum from each village and Rs. 2 per annum from each town school under their charge as contribution to Library Fund.

Village Teachers Committees were established to control these libraries. By one of the resolutions of these committees, the libraries were thrown open to anybody in the mofussil, who paid Re. 1 per annum, on the recommendation of a teacher. In 1869, 70 such libraries were established at Lucknow, Barabanki, Sitapur, Hardoi, Faizabad, Rai Bareli, Sultanpur and Pratapgarh" (Magnanand; 1965; p. 47).

In Uttar Pradesh State, several public libraries were started by voluntary efforts of the individuals with the support of the British Government. The most notable among them are: Allahabad Public Library (1864), Camerchial Library, Banaras (1872), Lyall Library and Reading Room, Meerut (1872), Bhartiy Bhavan Library, Allahabad (1886) and Arya Bharta Pushthagalaya, Banaras (1893). (Saxena; 1968; p.16). In the beginning of twentieth century, voluntary efforts made in Uttar Pradesh State resulted in the establishment of the following public libraries as seen below in the table.

TABLE 2.6

Early 20th Century Native General Libraries in Uttar Pradesh

Sl. No.	Name of Library	Place	Year
1.	Amir-ud-dullah Publich Library	Lucknow	1910
2.	Tilak Memorial Library	Mussourie	1920
3.	Mahatma Krishna Ram Public Library	Dehra Dun	1921
4.	Gaya Prasad Library and Reading Room	Kanpur	1921
5.	Ganga Prasad Memorial Library	Lucknow	1921

Baroda Library Movement

Maharaja Gaekward III. The library movement in India witnessed a significant development in Baroda at the dawn of the twentieth century. Maharaja Sayaji Rao Gaekward III of Baroda who came to the throne at the age of 15 in 1875 and reigned till 1939 had a vision of social development through the spread of education and public libraries. As an enlightened ruler, he formally introduced free and compulsory education in 1907 and sanctioned financial help in establishing rural libraries throughout Baroda State.

Role of W.A. Bordon. In 1910, Maharajah's scheme of a public library system for the whole State was put into operation. Any village or town which was ready to pay one third of the initial expenditure for starting a public library was granted two-thirds of the expenditure from Government funds. To coordinate and supervise the system, Maharaja brought W.A. Bordon, a leading American librarian, who had been a student of Charles Cutter and a lecturer associate of Melvil Dewey at Columbia's School of Library Economy. Bordon came to India in 1910 at the age of 57 with a good background and an experience of 23 years in library management in the Young Men's Insititute Library, Connecticut, U.S.A. The contributions of W.A. Bordon to this effect can be seen from the following paragraph :

"As Director of the newly created State Department of Libraries, Bordon planned a comprehensive network of libraries, constituting a State Central Library at Baroda, 4 District or Divisional Libraries, 45 town libraries and more than 1000 village libraries and travelling libraries—all integrated into one chain system". (Shah; 1985; p.12).

Central Library, Baroda. Nucleus of the collection of Central Library of Baroda came from the generous gift of the Maharaja himself who in 1910 donated over 20,000 volumes from his private palace library. Bordon planned a suitable building of fire proof construction with spacious reading rooms, women's library, children's library, lecture hall, library school and administrative offices for the central library.

Bordon has developed a special scheme for classification of books. He founded 'Library Miscellary', the earliest library journal in India which began publication from 1912. The first professional Library Training School in India was also started by him at Baroda. Bordon was fortunate to have a good native Assistant in Motibhai Amin who formed Mitra Mandal Libraries throughout the State. Amin was put in charge of the development of village libraries.

According to Sir V.T. Krishnamachary, the then Diwan of Baroda State, the Maharaja emphasized that, "Libraries should not limit their benefits to the few English readers but should see to it that vernacular libraries should be encouraged, so that every citizen in the State may enroll himself as a pupil in the People's University - the Library" (Philip; 1928; p.126). The Maharaja of Gaekward III deserves to be called as the pioneer of the public library movement in India since the Baroda State was the first to provide State-aided free public library services in this country.

The End of Baroda Movement. "The growth continued upto a certain stage but then stagnation developed during 1940 after the death of Sayaji Rao in 1939 as the movement is too dependent upon the personality of the Maharaja... The last blow to the Baroda Library System was the political merger of the Baroda State on May 1, 1949 into the province of Bombay which did not subscribe to the philosophy of public library service of Baroda" (Shah; 1985; p. 12).

Before Independence—Freedom Struggle

The rise of national spirit and the freedom struggle against alien rule in India contributed considerably to the development of public libraries in India. The Indian National Congress established in 1885 gave an opportunity to Indian nationals to look at themselves, their history, culture and customs with courage and conviction. By reversing the convention followed in the native general libraries in acquiring more English books, the natives procured more books in Indian languages for the newly established libraries with national spirit. Marathi Grantha Sanghralaya, Thane (1893), Mumbai Marathi Grantha Sanghralaya, Mumbai (1898), Pune Marathi Sanghralaya, Pune (1911) are some of the notable examples for such libraries established with the objectives of national spirit.

The role of national spirited youths in development of public libraries in Bengal is explained by Prof. Prabir Roy Chowdhry in the following words : "At the beginning of the twentieth century, the library movement in Bengal got special impetus from the freedom movement of our country. Hundreds of libraries were established in villages and towns, mainly at the initiatives of groups of young people. They organised these libraries with patriotic zeal. Many proscribed and revolutionary books were kept in those libraries which were secretly circulated among the youth people. Many of these libraries were frequently raided by the police forces of the imperialist power, their organisors were arrested and the books and other reading materials were taken away" (Choudhry; 1989; p.136).

The history of library movement in modern Andaman and Nicobar Islands is linked to Cellular Jail. A few talented political prisoners took an active interest in organising a library inside the Cellular Jail in 1911. More than 400 political prisoners became the active members on the library (Dutta; 1989; p. 29).

Congress Government—Fyzee Committee

An important turning point of the library movement began in 1937 when the Congress came to power in many provinces. In this stage, the government played a dominant role in setting up libraries for which there was a popular demand. The Congress Government of Bombay State, by a Government resolution dated 19 December 1939 appointed a committee under the Chairmanship of A.A.A. Fyzee, Principal, Government Law College, Bombay. The said Committee put forth a scheme of developing libraries in Bombay province in six stages:

Stage I : 1 Central Library and 3 Regional Libraries.
Stage II : 15 District Libraries in all Districts of Bombay Province.
Stage III : 167 Taluka or peta libraries and 100 Libraries in towns.
Stage IV : 979 Libraries for village of population 2,000 and more.
Stage V : 2,696 Libraries for villages of 1,000 to 2,000 population.
Stage VI : 17,753 Libraries for villages below 1,000 population.

"This was the first library development plan in India. At that period of time, the report was an ideal blueprint for a State run library system. Part of the recommendations were implemented" (Nagaraj; 1997; p. 13).

The elected Governments in various States have taken keen interest in developing libraries through various administrative measures. For example, the provincial government of Uttar Pradesh State gave as much attention to the spread of literacy as to its maintenance through a system of libraries and reading rooms in the State's programme of Adult Education. On the first Literacy Day (1938), 768 libraries and 3,600 reading rooms were opened in the rural areas. The number of libraries was increased to 1040 in 1941. Forty additional libraries were opened for women in 1941.

In addition, grants were given to about 500 private libraries in 1939 and 506 such libraries in 1940. The 250 libraries of Rural Development Department were also equipped with reading materials to facilitate the rural mass (Sohan Singh; 1957; p. 80).

The setting up of libraries through Government effort was given preference in several States. For example, in Travancore State, the State Education Department had set up 80 rural libraries in 1955 which was subsequently developed into a vigorous rural library movement in the State in future. Assam, Bihar, Bombay, Orissa, Punjab, Cochin and other provinces and States of India have set up large number of village libraries. It was estimated that in 1942, there were 13,000 village libraries in India (Sinha; 1959; p. 3).

After Independence

Public Library Acts. It has been universally accepted that library legislation guarantees the establishment, development and maintenance of public libraries in uniform manner. It ensures proper network of public libraries for the entire State. The pioneering role in library legislation was played by S.R. Ranganathan who drafted a 'Model Library Act' and presented it to the first All Asia Educational Conference held in Banaras in 1930. His draft Bill was presented for the first time in the Madras Legislature in 1933 without success. However, he succeeded in his third attempt during 1948 in independent India. When Madras Public Libraries Act, 1948 was passed thanks to the initiative of Shri Avinashilingam Chettyiar, the then Education Minister of Tamil Nadu, the Act became historic first Public Library Act in this country, as the seed for free public library movement was sown in Indian soil.

At present, 12 out of 25 States and 8 Union Territories in India have already enacted public library Acts as follows during a long time spell of fifty years, i.e., between 1948 to 1998 as reflected hereunder in Table 2.7 :

TABLE 2.7
Public Library Acts in India

Sl. No.	*Name of State*	*Year*
1.	Tamil Nadu	1948
2.	Andhra Pradesh	1960
3.	Karnataka	1965
4.	Maharashtra	1967
5.	West Bengal	1979

6.	Manipur	1988
7.	Kerala	1989
8.	Haryana	1989
9.	Mizoram	1993
10.	Goa	1993
11.	Orissa	2000
12.	Gujarat	2000

The Public Library Acts provide for the establishment of the Directorate of Public Libraries to administer the public libraries in the State; to make provision for funds either through Library Cess or Budget provision; and for the establishment and maintenance of a network of public libraries in the State such as State Central Library, District Central Library, Taluk Library, Branch Library, Village Library, etc., and to make these public libraries more user-friendly and responsive to the public need.

Further, Public Library Bills have been prepared and submitted to the State Governments for enactment in various States of India during the years mentioned below.

TABLE 2.8
Statewise Library Bills

Sl. No.	*Name of the State*	*Years*
1.	Assam	1964, 1972 and 1986
2.	Bihar	1973 and 1981
3.	Delhi	1955
4.	Himachal Pradesh	1982
5.	Jammu & Kashmir	1951 and 1975
6.	Madhya Pradesh	1946, 1950, 1958, 1959, 1968, 1970, 1978 and 1990
7.	Punjab	1980 and 1988
8.	Rajasthan	1965 and 1990
9.	Uttar Pradesh	1948, 1958, 1969, 1973, 1983 and 1993

(Kalia ; 1998; pp. 49-50).

The Role of Government of India. The Indian Union Government has been taking several measures for the development of public libraries in India. The Government of India passed the Imperial Library Act in 1948 changing the name of Imperial Library at Calcutta as the National Library of India.

The establishment of the Delhi Public Library with the assistance of UNESCO in 1951, the passing of Delivery of Books Act in 1954 as amended in 1956, establishment of Central Reference Library at Calcutta in 1955, formation of Advisory Committee for libraries under the chairmanship of K.P. Sinha in 1957, the establishment of Raja Rammohun Roy Library Foundation as a nodal agency to provide financial assistance to public libraries in 1972, formation of a committee on National Policy on Library and Information System under the Chairmanship of D.P. Chattopadhyaya in 1985 (which presented its report in May, 1986) are some of the notable actions of Government of India.

The most notable among the schemes of the Government of India is the scheme of 'Improvement of Library Service' implemented in the first three five year plans to establish State Central Libraries and District Libraries in each State. "As a result, 9 States in India established State Central Libraries and 254 District Libraries" (Thomas; 1997; p. 28).

The Role of Library Associations. The professional Library Associations formed at the national and the State levels have contributed considerably in motivating the public as well as the authorities in promoting the development of public libraries in India. A classic example is the role of Madras Library Association which played a crucial role in the enactment of Madras Public Library Act, 1948 through the Secretary of the Association, Dr. S.R. Ranganathan.

Some of the national and state level Library Associations who have had played a significant role in the development of public libraries in India are reflected in Tables 2.9 and 2.10 to make the subject more clear :

TABLE 2.9
National Level Library Associations

Sl. No.	*Year*	*Name of the Library Association*	*HQ*
1.	1919	All India Public Library Association	New Delhi
2.	1933	Indian Library Association	New Delhi
3.	1933	Association of Government Librarians and Information Scientists	New Delhi

4.	1955	Indian Association for Special Libraries and Information Centres	Kolkata
5.	1967	Indian Association for Teachers of Library and Information Science	Nagpur
6.	1975	Society for Information Science	New Delhi
7.	1980	Indian Public Library Association	Hyderabad
8.	1983	Medical Library Association of India	New Delhi

TABLE 2.10
State Level Library Associations

Sl. No.	*Year*	*Name of the Library Association*	*HQ*
1.	1910	Baroda Library Association	Baroda
2.	1919	Andhra Desa Library Association	Patamatalanka
3.	1921	Maharashtra Library Association	Mumbai
4.	1925	Bengal Library Association	Kolkata
5.	1928	Madras Library Association	Chennai
6.	1929	Punjab Library Association	Lahore
7.	1932	Bihar State Library Association	Patna
8.	1939	Assam State Library Association	Guwahati
9.	1944	Utkal Library Association, Orissa	Bhubaneswar
10.	1945	Kerala Library Association	Trivandrum
11.	1953	Gujarat Library Association	Ahmedabad
12.	1954	Delhi Library Association	Delhi
13.	1956	U.P. Library Association	Allahabad
14.	1957	M.P. Library Association	Bhopal
15.	1961	Maharashtra State Library Association	Nagpur
16.	1962	Mysore Library Association	Bangalore
17.	1962	Rajasthan Library Association	Jaipur
18.	1966	Jammu & Kashmir Library Association	Srinagar
19.	1969	Haryana Library Association	Kurukshetra
20.	1992	Tamil Nadu Library Association	Chennai

Thus, the year 1910 seems to have laid the milestone for true public library movement in India. Between 1910 and 1992, i.e., in a long time spell of 73 years, only 8 national level and 20 state level Associations have been formed to provide an effective leadership to the public library movement in the country. However, such a seven and half a decade long public library movement in India could succeed in enacting public library laws only in twelve States, leaving 23 per cent of the Indian States and U.Ts out of the ambit of the legislative support for good public library governance.

Role of Voluntary Organisations

Voluntary organisations are responsible for the establishment of large number of Public libraries in several States of India. Among them, the stellar role played by two organisations—Kerala Granthasala Sangham in Kerala State and Young Mizo Association in Mizoram State deserve special mention. However, the role of voluntary organisations in promoting public libraries in other states is very much limited compared to the role of the Associations in European countries.

The epoch-making event in the library movement in Kerala State was the convening of a conference of Kerala Granthasala Sangham in 1945 at the P.K. Memorial Library premises in Ambalapuzha. The conference resolved to develop the existing libraries and to establish new libraries in all parts of the State. P.N. Panicker was elected Secretary of the 14 Member Executive Committee and he continued in this position until the Managing Committee of the Sangham was taken over by the Control Board of the Government in 1977. During the conference, only 47 Public Libraries participated which became Members of the Sangham. The Committee Members of the Sangham under the leadership of Panicker visited every village of the State and promoted the growth of libraries in a big way.

Within a period of 32 years, the Sangham was responsible for the establishment of 4,500 libraries throughout Kerala inspiring enthusiastic voluntary workers to set up new libraries. When the Kerala Public Libraries (Kerala Granthasala Sangham) Act, 1989 was enacted, 5,239 Libraries run by Voluntary Organisations and promoted by Kerala Granthasala Sangham, were functioning in the State. Kerala Public Libraries Act itself was revolutionary in the sense that the Act does not stipulate the establishment of Government libraries but ensures development of the affiliated libraries through adequate funding collected by Library Cess and Budget allocation. (I have collected the particulars through personal visits to Kerala State and through discussions with the Library Information Science professionals).

In the State of Mizoram, situated in eastern India, Young Mizo Association has been playing a commendable role by running 341 libraries throughout the State providing Library services to the people. It should be mentioned that in the States of Kerala, Maharashtra, Gujarat, Orissa and to some extent in West Bengal, Voluntary Organisations are running most of the libraries while the role of Government libraries is supplementary in these States. From the available data, the number of libraries run by voluntary organisations in the following States are as follows:

TABLE 2.11
Number of Non-Government Libraries in Some States

Sl. No.	*Name of State*	*No. of Libraries*
1.	Andhra Pradesh	687
2.	Gujarat	7,154
3.	Kerala	5,785
4.	Maharashtra	6,138
5.	Mizoram	341
6.	Orissa	1,090

(Data collected through Questionnaires)

Growth of Libraries in India

Public libraries have been established and patronised in India since time immemorial. During the ancient and medieval period, the rulers of various princely States of India, as has been discussed earlier, have taken special interest in developing the public libraries. The Europeans settled in India joined hands with the Indians in founding large number of native general libraries in several towns of the western and eastern parts of India during the nineteenth century. Maharaja Sayajirao Gaekwad III established a network of public libraries in Baroda region during the early twentieth century. The rise of nationalism and the desire of the Indians to know more about the culture and traditions of India prompted the establishment of several public libraries with more books in Indian languages.

The Fyzee Committee Report brought out during the Congress Government in Bombay State in 1939 is a glowing example for the role of the elected Governments taking initiative in the establishment of public libraries in various States. After Independence, Public Library Acts have been enacted in 10 States leading to a comprehensive network of public libraries in the respective States.

As a result of all the developments seen so far, the public libraries have grown in large numbers. The Sinha Committee has recorded that at the end of March 1954, the country had nearly 32,000 libraries (Sinha; 1959; p. 5). UNESCO reported that over 28,000 libraries and reading rooms were in existence in 1974 in India (Campbell; 1982. p. 58). A Directory of public libraries in India brought out by Raja Rammohun Roy Library Foundation in 1986 listed 6,149 public libraries in various categories assisted by Foundation throughout India (Barua; 1986; p. 434).

In his book on Public Libraries in India, Pandey S.K. Sharma has estimated that 40,107 libraries were functioning in India in 1985 (Sharma; 1985; p. 156). As per the report of the working group on 'Libraries and Informatics' set up for the formulation of eighth Five Year Plan in India, there are 54,772 libraries in India out of which 47,684 are village libraries. (Kalia; 1988; p. 32).

D.R. Kalia states, "According to the data collected by me in July 1988, there was about 5,000 public libraries, which included (State) Central Libraries-30, Regional/Divisional Libraries-40, District Libraries-362 and City and Town Libraries-4,656. In addition, there were 50,884 village libraries" (Kalia; 1997; p. 6).

Survey of Public Libraries

I have surveyed the myriad categories of public libraries presently functioning in India through the Questionnaire circulated to the State Central Libraries of India. However, the survey could not be comprehensive due to two main factors. Firstly, only 27 State Central Libraries out of 30 units of States and U.T.s in India have returned the Questionnaires furnishing data. Secondly, some of the respondents have not properly filled-in the columns of number and category of public libraries functioning in their respective States/U.Ts.

This deficiency has been overcome by collecting the data from the secondary sources—published books and articles of the

TABLE 2.12
Public Libraries in India by Category

Sl. No.	State/Union Territory	State Central Library	Regional/ Divisional District/ Libraries	Sub Division/ Taluk/Tehsil/ Block/Circle Libraries	Municipal Town/City/ Branch Libraries	Rural/ Village/ Panchayat Libraries	Aided/ V.O. Libs	Others	Total
(1)	(2)	(3)	(4)	(5)	(6)	(7)	(8)	(9)	(10)
1.	Andaman and Nicobar Islands	1	13	—	—	—	11	8	33
2.	Andhra Pradesh	1	29	37	2,100	1,593	687	—	4,447
3.	Arunachal Pradesh	1	12	23	47	—	—	—	83
4.	Assam	1	22	16	1	204	—	4	248
5.	Bihar	1	31	465	69	4,000	—	—	4,566
6.	Chandigarh	1	—	—	6	—	—	2	09
7.	Dadra & Nagar Haveli	1	2	—	—	7	—	—	10
8.	Daman and Diu	—	—	—	2	—	—	—	02
9.	Delhi	1	1	—	35	27	—	41	105
10.	Goa	1	—	5	6	64	55	—	131
11.	Gujarat	1	19	84	582	—	6,760	254	7,700
12.	Haryana	1	12	12	26	—	—	—	51
13.	Himachal Pradesh	1	12	15	8	—	—	424	460
14.	Jammu & Kashmir	1	15	18	51	—	—	—	85
15.	Karnataka	1	37	—	449	3,668	60	—	4,215
16.	Kerala	1	14	—	—	—	5,785	—	5,800
17.	Lakshadweep	1	—	—	—	9	—	—	10
18.	Madhya Pradesh	1	49	—	109	15,800	80	6	16,045

(1)	(2)	(3)	(4)	(5)	(6)	(7)	(8)	(9)	(10)
19.	Maharashtra	1	23	—	—	—	6,584	32	6,640
20.	Manipur	1	5	—	1	—	120	—	127
21.	Meghalaya	1	4	—	—	—	—	—	05
22.	Mizoram	1	2	3	—	—	341	—	347
23.	Nagaland	1	8	—	2	—	178	—	189
24.	Orissa	1	13	4	15	—	3,500	—	3,533
25.	Pondicherry	1	3	—	70	—	—	—	74
26.	Punjab	1	11	—	90	1,045	—	—	1,147
27.	Rajasthan	1	34	9	40	2,500	—	—	2,584
28.	Sikkim	—	4	—	—	—	—	—	04
29.	Tamil Nadu	1	29	—	1,568	524	—	661	2,783
30.	Tripura	1	04	40	—	—	—	—	45
31.	Uttar Pradesh	1	59	13	69	1,500	180	—	1,822
32.	West Bengal	1	26	—	334	2,286	3,000	—	5,647
	Total	30	493	744	5,680	33,227	27,341	1,432	68,947

At the dawn of 21st century, the Chief Minister of Tamil Nadu has announced the establishment of Village Libraries in each Panchayat named as 'Ayyan Thiruvalluvan Library' in Tamil Nadu State and allocated Rs. 5,000 for each Library as per the orders of Govt. of Tamil Nadu in G.O.Ms. No. 1 (Rural).

senior library professionals in the field. Annual Reports and Status Reports of the Departments of Public Libraries of various States have also been consulted and used to update the data.

The estimates on number of public libraries in India made by Prof.D.R.Kalia (Kalia; 1998; p. 32) and Dr.V.K.Thomas (Thomas; 1997; pp. 22-66) have been used to fill up the gaps in the survey. From the survey conducted by it is assessed that the total number of public libraries in India comes to 68,947.

The Statewise and categorywise list of Public Libraries in India is provided in Table 2.12 for a comparative view.

The total number of public libraries in India, for the purpose of the present investigation, has been categorised under seven broad groups including the SCLs. While Madhya Pradesh has the largest number of public libraries (16,045), Daman and Diu has the least number of public libraries (02). Analysis by the category of public libraries shows that, out of a total of 68,974 public libraries spread over seven broad categories, State Central Libraries constitue 0.04 per cent (30); followed by Regional/Divisional/ District Libraries 0.71 per cent (493); Sub Divisional/Taluk/ Tehsil/Block/Circle Libraries 1.08 per cent (744); Municipal/ Twon/Branch/City Libraries 8.24 per cent (5680), Aided and Voluntary Organisation Libraires 39.66 per cent (27, 341); Rural/ Village public libraries 48.19 per cent (33, 227); and other categories of public libraries constitute only 2.08 per cent (1432) of the total public libraries functioning in India.

Interestingly, the strength of rural libraries 933,227) is nearly six times higher than the strength of Town/City Libraries (5680) in the Public Libraries map of the country. Suprisingly, one state and one UT, namely, Sikkim and Daman and Diu do not have State Central Libraries at their credit.

In order to provide a bird's eyeview of public libraries of India, a public library map indicating the number of public libraries functioning in various States/Union Territories of India is drawn and presented in Map. 2.1.

Genesis of State Central Libraries in India

After independence, the public libraries originated through various sources and methods have been brought into a system. A network of public libraries with State Central Libraries at the top of a pyramid followed by Regional/Divisional libraries, District

MAP 2.1
Public Library Map of India

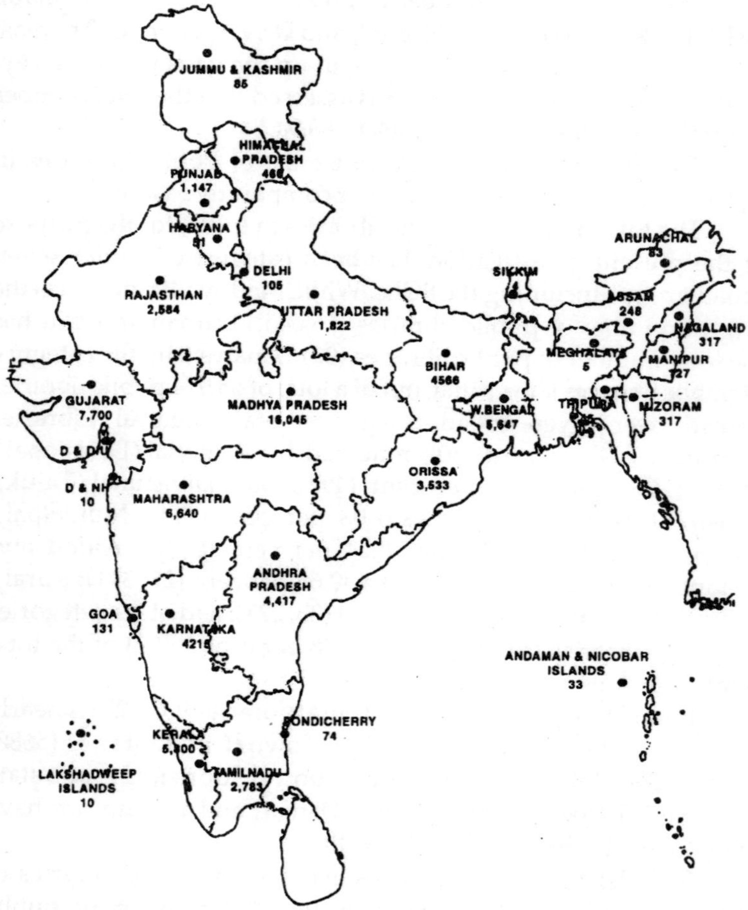

Central Libraries, Taluk Libraries, Branch Libraries, etc as the lower orders of the hierarchy with village libraries forming the base and the bottom of the pyramid has been structured either by Public Library Acts or through administrative orders. At present, 30 State Central Libraries are functioning in 24 States and 6 Union Territories of India.

The genesis of State Central Libraries in India depicts myriad patterns of State Central Library system as reflected hereunder:

(i) Recognising an existing reputed library in the State Capital as State Central Library;

(ii) Establishing new State Central Libraries as per the schemes of Government of India/States;

(iii) Starting State Central Libraries where there were no reputed libraries; and

(iv) Upgrading an existing library as State Central Library owing to reorganisation/ formation of new States.

Recognising an Existing Reputed Public Library as State Central Library

Reputed Public Libraries functioning in the State Capitals were recognised as State Central Libraries either by Public Library Acts or through executive actions.

Andhra Pradesh

Asafia Library, established in 1891 in Hyderabad was declared as the State Central Library of Andhra Pradesh as per the Hyderabad Public Libraries Act of 1955. The establishment of this library was due to the sustained efforts of Moulvi Syed Hussain Bilgrami, the then Director of Public Instruction in the Government of Hyderabad Nizam. The personal Library of this great scholar formed the initial corpus of the State Central Library. It was then known as Asafia State Library (or Kutub Khana Asafia) after the name of Asaf Jha Dynasty. Syed Tassadug Hussain, an eminent scholar of eastern languages, was appointed as Superintendent of this library. Originally, the library was intended to preserve the rare manuscripts and printed books now extinct and books on Islamic and Hindu culture and civilisation primarily for the use of research scholars and the general public. Asafia State Library was then considered as one of the best among the famous manuscript libraries in India.

Kerala

Trivandrum Public Library established in 1829 by His Highness Swathy Thirunal, Maharaja of Travancore was recognised as State Central Library of Kerala State. The task of organising the Library was entrusted to Lt. Col. Cadogan, the then British Resident in Travancore State. In those days, Trivandrum Public Library served as a Palace Library in which admission was restricted to those who were invited to attend the Durbar of His Highness, the Maharaja. During the year 1898, the Trivandrum Public Library was brought under the administrative control of the Government and the doors of the Library were thrown open to the public from 1899. From 1948, the Government of Kerala recognised the library as State Central Library.

Tamil Nadu

The Connemara Public Library, Chennai established in 1896 by the Government of Madras was designated as State Central Library of Tamil Nadu State in terms of Madras Public Library Act, 1948 and renamed as Connemara (State Central) Public Library. The nucleus of Connemara Public Library, the State Central Library of Tamil Nadu State, however, began as a small Museum Library in 1860, owing to the efforts of Captain Jesse Mitchell, the then Superintendent of the Museum of Madras.

The Library, so founded was shifted to its own building in September 1896 and named after Lord Connemara, to perpetuate his memory in recognition of his efforts for the purpose. The Library was formally opened for the public from 5th December 1896 by the then Governor, Sir Arthur Elbank Havelock, who succeeded Lord Connemara. (I have personally visited the above mentioned three State Central Libraries and collected the data through discussions with the Library Authorities and Annual Reports of the respective libraries).

Bihar

"Sachidananda Sinha Public Library established by Dr. Sachidananda Sinha, the first great journalist of Bihar in 1924 was converted to the status of the State Central (Public) Library by a Deed of Agreement between the Trustees of the Library and the Government of Bihar on November 24, 1955. Later, this Library was donated as a gift to the State of Bihar by Dr. Sachidananda Sinha" (Esperanza; 1996; p. 258).

Goa

Central Public Library at Panaji established as early as 1832 as 'Publica Livaria' by Viceroy Dom Manvel De Portugal Castro is made as State Central Library in accordance with the legislation passed in 1993. The Library was originally attached to 'Academia Militar', a military training institution. In 1836, the name of the library was changed to 'Bibliotheca Publica'. On February 15, 1897 the status of the said library was raised to that of a National Library and renamed as 'Bibliotheca Nacional de Nova-Goa'.

In March 1925, it was annexed to the academic and cultural institution 'Instituto Vasco de Gama' and redesignated as 'Bibliotheca Nacional Vasco de Gama'. By a decree of law dated, March 18, 1956 the privilege of 'Deposito Legal Portuguese Book Delivery Act' was made applicable to this library. As a result, the library received not only books published in Goa, but also from the Portugal and all other nations coming under the Portuguese Overseas Provinces.

In 1941, a spacious well-ventilated Reading Hall with wooden cupboards along the wall for shelving of books was provided to the library. From September 1959, it was detached from 'Instituto Vasco de Gama' and hence renamed as 'Bibliotheca Nacional de Goa'. Since then, the library continues to be the State Central Library of Goa.

Records indicate that as early as 1833, the library was kept open to the public upto 10.00 p.m. A printed author catalogue was published in 1920 and a card catalogue, with author and title access, was made available towards the end of 1930's (Rodriques; 1996; p. 271).

Karnataka

The Bangalore Public Library popularly known as Sir Seshadri Iyer Memorial Library, established in 1915, was designated as the State Central Library of Karnataka State on 5th December 1966 (as per Karnataka Public Libraries Act, 1965). The library is housed in a beautiful building of its own in Cubbon Park, Bangalore. The building was constructed in 1876 through the efforts of Col. Richard Meade, the British Commissioner of the princely State of Mysore. Many Government Offices of Mysore State were housed in this building including the Athara Khacheri

(Secretariat). When the Bangalore Public Library was established in 1915, the Seshadri Iyer Memorial Hall was converted as the library building. The library was rechristened as State Central Reference Library in 1966 *(Ijari and Khan; 1996;* p. *295).*

Pondicherry

'Bibliotheque Publique' (Public Library), established in 1827 by Eugine Desbeissys de Richmont, the then Governor of Pondicherry was renamed as Romain Rolland Library during the birth centenary of the great French scholar Romain Rolland in 1966 and declared as State Central Library of Pondicherry by an administrative order (Sounderrajan; 1996; p. 302).

Establishing New State Central Libraries as per the Government of India Schemes

In the first and second Five Year Plans, the Government of India have formulated Central Schemes called as *Promotion of Arts and Culture and setting up of Public Libraries in States* and *Integrated Library Services.*

It has been the primary objective of the schemes to establish Integrated Public Library System in every State constituting a pyramidical structure with Village Libraries at the base and the State Central Library at the apex of the system.

Under these schemes, new State Central Libraries were started in the States/Union Territories where there were no State Central Libraries. By utilising the Plan assistance under the schemes, new State Central Libraries were established in Allahabad (1949), Chandigarh (1955), Kolkata (1956), Jaipur (1956) and Bhubaneswar (1967) respectively in the States/Union Territories of Uttar Pradesh, Chandigarh, West Bengal, Rajasthan and Orissa.

Starting State Central Libraries in the States where there was no Reputed Library

State Central Libraries were started in the States where there were no reputed Public Libraries fit to be declared as State Central Libraries.

Delhi

In Delhi Union Territory, the Delhi Public Library was started by the Government of India in 1951 as a Pilot Project of UNESCO to serve as a model for public libraries in South East Asia.

Gujarat

In Gujarat State, a State Central Library was established in the newly formed capital city Gandhinagar in 1982.

Upgrading an Existing Library as State Central Library Owing to Reorganisation/Formation of New States

When a new State was created through reorganisation of States or formation of new States by bifurcation or due to elevation of a Union Territory as an independent State, the District Library or any other reputed Library functioning in the State Capital is upgraded as State Central Library.

Andaman and Nicobar Islands

In the Union Territory of Andaman and Nicobar Islands, the Hindi Library at Port Blair established in 1959 under the National Language Teaching Scheme was converted into a District Library which was later upgraded as State (Central) Library in 1974 (Dutta; 1989; p. 29).

Arunachal Pradesh

Owing to the creation of Arunachal Pradesh State by upgrading the Union Territory of North Eastern Frontier Agency (NEFA) in 1987, the Secretariat Library of NEFA situated in Shillong was shifted to the new capital Itanagar and developed as State Central Library (Adhikari; 1989; p. 161).

Assam

Due to the creation of Meghalaya State in 1972 by bifurcating Assam State, the existing State Central Library of Assam at Shillong has been transferred to Meghalaya State. Hence, the District Library of Guwahati was upgraded as State Central Library.

Haryana

When the State of Haryana was carved out of the erstwhile State of Punjab during 1966, the newly formed State of Haryana has upgraded the District Library of Ambala as the State Central Library of Haryana in 1967.

Manipur

Manipur District Library, established in 1958 has been elevated to the status of State Central Library when the Union Territory was promoted as a State.

Origins of State Central Libraries

From the Questionnaires collected from the 27 State Central Libraries of India, the year of origin of the State Central Libraries can be arranged in the following order:

TABLE 2.13

Ranking of State Central Libraries in Chronological Order

Ranking	*Year of Origin*	*Place of Functioning*	*State / U.T.*
1.	1827	Pondicherry	Pondicherry
2.	1829	Trivandrum	Kerala
3.	1832	Panaji	Goa
4.	1891	Hyderabad	Andhra Pradesh
5.	1896	Chennai	Tamil Nadu
6.	1915	Bangalore	Karnataka
7.	1924	Patna	Bihar
8.	1949	Allahabad	Uttar Pradesh
9.	1951	Delhi	Delhi
10.	1954	Guwahati	Assam
11.	1955	Bhopal	Madhya Pradesh
12.	1955	Chandigarh	Chandigarh
13.	1956	Calcutta	West Bengal
14.	1956	Itanagar	Arunachal Pradesh
15.	1956	Jaipur	Rajasthan
16.	1956	Patiala	Punjab
17.	1957	Ambala	Haryana
18.	1958	Kavaratti	Lakshadweep
19.	1958	Imphal	Manipur
20.	1958	Shillong	Meghalaya
21.	1959	Solan	Himachal Pradesh
22.	1959	Port Blair	Andaman and Nicobar Islands
23.	1967	Bhubaneswar	Orissa
24.	1981	Kohima	Nagaland
25.	1982	Gandhinagar	Gujarat
26.	1984	Aizwal	Mizoram
27.	1994	Mumbai	Maharashtra

Table 2.13 clearly indicates that, the emergence of 27 State Central Libraries took a long history of 67 years beginning from 1827 through 1994. Surprisingly, Pondicherry being a tiny State-alike became the first Union Territory (though not having statehood) to realise the concept of a State Central Library in its

soil. All these State Central Libraries owe their existence to the public libraries of some kind, have come up amidst a mixed kit of political and social environment different from each other.

Role of State Central Libraries

The State Central Library, as the apex library of a State, can play a crucial role in several non-library activities such as the promotion of literacy, developing the reading habits among the people and in preserving the State's tradition and cultural heritage which may ultimately lead to the increased use of public libraries in the State.

Promotion of Literacy

Illiteracy is a major barrier for the effective use of library by all the people. The Central and State Governments are giving considerable priority for the removal of illiteracy which stands at 34.62 per cent (*Manorama Yearbook,* 2002; p. 273). The usage of public libraries shall definitely increase manifold if the literacy level increases. Hence, the State Central Libraries should take a lead in the promotion of literacy among the people.

Promotion of literacy should be predominant in the activities of the State Central Libraries. This activity can be effectively performed by the State Central Library by way of motivating the Librarians of grassroot libraries such as Branch Libraries, Village Libraries, etc., to take part in literacy missions.

The Questionnaires collected from 27 State Central Libraries of India reveal that atleast 7 State Central Libraries at Andaman & Nicobar Islands, Andhra Pradesh, Gujarat, Himachal Pradesh, Lakshadweep, Madhya Pradesh and Punjab have engaged themselves in adult education and promotion of literacy in the respective States/U.Ts.

Developing the Reading Habit

Even among the literate population, the reading habit is dwindling due to various factors such as invasion of television in the drawing room of every household, the inability of the individuals to allocate sufficient time for reading, the absence of motivation for reading, etc. Hence, the State Central Library can play a positive role in inculcating the reading habit among the literate population of the State by adopting various methods.

The reading habit can be easily cultivated right from the school days among the young ones. The school drop-outs can also be pursuaded to continue their reading habit by enrolling them in the public libraries of the State. Reading competitions can be arranged and prizes awarded for those who evince keen interest in reading.

If the reading habit is gradually developed among the potential users of the libraries, the public libraries in the States shall have the optimum utilisation of library resources which should be one of the vital aims and objectives of the State Central Library.

Preserving the Cultural Heritage of the State

Every State is unique in some way. The general public living in a State shall normally feel proud in preserving their customs, traditions, cultural heritage, etc. The State Central Library being the apex library of the State can play a vital role in preserving the cultural heritage of the State. For this purpose, the State Central Library can develop a special collection of books on the customs, traditions and cultural heritages of the State. The State Central Library can acquire all relevant books on the cultural tradition of the State published in and outside the State in any language.

It may also conduct exhibitions and competitions on the myriad cultural aspects of the State. A special State Bibliography or Compendium on the literature available in the State Central Library relating to the cultural heritage of the State can be brought out to stimulate further reading on the subject.

In these ways, the State Central Libraries have a definite role in promoting the literacy, inculcating the reading habits among the people and in preserving the cultural heritage of the State.

As per the information furnished by the Librarians of the State Central Libraries in the Questionnaire collected by me the State Central Libraries of nine States/U.Ts of Andaman and Nicobar Islands, Arunachal Pradesh, Bihar, Goa, Himachal Pradesh, Lakshadweep, Maghalaya, Orissa and Pondicherry have been maintaining special collections of books in their libraries which reflect the cultural heritage and local traditions of the respective States/Union Territories.

Role of Various Agencies

The Role of State Government. The State Central Libraries are usually funded and managed by the respective State Governments as per the provisions of the Public Library Acts. In the States where there are no Public Library Acts, it becomes the responsibility of the State Governments to maintain the State Central Libraries which function as a separate unit in some States.

In majority of the States, the State Central Library is an integral part of the Department of Public Libraries or Department of Education/Art and Culture of the State. In both the cases, the State Central Libraries are under the control of the State governments of the respective State.

Hence, it is the primary responsibility of the State Governments to administer the State Central Libraries. The State Governments have a larger role in properly directing the State Central Libraries to perform the duty of the apex library of the State in evolving a uniform pattern of providing Public Library services. If the State Central Libraries are not performing the expected functions of the apex library, the responsibility for such lapses should squarely lie on the State Governments which are the controlling authorities of the State Central Libraries.

The Role of Central Government and Raja Rammohun Roy Library Foundation (RRRLF)

The Central Government has directly established only one State Central Library in India, i.e., Delhi Union Territory in view of its special status as National Capital Territory of India. In 1951, the Government of India started Delhi Public Library in collaboration with UNESCO as a pilot project which has since been developed into 1 Central Library, 1 Zonal Library, 55 Branch and Community Libraries, 1 Braille Library, 32 Resettlement Colony Libraries, 3 Sports Complex Libraries, 2 Hospital Libraries, 1 Prisoner's Library and a network of mobile serving stations covering 70 areas and 22 deposit stations in the capital city of India (India; 1998; p.102) .

Raja Rammohun Roy Library Foundation (RRRLF), established as an autonomous body in 1972 at Calcutta, is the funding body and the nodal agency for the Government of India for implementation of the various schemes of the Central

Government in the field of public libraries. Since the subject of 'Libraries' is placed in the State List as per the Constitution of India, Raja Rammohun Roy Library Foundation or the central Government cannot establish or manage public libraries in any State/U.T. Under the circumstances, the Raja Rammohun Roy Library Foundation can play only a catalytic role in developing the State Central Libraries from the outside.

Since 1972, Raja Rammohun Roy Library Foundation has been regularly supplying large number of books at free of cost to all the State Central Libraries of India under the 'Central Book Selection Scheme' of Raja Rammohun Roy Library Foundation. In order to cope up with the modern technological advancement, Raja Rammohun Roy Library Foundation is proposing a scheme for computerisation and networking of all State Central Libraries of India (RRRLF; 1997; p. 2).

The Role of Voluntary Agencies

The voluntary agencies are non-government organisations which are not run for the profit of any individual or group of individuals. In many spheres of human activities, for example, health, education, etc., voluntary agencies are playing a dominant role in India. However, as far as State Central Libraries are concerned, the role of voluntary agencies is felt only in Bihar and Maharashtra.

The State Central Library of Bihar State at Patna was developed by the Trustees of Sachidananda Sinha Library and later the library was donated as a gift to the State of Bihar for converting as a State Central Public Library by a Deed of Agreement between the Trustees of the Library and the Government of Bihar on November 24, 1955 (Esperanza; 1996; p. 258).

The second instance is related to the State Central Library of Maharashtra State at Mumbai. The present State Central Library at Mumbai was established by the State Government very recently in the year 1994. However, since the enactment of Maharashtra Public Library Act in 1967, till the establishment of State Government funded State Central Library in 1994, the Library of Asiatic Society of Bombay established in 1804 functioned as the State Central Library of Maharashtra. The Society has managed the Central Library of Maharashtra State from 1967 until the State

Central Library was separately established by the Government of Maharashtra in the year 1994.

Organisational Structure of State Central Libraries

An analysis of the organisational structure prevailing in the State Central Libraries of India, as seen from the Questionnaires collected, depict different patterns. However, the typical structure prevalent in most of the State Central Libraries begin from the Director of the Controlling Department at the top, followed by the Chief Librarian/Director of the State Central Library leading to the Deputy Librarian, Assistant Librarian, Library Assistant/ Clerk, in the hierarchical order ending with the Library Attendant/ Binder/Xerox Operator at the bottom of the organisational structure of the existing State Central Libraries in India.

CHART 2.1

Organisational Structure of the Existing SCLs in India

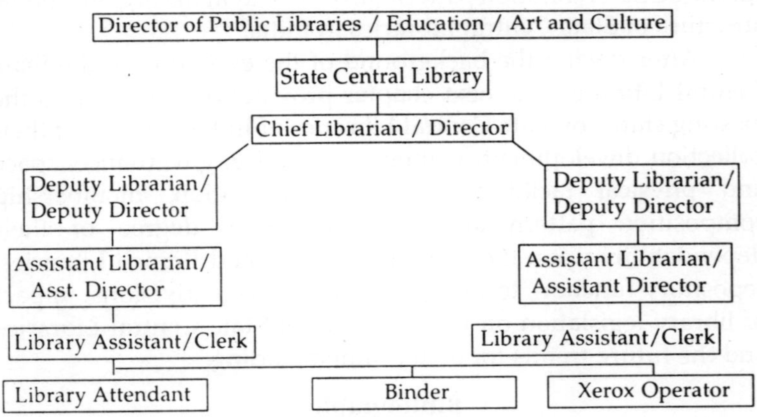

(Collected from the filled - in Questionnaires).

Conclusion

The existence of libraries in India dates back to Indus Valley Civilization. The ancient, medieval and modern rulers have consciously developed public libraries in India. During the colonial rule, the Europeans settled in India played a commendable role in establishing native general libraries by coordinating with Indian natives. While Baroda Maharaja's rule, Fyzee Committee Report, and freedom struggle made a commandable contribution for the development of libraries during pre-independence period, the Public Library Acts, Central Government, State Government, Professional Library Associations and Voluntary Organisations are responsible for the proliferation of public libraries during the post-independence period. It is estimated that there are over 68,947 public libraries functioning in India at present.

The State Central Libraries have been established in 24 States and 6 Union Territories either by recognising a reputed public library in the State capital or by establishing a new one or by upgrading a District Library into a State Central Library. The State Central Libraries can play an important role in literacy movement, developing the reading habits among the people and in preserving the traditions and cultural heritage of the States. The State Governments are largely responsible for the establishment and maintenance of State Central Libraries whereas the Central Government, RRRLF and voluntary agencies are also contributing for the SCLs. A common pattern can be found in the organisational structure of State Central Libraries in India.

After tracing the background of the evolution of the State Central Libraries, the next chapter provides an insight into the existing status of State Central Libraries of India in terms of their collection development, manpower, finance, governance, space and physical facilities, areas of automation, membership composition pattern and its domination, degree of their dependability upon the National, District and Branch Libraries, repository function, technical status, language divisions, impact of library legislation on the life-styles of State Central Libraries and the future trends for better understanding.

Bibliography

1. Adhikari, A.K. Library Movement in Arunachal Pradesh. In Saha, Ramakrishna, *ed. Library Movement in India.* 1989. Bengal Library Association; Calcutta, pp. 135-48.
2. Asundi, A.Y. Library Scene in Karnataka :Nineteenth Century and Earlier. *In* Gupta, B.M., *ed. Handbook of Libraries, Archieves and Information Centres in India.* V. 16. Library Development in India, 1996. Segment Books; New Delhi, pp. 119-28.
3. Baba, Abdul Majid. Library Movement in Jammu and Kashmir: Problems and Prospects. *Souvenir of All India*

Library Conference, 39th, Bangalore. 1994, Indian Library Association; Delhi, pp. 144-49.

4. Barua, B.P. *Directory of Public Libraries*, 1986. Naya Prakash; Kolkata, p. 520.
5. Barua, B.P. Rural Library Services in India. *In* George, K.M., *ed. Indian Libraries: Trends and Perspectives.* 1985. Orient Longman; Hyderabad, pp. 163-78.
6. Barua, Dilip Kumar. Libraries in Aparanta. *Herald of Library Science.* April-July 1977, Vol. 16, No. 23, p. 191.
7. Bhattacharya, G. West Bengal. *In* Ranganath, S.R. etc., *Ed. Free Book Service for All: An International Survey.* 1968. Mysore Library Association; Mysore, p. 172.
8. Buragohain, Alaka. Library Situation in the State of Assam: A Status Report. *In* Saha, Ramakrishna, *ed. Library Movement in India.*, 1989. Bengal Library Association; Calcutta, p. 39.
9. Campbell, H.C. *Developing Public Library Systems and Services.* Unesco; Paris, p. 186.
10. Choudhary, Prabhir Roy. Public Library Development in West Bengal: A Review. *In* Saha, Ramakrishna, *ed. Library Movement in India,* 1989, Bengal Library Association; Calcuta, pp. 135-48.
11. Dutta, Ajit Kumar. Andaman and Nicobar Islands: Marching towards Modernised Public Library Movement in India. *In* Saha, Ramakrishna, *ed. Library Movement in India.* 1989. Bengal Library Association; Calcutta, pp. 29-30.
12. Esperanza, A.C., The State Central Library, Patna. *In* Gupta, B.M., *ed. Handbook of Libraries, Archieves and Information centres in India.* Vol. 16. Library Development in India, 1996. Segment Books; New Delhi, pp. 258-70.
13. Giridhari Singh, N. Development of Libraries in Manipur. *In* Saha, Ramakrishna, *ed. Library Movement in India,* 1989. Bengal Library Association; Kolkata, p. 95.
14. Ijari, S.R. Library Movement in Karnataka; *In* Gupta, B.M., *ed. Handbook of Libraries, Archives and Information Centres in India.* Vol. 16. Library Development in India, 1996. Segment Books; New Delhi, pp. 174-208.
15. Ijari, S.R. and Khan, H.A. State Central Reference Library, Karnataka. *In* Gupta, B.M., *ed. Handbook of Libraries, Archieves and Information Centres in India.* V. 16. Library Development in India, 1996. Segment Books; New Delhi, pp. 293-301.

16. Inamdar, N.B. Development of Public Libraries in Andhra Pradesh. *Granthana: Indian Journal of Library Studies,* July 1992. Vol. III. No. 2. pp. 115-28.
17. Inamdar, N.B. and Shakira, A.W. Management of Libraries in the State of Hyderabad: An overview. *In* Gupta B.M., *ed. Handbook of Libraries, Archieves and Information Centres in India.* Vol. 16. Library Development in India. 1996. Segment Books; New Delhi, p. 89.
18. India. Research, Reference and Training Division. India 2002: A Reference Annual. 2002. Publication Division; New Delhi, p. 102.
19. Kalia, D.R. Public Libraries. *In* Jain, M.K, *ed. 50 years Library and Information Services in India,* 1998, Shipra Publications; New Delhi, pp. 19-30, 32.
20. Kalia, D.R. *Report of the Sub-Group on Public Library System of the Working Group on Libraries and Informatics,* 1988, Planning Commission. New Delhi.
21. Kalia, D.R. Scenario of Public Libraries in the 21st Century in the Global and Indian Context. Paper presented at the National Seminar on 'Public Library Scenario in 21st Century' conducted by Raja Rammohun Roy Library Foundation during 22-23, May 1997 at Kolkata. (unpublished).
22. Karisidappa and Kumbar. Library Development in India. In Gupta, B.M., ed. *Handover of Libraries, Achives and Information Centres in India.* Vol. 16. Library Development in India, 1966, Segment Books; New Delhi, pp. 200-7.
23. Kaula, P.N. Libraries in India. *Herald of Library Science.* Vol. 16. No. 2-3, Apr-June 1977, p. 165.
24. Maganand. Growth of Public Libraries in Uttar Pradesh. *In* Sen, N.B., *ed. Development of Libraries in New India,* 1965, New Book Society of India; New Delhi, pp. 47-61.
25. Manorama Year Book, 2002, Malayala Manorama Press; Kottayam, p. 272.
26. Mookerjee, Subodh Kumar and Sengupta, Benoyendra. *Library Organisation and Administration,* 1977, The Worldpress; Kolkata, pp. 23-46.
27. Nagaraj, M.N. Milestones in the path of Library Service of India. Paper presented during the National Seminar or

"Scenario of Public Libraries in 21st Century" held at during May 22-24. 1997; Kolkata pp. 1-33 (unpublished).

28. Philip, Sergeant W. *The Ruler of Baroda: an account of the life and work of the Maharaja Gaekwad,* 1928, J. Murray; London, p. 126.
29. Raja Rammohun Roy Library Foundation. *RRRLF Newsletter.* XVII (2) April 1997, p. 2.
30. Raman Nair. Public Library Systems in Ancient South India. *In* Gupta, B.M., *ed. Handbook of Libraries, Archieves and Information Centres in India.* Vol. 16. Library Development in India, 1996, Segment Books; New Delhi, p. 131.
31. Rodriques, Pia De Menezes. Goa State Central Library: past, present and future. *In* Gupta, B.M., *ed. Handbook of Libraries, Archieves and Information Centres in India.* Vol. 16. Library Development in India, 1996, Segment Books; New Delhi, p. 271.
32. Saxena, R.S. Uttar Pradesh. *In* Ranganathan. *ed. Free Book Service for all: An International Survey,* 1968, Asia Publishing House; Bombay, pp. 163-71.
33. Shah, P.R. The Genesis of Public Library Movement in Baroda and Sir Sayaji Rao Gaekwad-The genius. *Souvenir of the platinum Jubilee of Central Library-Baroda and All India Library Conference,* 31st, Baroda, 1-4 November 1988. Government of Gujarat; Baroda, pp. 10-13.
34. Sharma, Narendra. Library Developments in Rajasthan, *In* Gupta, B.M., *ed. Handbook of Libraries, Archieves and Information Centres in India.* Vol. 16. Library Development in India, 1996, Segment Books; New Delhi, pp. 226-27.
35. Sharma, O.P. Literature of the history of Library movement in India. *Herald of Library Science.* Vol. 6; No. 1. January 1968, p. 9.
36. Sharma, Pandey S.K. *Public Libraries in India,* 1985, Ess Ess Publication; New Delhi, pp. 15-61.
37. Sinha, K.P. Report of Advisory Committee for Libraries, 1959. Government of India, Ministry of Education; New Delhi, pp. 1-115.
38. Sohan Singh. *History of Adult Education during British Period.* 1957. Indian Adult Education Association; Delhi, p. 80.
39. Sounderrajan, K. Romain Rolland Library, Pondicherry. *In* Gupta, B.M., *ed. Handbook of Libraries, Archieves and*

Information Centres in India. Vol. 16. Library Development in India, 1996, Segment Books; New Delhi, pp. 302-6.

40. Singh Sukhdev. History of Library Movement in Punjab. *In* Gupta, B.M., *ed. Handbook of Libraries, Archieves and Information Centres in India.* Vol. 16. Library Development in India, 1996.Segment Books; New Delhi, p. 205.
41. Surya Rao, G., and Babu Rao, C. Library Movement in India: A historical perspective. *In* Vashisth, C. *ed. Library Movement and Library Development in India*, 1994. Indian Library Association; Delhi, p. 23-31.
42. Thomas, V.K. *Public Libraries in India; Development and Finance.* Vikas Publishing House, 1997; New Delhi, pp. 22-66.
43. Tomar, Surendra Singh. Public Library System in Madhya Pradesh. *Library Herald.* Apr-Sep 1992. Vol. 31. No. 1-2. pp. 45-51.
44. Trehan, G.L. *Modern Public Library: Movement and Services in India.* 1982. Library Literature House; Chandigarh, p. 6.
45. Venkatachalappa, M. Bihar. *In* Ranganathan, S.R. etc., *ed. Free Book Service for All: An International Survey*, 1968. Mysore Library Association; Mysore, p. 69.
46. Venkatappaiah, V. Andhra Pradesh. In Ragana, R. etc. *Free Book Service for all: An International Survey,* 1968. Mysore Library Association; Mysore, p. 52.
47. Venkatappaiah, Velaga. Public Library Movement before Independence in Andhra Pradesh. *In* Gupta, B.M., *ed. Handbook of Libraries, Archieves and Information Centres in India.* Vol. 16. Library Development in India, 1996, Segment Books; New Delhi, pp. 138-45.
48. Wadikar, A.L. Library Service in Madhya Pradesh. *In* Saha, Ramakrishna, *ed. Library Movement in India,* 1989, Bengal Library Association; Calcutta, p. 84.

3

The Existing Status of State Central Libraries in India

Introduction

After tracing the background of the evolution of public libraries in India in general and the State Central Libraries in India in particular, the present chapter depicts the existing status of SCLs in India. The current conditions of SCLs in terms of their collection development, manpower, finance, governance, space and building, physical conditions, areas of automation, membership composition pattern and its domination are analysed in this Chapter. Further, the influence of SCLs on other categories of libraries such as National Library, District Library and Branch Libraries have also been probed. The repository function of the SCLs, their technical status, language divisions, etc. have been explained and the future trends of the SCLs are sensibly predicted.

Collection Development

Nature of Collection. The collection development, storage, and dissemination of reading materials are the three most important functions of a library. Among the three, collection development occupies the pivotal position. A library cannot serve its clientele properly without a strong and balanced collection. The efficiency and effectiveness of a library depends largely on the quantity and quality of its collection. Mere numerical value of the collection is not the decisive factor.

In a public library, collection development should be undertaken as per the needs and requirements of its users. To meet the information needs of its clientele, the public library has to cover the whole gamut of Universe of knowledge. The clientele of a public library vary from a neo-literate to a doctoral scholar, from

TABLE 3.1
State of Collection—Book Materials

Sl. No.	Name of State/U.T.	Books	Reference	Back Volumes	Reports of Commissions	Reprints	Patents/ Standards	Current Journals	Newspaper Subscribed	Total Collection	Rank
(1)	(2)	(3)	(4)	(5)	(6)	(7)	(8)	(9)	(10)	(11)	(12)
1.	Andaman & Nicobar Islands	69,825	5,450	—	45	—	—	—	28	75,320	19
2.	Andhra Pradesh	3,97,113	—	4,500	—	—	—	287	44	4,01,613	4
3.	Arunachal Pradesh	26,393	2,300	—	25	—	10	—	13	28,728	26
4.	Assam	77,317	—	1,050	—	—	—	51	24	78,367	18
5.	Bihar	1,45,454	—	—	—	—	—	41	—	1,45,454	10
6.	Chandigarh	1,34,999	501	4,000	—	—	—	100	20	1,40,000	11
7.	Delhi	14,80,175	—	—	500	—	—	400	34	14,80,675	1
8.	Goa	1,40,000	—	—	—	—	—	—	—	1,40,000	12
9.	Gujarat	39,016	40,237	—	—	—	—	35	26	79,253	17
10.	Haryana	47,675	10,000	—	—	—	—	20	11	57,675	22
11.	Himachal Pradesh	87,808	2,142	1,674	—	—	—	16	28	91,648	16
12.	Karnataka	2,15,148	25,000	—	24	—	—	216	—	2,40,172	7
13.	Kerala	2,47,794	—	9,000	—	—	—	472	29	2,56,794	6

(*Contd.*)

(1)	(2)	(3)	(4)	(5)	(6)	(7)	(8)	(9)	(10)	(11)	(12)
14.	Lakshadweep	30,000	—	—	—	—	—	—	12	30,000	25
15.	Madhya Pradesh	62,507	—	—	—	—	—	—	—	62,507	21
16.	Maharashtra	6,55,425	4,381	50,000	—	—	—	5,922	—	7,09,806	2
17.	Manipur	1,24,638	—	500	—	—	—	85	27	1,25,138	13
18.	Meghalaya	1,70,000	—	—	—	—	—	75	25	1,70,000	9
19.	Mizoram	17,000	—	—	—	—	—	50	18	17,000	27
20.	Nagaland	39,000	—	—	—	—	—	—	—	39,000	23
21.	Orissa	2,00,000	—	—	—	—	—	82	18	2,00,100	8
22.	Pondicherry	2,72,867	18,170	850	—	—	—	128	20	2,91,887	5
23.	Punjab	1,09,837	7,000	—	50	—	—	115	18	1,16,887	14
24.	Rajasthan	35,488	—	—	—	—	—	05	11	35,504	24
25.	Tamil Nadu	4,00,000	30,000	40,000	1,000	50,000	1,000	3,000	06	5,25,000	3
26.	Uttar Pradesh	62,650	—	—	—	—	—	—	15	62,650	20
27.	West Bengal	1,00,000	500	4,350	100	—	50	138	14	1,05,152	15
	Total	54,65,109	1,45,681	1,15,924	1,744	50,000	1,060	10,493	413	57,06,314	

a layman to a lawyer and from a small child to an aging senior citizen. The collection development policy of a public library should be motivated to acquire relevant reading materials such as printed books, rare manuscripts, periodicals, government publications, newspapers, pamphlets, microdocuments, digital documents and any other relevant materials required to satisfy the needs of its users.

Carnousky defines collection development as, "the effective and timely selection of library materials forming carefully constructed areas and subject collection shaped overtime by bibliographic experts. It is the synopsis, linking thousands of decisions into sensitive provision of needed research materials, the capacity to make the parts fit the needed whole" (Carnousky; 1953; p. 463).

Collection of Books in SCLs of India. The number and categories of book materials available in State Central Libraries of India are furnished in Table 3.1.

Thus, at the collection front, 27 out of 30 SCLs in India, possess a total bookstock of 54,65,109 volumes; followed by 1,45,681 reference tools; 1,1[illegible]24 back volumes; 1,744 commission reports; 50,000 reprints; 1060 patents and standards; 10,493 current journals; and subscribes to 413 titles of newspapers.

From the table, it can be assessed that the total number of collection of SCLs ranges from 17,000 at Mizoram to 14,80,675 at Delhi. From among the various categories of book materials collected in SCLs, reference tools are stored in 12 libraries, back volumes have been added in 10 libraries, reports of commissions and committees are kept in 7 libraries, patents/standards are available in 3 libraries and only 1 library has a separate collection of reprints.

The descending order of number of books stocked in SCLs of various States/U.Ts proceeds as follows : (1) Delhi (14,80,675), (2) Maharashtra (7,09,806), (3) Tamil Nadu (5,25,000), (4) Andhra Pradesh (4,01,613), (5) Pondicherry (2,91,887), (6) Kerala (2,56,794), (7) Karnataka (2,40,172), (8) Orissa (2,00,000), (9) Meghalaya (1,70,000), (10) Bihar (1,45,454), (11) Chandigarh (1,40,000), (12) Goa (1,40,000), (13) Manipur (1,25,138), (14) Punjab (1,16,887), (15) West Bengal (1,05,152), (16) Himachal

Pradesh (91,648), (17) Gujarat (79,253), (18) Assam (78,367), (19) Andaman and Nicobar Islands (75,320), (20) Uttar Pradesh (62,650), (21) Madhya Pradesh (62,507), (22) Haryana (57,675), (23) Nagaland (39,000), (24) Rajasthan (35,488), (25), Lakshadweep (30,000), (26) Arunachal Pradesh (28,728) and (27) Mizoram (17,000).

The higher growth of collection for the first three ranked SCLs in the list can be partly attributed to their status as the recipient libraries under the provisions of the Delivery of Books Act, 1954.

Journals

The number of current Journals received in State Central Libraries of India varies from 05 at Rajasthan to 5,922 at Maharashtra State. Regarding the newspapers subscribed, Andhra Pradesh subscribes to a larger number of 44 titles whereas Tamil Nadu SCL subscribes only 06 newspapers.

Annual Growth of Book Collection. An attempt has been made to study the annual growth of collection of books in SCLs of India which is tabulated in Table 3.2.

Table 3.2 indicates the total books added in a year on purchase or received as gifts or on exchange basis or as per the provisions of the Delivery of Books Act, 1954 or under the benefit of the Press and Registration of Books Act, 1867. The annual growth rate is compared with the total collection, based on which the percentage of growth is arrived.

In all, 99,597 books were added on purchase ; 17,399 volumes were received as gifts or complimentary copies; 225 volumes were collected on exchange basis; 55,089 volumes were received as per the Delivery of Books Act, 1954 and the Press and Registration of Books Act, 1867 thereby adding to a total number of 1,77,898 books in a year in all the SCLs put together.

The percentage of annual collections compared with the total collections of SCLs of all States/U.Ts works out to 3.12 per cent. The top 10 SCLs where the percentage of annual growth of collection is higher is listed in Table 3.3.

TABLE 3.2
Annual Growth of Collection of State Central Libraries

Sl. No.	Name of State/U.T.	Vols recd on Purchased	Vols recd as Gifts	Vols recd on Exchange	Vols recd on DB Act/ RB Act	Total books added	Total Collection	Percentage of Growth	Rank
1.	Andaman & Nicobar Islands	2,000	500	—	—	2,500	75,320	3.32%	7
2.	Andhra Pradesh	2,500	1,800	—	1,200	5,500	4,01,613	1.38%	18
3.	Arunachal Pradesh	131	649	—	—	780	28,728	2.79%	12
4.	Assam	600	150	—	—	750	78,367	0.96%	22
5.	Bihar	160	1,564	—	—	1,724	1,45,454	1.19%	20
6.	Chandigarh	4,000	400	—	—	4,400	1,40,000	3.14%	8
7.	Delhi	56,000	4,000	—	15,000	75,000	14,80,675	5.07%	2
8.	Goa	2,000	600	200	66	2,866	1,40,000	2.07%	16
9.	Gujarat	1,100	300	25	1,315	2,740	79,253	3.46%	5
10.	Haryana	75	600	—	—	675	57,675	1.17%	21
11.	Himachal Pradesh	650	500	—	—	1,150	91,648	1.25%	19
12.	Karnataka	2,000	150	—	14,408	16,558	2,40,172	6.89%	1
13.	Kerala	3,500	2,000	—	—	5,500	2,56,794	2.14%	14
14.	Lakshadweep	1,000	10	—	—	1,010	30,000	3.37%	6

(Contd.)

15.	Madhya Pradesh	—	—	—	—	—	62,507	—	—
16.	Maharashtra	4,381	2,094	—	13,800	20,275	7,09,806	2.86%	10
17.	Manipur	200	350	—	—	550	1,25,138	0.44%	23
18.	Meghalaya	4,500	300	—	—	4,800	1,70,000	2.82%	11
19.	Mizoram	100	550	—	—	650	17,000	3.82%	3
20.	Nagaland	—	—	—	—	—	39,000	—	—
21.	Orissa	5,000	2,000	—	300	7,300	2,00,000	3.65%	4
22.	Pondicherry	6,000	700	—	—	6,700	2,91,887	2.30%	13
23.	Punjab	200	1,800	—	—	2,000	1,16,887	1.71%	17
24.	Rajasthan	—	—	—	—	—	35,488	—	—
25.	Tamilnadu	3,000	1,200	—	7,000	11,200	5,25,000	2.13%	15
26.	Uttar Pradesh	—	—	—	—	—	62,650	—	—
27.	West Bengal	500	550	—	2,000	3,050	1,05,000	2.90%	9
	Total	99,597	17,399	225	55,089	1,77,898	57,06,062	3.12%	

CHART 3.1
Growth of Collection in SCLs of India
(States with Library Acts)

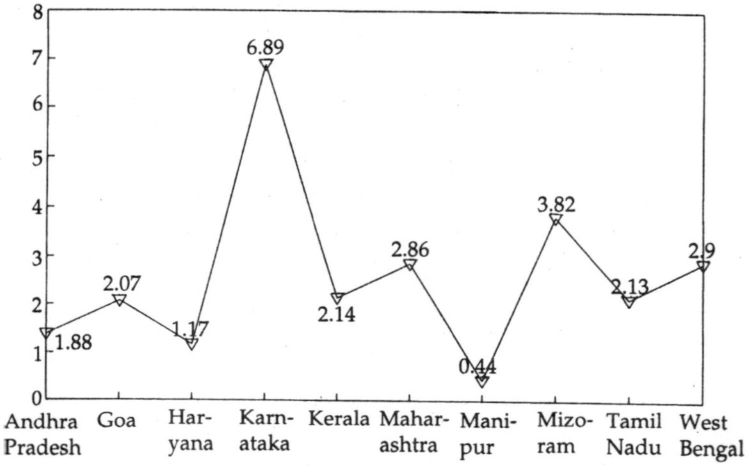

CHART 3.2
Growth of Collection in SCLs of India
(States/UTs without Library Acts)

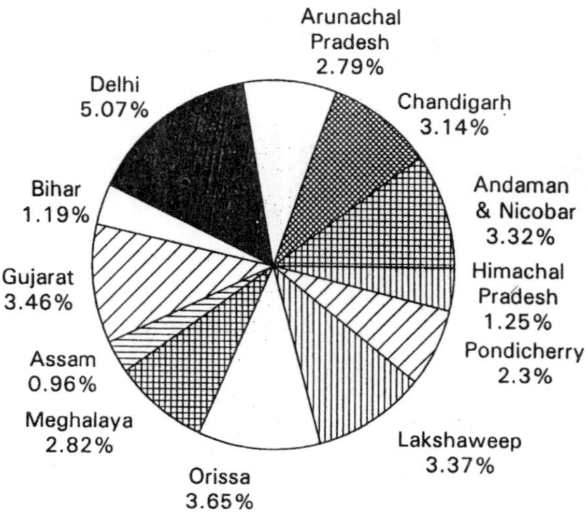

TABLE 3.3
Top 10 SCLs with Higher Annual Growth of Collection

Sl. No.	*Name of State/U.T.*	*% of Annual Growth*
1.	Karnataka	6.89%
2.	Delhi	5.07%
3.	Mizoram	3.82%
4.	Orissa	3.65%
5.	Gujarat	3.46%
6.	Lakshadweep	3.37%
7.	Andaman & Nicobar Islands	3.32%
8.	Chandigarh	3.14%
9.	West Bengal	2.90%
10.	Maharashtra	2.86%

The annual growth is a measure by which the rate of additions to a library in comparison with the available stock is valued. This shows the seriousness with which the acquisition policy is pursued and the funds allotted for the collection development of the library. The growth of collection is maximum (6.89 per cent) in Karnataka, followed by Delhi (5.07 per cent) Mizoram (3.82 per cent) and Orissa (3.65 per cent) while Maharashtra ranks tenth with only 2.86 per cent increase in annual growth of collection. The annual growth of collection of SCLs of 27 States/U.Ts. has also been analysed on the basis of classification of States having passed Public Library Acts and, States without Library Acts in the following Table 3.4 and Charts 3.1 and 3.2.

TABLE 3.4
Growth Rate of Collection

States/UTs with Library Act		*States/U.Ts without Library Act*	
Name of State	*Percentage*	*Name of States/U.T.*	*Percentage*
Karnataka	6.89 %	Delhi	5.07 %
Mizoram	3.82 %	Orissa	3.65 %
West Bengal	2.99 %	Gujarat	3.46 %
Maharashtra	2.86 %	Lakshadweep	3.37 %
		A. & N. Islands	3.32%

(Contd.)

States/UTs with Library Act		*States/U.Ts without Library Act*	
Name of State	*Percentage*	*Name of States/U.T.*	*Percentage*
Kerala	2.14 %	Chandigarh	3.14 %
Tamilnadu	2.13 %	Meghalaya	2.87 %
Goa	2.07 %	Arunachal Pradesh	2.79 %
Andhra Pradesh	1.38 %	Pondicherry	2.30 %
Haryana	1.17 %	Punjab	1.71%
Manipur	0.44 %	Himachal Pradesh	1.25 %
Average	2.59 %	Bihar	1.19 %
		Assam	0.96 %
		Average	2.69 %

From the above table, it can be seen that among the States having Public Library Acts, Karnataka State with 6.89 per cent tops the list of annual growth rate of book collection. Manipur State, even though having passed Public Library Act, registered the lowest annual growth rate among the SCLs of all States/U.Ts in India. From the list of States/U.Ts without Public Library Acts, it is found that, Delhi (5.07 per cent) is the topmost in regular collection development every year while the collection of the State Central Library of Assam grows at a snail's pace of only 0.96 per cent annually. The average percentage of the States without Public Library Act is 2.69 per cent, a little higher than (0.10 per cent) the average growth of collection of the States having Public Library Acts (2.59 per cent). This also indicates that, the growth of collection is in no way better in the States having Public Library Act.

Special Collections

In addition to the general collection of books on various subjects in different languages available in SCLs, many SCLs have acquired/developed special collections of books. These special collections are either bulk donation by some eminent writers/social personalities or a carefully developed collection on local history, local leaders, rare books and the like.

The number of books forming part of special collections in each State Central Library is listed in Table 21 as follows:

TABLE 3.5
Special Collections of State Central Libraries

Sl. No.	Name of State/U.T.	No. of Volumes of Special Collections	Total Collection	% of Total	Ranking Collection
1.	Andaman & Nicobar Islands	235	75,320	00.31%	15
2.	Andhra Pradesh	—	4,01,613	—	—
3.	Arunachal Pradesh	—	28,728	—	—
4.	Assam	10,603	78,367	13.53%	3
5.	Bihar	3,451	1,45,454	02.37%	7
6.	Chandigarh	1,500	1,40,000	01.07%	10
7.	Delhi	14,242	14,80,675	00.96%	12
8.	Goa	—	1,40,000	—	—
9.	Gujarat	—	79,253	—	—
10.	Haryana	—	57,675	—	—
11.	Himachal Pradesh	50	91,648	00.05%	16
12.	Karnataka	2,000	2,40,172	00.83%	13
13.	Kerala	10,418	2,56,794	04.05%	6
14.	Lakshadweep	100	30,000	00.33%	14
15.	Madhya Pradesh	—	62,507	—	—
16.	Maharashtra	—	7,08,806	—	—
17.	Manipur	10,500	1,25,138	08.39%	4
18.	Meghalaya	—	1,70,000	—	—
19.	Mizoram	6,994	17,000	40.00%	1
20.	Nagaland	—	39,000	—	—
21.	Orissa	50,000	2,00,000	25.00%	2
22.	Pondicherry	29,500	2,91,887	01.01%	11
23.	Punjab	2,718	1,16,887	02.32%	8
24.	Rajasthan	—	35,488	—	—
25.	Tamil Nadu	27,000	5,25,000	05.14%	5
26.	Uttar Pradesh	—	62,650	—	—
27.	West Bengal	1,900	1,05,000	01.81%	9
	Total	1,71,200	57,06,062	03.02%	

A cursory glance at the Table 3.5 reveals that the number of books available under special collection ranges from a minimum number

TABLE 3.6
Strength of Collection by Discipline

Sl. No.	*Name of State/U.T.*	*Subject of Collection which is stronger*	*Weaker Subject*	*Subjects Receiving Utmost Attention*	*Subjects Receiving Least Attention*
1.	Andaman and Nicobar Islands	Science and Technology	Medical Science	Fiction	Social Science
2.	Andhra Pradesh	Social Science	Useful Arts	Literature	Philosophy & Religion
3.	Arunachal Pradesh	Sociology	Science and Technology	Current Topics	Linguistics
4.	Assam	History and Anthropology	Law and Applied Science	Literature	Philosophy
5.	Bihar	Social Science and Humanities	Science and Technology	—	Technology
6.	Chandigarh	Social Science and Fiction	Fine Arts	Fiction	Poetry
7.	Delhi	Technology	Fine Arts	Technology	Fine Arts
8.	Goa	History	Philosophy	Fiction	Metaphysics
9.	Gujarat	Reference		Computer Science	Geography
10.	Haryana	Hindi	Reference	Hindi Literature	Urdu
11.	Himachal Pradesh	English Fiction	Reference	English Fiction and Computer Science	Urdu/Punjab
12.	Karnataka	Social Science	Computer Science	Social Science	Geology

(Contd.)

Sl. No.	Name of State/U.T.	Subject of Collection which is stronger	Weaker Subject	Subjects Receiving Utmost Attention	Subjects Receiving Least Attention
13.	Kerala	Literature	Science and Technology	Fiction	Law
14.	Lakshadweep	Reference	Nil	Fiction	Hindi
15.	Madhya Pradesh	—	—	—	—
16.	Maharashtra	Social Science and Humanities	Science and Technology	Literature	Science and Technology
17.	Manipur	Literature	Science	Literature	Science and Technology
18.	Meghalaya	General	—	—	—
19.	Mizoram	Literature	General Science	Literature	Science
20.	Nagaland	History and Science	Science and Technology	Fiction	Hindi
21.	Orissa	History and Culture	Technology and Medicine	—	—
22.	Pondicherry	Literature	Law and Arts	Fiction	Law and Religion
23.	Punjab	Philosophy and Religion	Science and Technology	Fiction	Linguistics
24.	Rajasthan	Hindi Literature	Foreign Languages	General Knowledge	Languages
25.	Tamil Nadu	History	General Science	Social Science	Geology
26.	Uttar Pradesh	—	Text Books	Text book	—
27.	West Bengal	Literature and Social Science	Technology and Competitive Exams	Literature and Social Science	—

of 50 in Himachal Pradesh to 50,000 in Orissa. But, the comparative figure of number of books collected through special collections and general collections indicate that in Mizoram State's collection, special collection forms 40 per cent, followed by Orissa State which has 25 per cent of total books as special collection, and Assam State has 13.53 per cent share in this regard.

The percentage of special collection available in other SCLs appears insignificant, the least being in Himachal Pradesh where only 0.05 per cent of its total collection comprises special collection. There are 1,71,201 books in special collection in all SCLs forming 3.02 per cent of the total collection. The most significant aspect of the special collections is that books on local history form the special collection in State Central Libraries of 8 States/U.Ts, viz. Andaman & Nicobar Islands, Arunachal Pradesh, Goa, Lakshadweep, Orissa, Pondicherry and West Bengal. The rare books are kept as special collections in the States/U.Ts of Karnataka, Punjab and Tamil Nadu.

Collection by Discipline

Stronger/Weaker. The Respondents were requested to state the strength of collection in their respective SCLs by discipline by mentioning the subject they feel stronger and the one weaker. From the experience of supervising the SCLs, the librarians of the respective SCLs have been asked to state the subject that receives utmost attention and the one that receives the least attention.

The opinions of the Respondents in this direction are presented in the following Table 22. Among the 27 State Central Libraries, the subjects of Social Science and Humanities are stronger in 8 states viz., Andhra Pradesh, Arunachal Pradesh, Bihar, Chandigarh, Karnataka, Maharashtra, Nagaland and West Bengal. The subject of literature is stronger in the collections of 7 States of Kerala, Manipur, Mizoram, Pondicherry, Rajasthan, Tamil Nadu and West Bengal. The Library collections on the subjects of History, Sociology and Culture are found to be stronger in 4 States at Assam, Goa, Nagaland and Orissa. While the reference tools are stronger in the States of Gujarat and Lakshadweep U.T, the collection of Philosophy and Religion is more in Punjab and General collection is stronger in Meghalaya. The Chief Librarians of the State Central Libraries of the States of Madhya Pradesh and Uttar Pradesh have not indicated the stronger subjects in their libraries.

The books on the subjects of Science and Technology are poorly represented in 10 out of 27 State Central Libraries at Arunachal Pradesh, Bihar, Kerala, Maharashtra, Mizoram, Nagaland, Orissa, Punjab, Tamil Nadu and West Bengal. The subject of Fine Arts is weak in Chandigarh and Delhi whereas the shortage of reference collection is felt by the Librarians of Haryana and Himachal Pradesh. The collection position of books on Computer Science is found inadequate in the States of Karnataka and West Bengal. The subjects of Medical Science, Useful Arts, Law, Philosophy and Foreign Languages are found to be weaker in 1 State each, whereas Textbooks are very less in 1 State only.

The Chart 3.3 drawn below indicates the stronger and weaker subjects in the various State Central Libraries of India as per the opinions of the Librarians of the State Central Libraries.

CHART 3.3
Stronger Subjects in SCLs of India

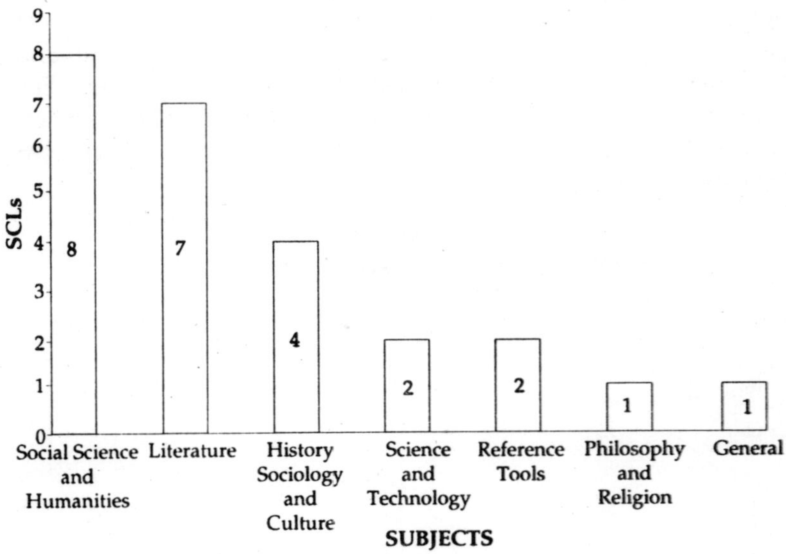

Collection Receiving Utmost/Least Attention. Further, the analysis on the subjects receiving utmost attention in the SCLs of Indian States/Union Territories indicates that the most dominant subject is literature including fiction. Among the 27 SCLs analysed in this project, 16 SCLs (59 per cent) receive utmost attention from their readers in respect of their collection on Literature.

The State Central Libraries of the States/U.Ts of Andaman and Nicobar Islands, Andhra Pradesh, Assam, Chandigarh, Goa, Haryana, Himachal Pradesh, Kerala, Lakshadweep, Maharashtra, Manipur, Mizoram, Nagaland, Pondicherry, Punjab and West Bengal come under this category. The subject categories of Technology including Computer Science, Current topics including General Knowledge and Social Sciences are receiving utmost attention only in 2 States respectively. Textbooks are received better in the State of Uttar Pradesh. The data on the subjects receiving utmost attention are not available for 4 SCLs.

The Chart 3.4 offers graphical presentation of the subject collection receiving utmost attention in the SCLs of India. Among the subjects which receive least attention, the subjects of Science and Technology are not the preferred subjects in 4 SCLs of Bihar, Maharashtra, Manipur and Mizoram States. The collection of Philosophy and Religion are not frequently referred by the readers of the SCLs of Andhra Pradesh and Assam States. The subjects of Geology, Law, Linguistics and the language books of Hindi and Urdu languages are receiving least attention in 2 SCLs each. The subjects not preferred vary in the remaining States. The subjects such as Social Science, Poetry, Fine Arts, Metaphysics, Geography, Punjabi and Foreign Languages fall under this category.

CHART 3.4
Subjects Receiving Utmost Attention in SCLs

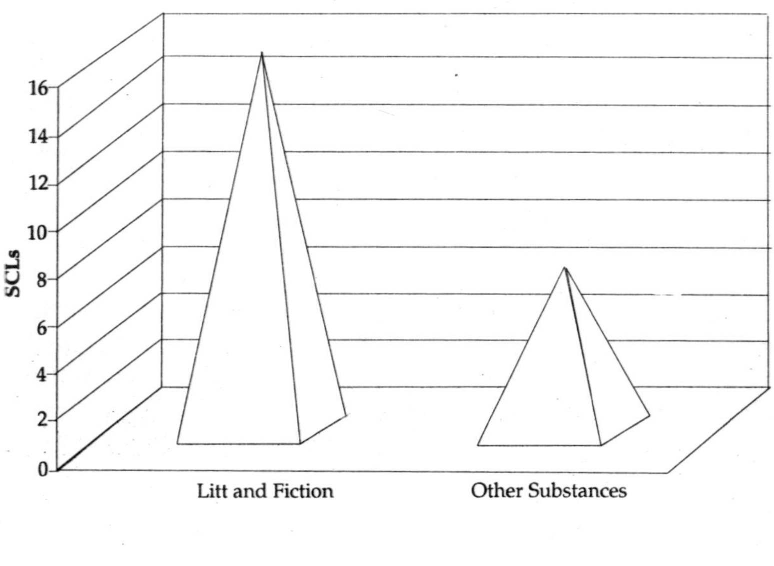

Collection of Non-Book Materials

The basic functions of a library are the collection, processing and utilisation of documents. However, the print medium documents have been dominating the libraries so far all over the world. This is natural due to the long history of writing which began with the cuneiform system in Mesopotamia since 3,000 B.C.

After the invention of codex with pages like those of a book evolved in the first century A.D. this single form of printing dominated the preservation of knowledge and dissemination of information in the civilised society for quite a very long period. The invention of printing process in 15th century created a revolution in thought through the spread of multiple copies. The printed books constitute the majority of collection in most of the libraries. The non-book materials used in the libraries have been the result of inventions of the late 19th and 20th century. Traditionally, the term 'non-book materials' shall include all those materials which are not bound as a book. However, in the present situation it denotes any material brought out in the form of a pamphlet, tablet, maps and atlases, manuscripts, palm leaves, videotapes, microdocuments, slides, films and the electronic materials like floppies, CD-ROMs, tapes, etc.

The Table 3.7 shown on next pages tabulates the various categories of non-book materials available in different State Central Libraries of India. Among the non-book materials, maps and atlases are available in 17 libraries. Other non-book materials available in various SCLs are as follows : Manuscripts (07), Palmleaves (02), Videotapes (09), audio-cassettes (09), floppies (04), CD-ROMs (05), microfilms (03), microfiches (03) and Gramophones and films (01).

The percentage of non-book materials compared to the total collection of State Central Libraries is insignificant in most of the libraries. The percentages are below 1 in all, but two of the States—Pondicherry (2.38 per cent) and West Bengal (1.07 per cent). The percentage of non-book materials in all SCLs compared to the total book collection comes to a mere 0.17 per cent. The analysis shows that, the collection of the State Central Libraries comprise mostly of book materials. The non-book materials are not significant, compared to book materials. There are only 9,863 items of non-book materials as per the categories mentioned below. The number

TABLE 3.7
State of Collections—Non Book Materials

Sl. No.	Name of State/U.T.	Maps/ Atlases	Manu scripts	Palm leaves	Video tapes	Audio casse-ttes	Flopp-ies	CD-ROMs	Micro films	Micro fiches	Anyother form	Total Non-book materials	Library Collection	% of Non-book Materials
(1)	(2)	(3)	(4)	(5)	(6)	(7)	(8)	(9)	(10)	(11)	(12)	(13)	(14)	(15)
01.	Andaman and Nicobar Islands	35	—	—	—	—	—	—	—	—	—	35	75,320	0.05%
02.	Andhra Pradesh	—	—	—	—	—	—	—	—	—	—	—	4,01,613	—
03.	Arunachal Pradesh	—	03	—	—	—	—	—	—	—	—	03	28,728	0.0001%
04.	Assam	35	05	—	—	—	—	—	—	—		40	78,367	0.001%
05.	Bihar	—	—	—	—	—	—	—	—	—	—	—	1,45,454	—
06.	Chandigarh	100	—	—	559	32	—	—	—	—	—	691	1,40,000	0.49%
07.	Delhi	09	—	—	11	944	02	—	—	—	—	966	14,80,675	0.065%
08.	Goa	10	50	—	—	—	—	—	—	—	—	60	1,40,000	0.043%
09.	Gujarat	25	—	—	—	03	06	16	—	280	—	330	79,253	0.42%
10.	Haryana	—	—	—	—	—	—	—	—	—	—	—	57,675	—
11.	Himachal Pradesh	20	23	—	04	—	08	—	—	—	—	55	91,648	0.06%
12.	Karnataka	10	—	—	—	—	—	20	—	—	—	30	2,40,172	0.01%
13.	Kerala	120	25	04	—	28	—	—	40	600	—	817	2,56,794	0.32%
14.	Lakshadweep	50	—	—	150	—	—	55	—	—	—	255	30,000	0.55%

(Contd.)

(Contd.)

(1)	(2)	(3)	(4)	(5)	(6)	(7)	(8)	(9)	(10)	(11)	(12)	(13)	(14)	(15)
15.	Madhya Pradesh	—	—	—	—	—	—	—	—	—	—	—	62,507	—
16.	Maharashtra	1,500	—	—	—	—	—	—	1	—	—	1,501	7,09,806	0.21%
17.	Manipur	10	15	—	60	15	—	—	—	—	—	100	1,25,138	0.08%
18.	Meghalaya	—	—	—	30	—	—	—	—	—	—	30	1,70,000	0.02%
19.	Mizoram	05	—	—	—	—	—	—	—	—	—	05	17,000	0.003%
20.	Nagaland	—	—	—	—	—	—	—	—	—	—	—	39,000	—
21.	Orissa	300	—	—	—	050	200	—	—	—	—	550	2,00,000	0.28%
22.	Pondicherry	—	—	—	—	—	—	—	—	—	—	—	2,91.887	—
23.	Punjab	50	2,718	01	06	01	—	01	—	—	—	2,777	1,16,887	2.38%
24.	Rajasthan	—	—	—	—	—	—	—	—	—	—	—	35,488	—
25.	Tamil Nadu	250	—	—	75	50	—	04	90	25	—	494	5,25,000	0.09%
26.	Uttar Pradesh	—	—	—	—	—	—	—	—	—	—	—	62,650	—
27.	West Bengal	100	—	—	48	19	—	—	79	—	878	1124	1,05,000	1.07%
	Total	2,629	2,839	05	943	1,142	216	96	210 Rolls	905	878 GR Record	9,863	57,06,062	0.16%

and categories of non-book materials available in all SCLs in India are depicted in Table 3.8 below:

TABLE 3.8
Non-Book Materials in SCLs of India

Sl. No.	*Category*	*Number*
1.	Maps / Atlases	2,629
2.	Manuscripts	2,839
3.	Palmleaves	05
4.	Videotapes	943
5.	Audio Cassettes	1,142
6.	Floppies	216
7.	CD-ROMs	96
8.	Microfilms	131
9.	Microfiches	905
10.	Gramophone Records	878
	Total	9,863

Manpower

Professionally trained manpower is a pre-requisite factor for effective and efficient functioning of any organisation. The term, 'manpower', usually, denotes the entire staff serving an organisation. The success of a library would, primarily, depend upon the quality, expertise and aptitude of the manpower working in the library. The management of manpower involves—arriving at a decision of the manpower required, selecting those who are considered as the best suitable candidates for recruitment, preparing them for efficient service in the organisation and, keeping them in the service of the organisation as long as their services are mutually beneficial and obligatory. The size of manpower of a public library depends primarily on the volume of its stack and the scope of its services to the users. There should be sufficient number of competent staff to provide a variety of services to satisfy the wide ranging demands of the multi-faceted clientele of a Public Library.

TABLE 3.9
Manpower of State-Central Libraries

Sl. No.	Name of State/U.T.	Prof.	Semi Prof.	Non Prof.	Total	Ratio of Prof. and Non-Prof.	Ratio of Manpower and Collection	Promotion	Pay Scales
1.	Andaman and Nicobar Islands	4	1	7	12	1:1.3	1:6,400	No	State Govt.
2.	Andhra Pradesh	13	20	100	133	1:3	1:3,000	Dept Promotion	State Govt.
3.	Arunachal Pradesh	8	4	4	16	1:1	1:4,000	Dept Promotion	State Govt.
4.	Assam	3	–	5	8	1:2	1:10,000	Dept Promotion	State Govt.
5.	Bihar	2	3	20	25	1:4	1:5,769	No norms	State Govt.
6.	Chandigarh	19	29	46	94	1:1	1:1,474	No norms	UGC/State Govt.
7.	Delhi	200	98	103	401	1:1	1:3,283	Dept Promotion	Central Govt.
8.	Goa	8	6	20	34	1:13	1:10,000	Dept Promotion	State Govt.
9.	Gujarat	13	3	8	24	2:1	1:5,000	Dept Promotion	State Govt.
10.	Haryana	2	3	9	14	1:1.8	1:12,000	Dept Promotion	State Govt.
11.	Himachal Pradesh	5	5	20	30	1:2	1:3,000	Dept Promotion	State Govt.
12.	Karnataka	8	6	12	26	1:09	1:12,000	Dept Promotion	State Govt.

(Contd.)

(Contd.)

13.	Kerala	20	15	29	64	1.2:1	1:7,500	Dept Promotion	State Govt.
14.	Lakshadweep	4	00	4	08	1:1	1:3,750	Dept Promotion	Central Govt.
15.	Madhya Pradesh	1	4	2	07	2.5:1	1:8,928	Dept Promotion	State Govt.
16.	Maharashtra	20	—	56	76	1:2.8	1:10,000	Dept Promotion	State Govt.
17.	Manipur	10	5	20	35	1:1.3	1:3,580	Dept Promotion	State Govt.
18.	Meghalaya	5	6	22	33	1:2	1:5,152	Dept Promotion	State Govt.
19.	Mizoram	2	3	7	12	1:1.3	1:1,000	Dept Promotion	State Govt.
20.	Nagaland	2	2	10	14	1:2.2	1:2,786	No norms	State Govt.
21.	Orissa	42	2	18	62	2:1	1:2,493	Dept Promotion	State Govt.
22.	Pondicherry	3	3	15	21	1:3	1:15,000	Dept Promotion	Central Govt.
23.	Punjab	8	7	22	37	1:1.5	1:3,160	Dept Promotion	UGC/State Govt.
24.	Rajasthan	7	—	12	19	1:1.8	1:1,870	Dept Promotion	State Govt.
25.	Tamil Nadu	13	44	62	11.9	1:1.2	1:5,000	Dept Promotion	State Govt.
26.	Uttar Pradesh	7	5	15	27	1:1.2	1:2,320	Dept Promotion	State Govt.
27.	West Bengal	14	2	20	36	1:1.5	1:3,000	Dept Promotion	State Govt.
	Total	443	276	668	1,387	1:1.08	1:5,600		

The American Library Association Committee on Post-War planning lays down certain broad principles for determining the number of staff required for a public library as : "The number of staff members in a Public Library should be sufficient to provide consistently efficient service at all hours when the library is open to the public, and to perform the duties involved in assembling, organising and interpreting the materials required by the programme of the library. The size of the staff for any library or library system must be based upon the program of service adopted by the library, the population and size of the service area, the financial support, and more specifically the number of departments, branches and other organised units, the amount of circulation and reference service, the plans of the library buildings, the hours of opening and other factors. All hours when the library is open, professional members of the staff should be in charge of public services requiring professional preparation and skill" (A.L.A; 1942, p. 7).

The number of staff members required for a public library should also be limited to the total user population of the library. "1996 ALA standards (for USA) recommend one staff member per 2,000 population. The Roberts Committee (UK) recommends that the staff for an average system in urban libraries excluding the Chief Librarian should be employed on the basis of atleast 1 Assistant per 3,000 population in the community served" (Mookerjee and Sengupta;1972; p. 408).

The Indian Standards for staff formula for public libraries has been suggested by S.R. Ranganathan which are reproduced below: "A statement of the staff requirements for a public library is given below in simple terms" :

1. Book Section : 1 person for every 6,000 volumes added in a year.
2. Periodical Publication Section: 1 person for every 1,000 periodicals currently taken
3. Classification and Cataloguing section : 1 person for every 2,000 volumes added in a year.
4. Maintenance Section : 1 person for every 2,000 volumes added in a year and 1 person for every 50,000 volumes in the library.
5. Publicity Section: Minimum 1 artist.
6. Administrative Section : Minimum 1 Library Accountant, 1 Stenotypist and 1 Correspondence Clerk.
7. Reference Section : 1 person for every 50 readers using the library in a day.

8. Circulation Section : 1 person for every 1,500 hours for which one wicket gate of the library has to be kept open in a year.
9. Supervising Section : Librarian and 1 Deputy Librarian".

(Ranganathan; 1988; p. 43).

The total manpower scenario of SCLs of 27 States/U.Ts surveyed for this project is presented in Table 25 under three broad categories, namely, professional, semi-professional, and non-professional. The same is reflected in Chart 3.5.

The staff strength ranges from a mere 7 Members in Madhya Pradesh State to a larger number of 401 staff members in Delhi Union Territory. Among the total number of 1,387 staff members in 27 SCLs of India, 443 (32 per cent) are professional staff, 276 (20 per cent) are semi-professionals and there are 668 (48 per cent) non-professional staff. The ratio of professional and non-professional staff varies from 1:3 in Pondicherry to 2.5:1 at Madhya Pradesh State. The trend of the total strength of non-professionals being predominant over the professionals seems to be unhealthy.

It is needless to emphasize that only a qualified professional Librarian should head the apex library of the State. However, due to the administrative or other reasons, some controlling authorities of the SCLs fail to see the reason behind this necessity. In this analysis, it is ascertained that only 23 States (85 per cent) have provided the professional Chief Librarians for State Central Libraries. In 4 States (15 per cent), viz., Goa, Nagaland, Orissa and Uttar Pradesh the States Central Libraries are headed by non-professional officials.

The ratio of manpower compared to the library collection is also varying. There is 1 staff member for every 1,000 books available in Mizoram State whereas 1 staff member has to take care of 12,000 books in Karnataka State. Among all SCLs, only 2 libraries have recruited any staff member in the last 5 years. In 6 SCLs, staff members were deputed for training programmes and refresher courses so that they are informed of the latest technology in order to keep pace with the emerging needs.

The job satisfaction and motivation among the manpower of the SCLs can be attained only when there are adequate promotional avenues and attractive pay scales. It is ascertained from the survey

CHART 3.5
Manpower of SCLs of India

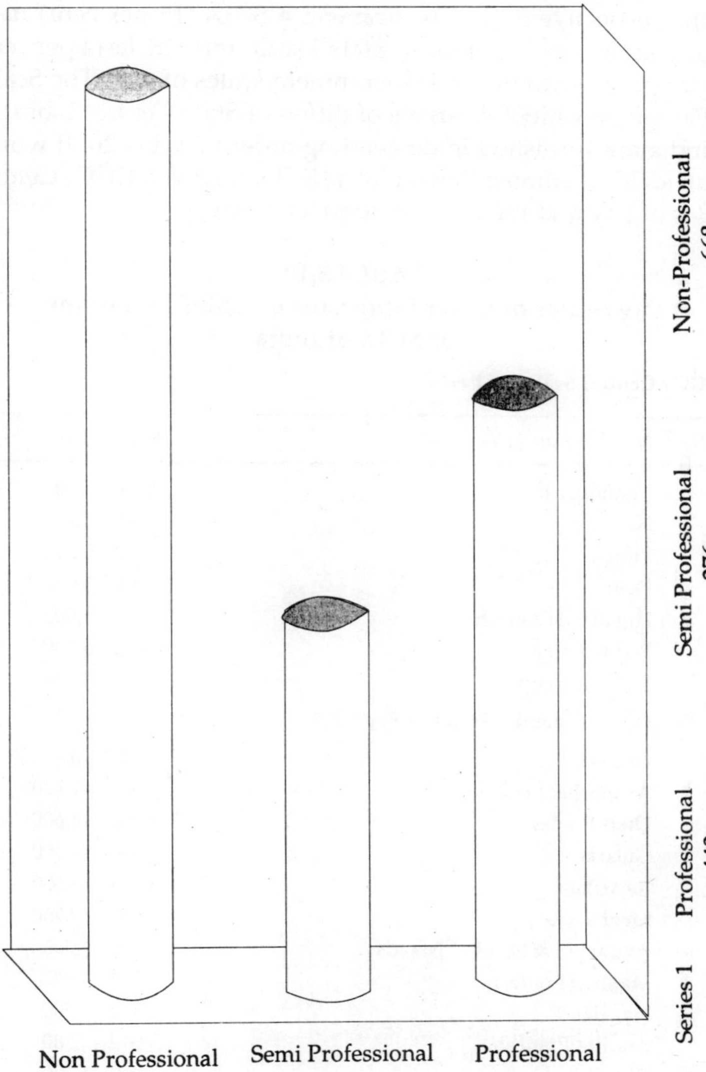

that in 4 SCLs out of 27 (15 per cent), there are no norms for promotion and in other libraries, departmental promotion is available. The salary structure of the staff of SCLs is almost uniform.

Among the 27 SCLs, 20 SCLs (74 per cent) have the payscales of the respective State Government, 4 SCLs (15 per cent) have U.G.C. scales implemented as State's scale and 3 SCLs (4 per cent) are favoured with Central Government scales of pay. The Scales of Pay of the Chief Librarians of different State Central Libraries of India are furnished in descending order in Table 26. It would be an ideal situation if the staff of all SCLs are given UGC/Central scales of pay and regular promotional avenues.

TABLE 3.10
Pay Scales of Chief Librarians of Chief Librarians of SCLs of India

I UGC / Central Scales of Pay

Sl. No.	*Name of State/U.Ts*	*Scale of Pay*
1.	Chandigarh	3,700 - 5,700
2.	Haryana	3,700 - 5,700
3.	Punjab	3,700 - 5,700
4.	Delhi	3,700 - 5,000
5.	Himachal Pradesh	3,000 - 5,000
6.	Pondicherry	2,000 - 3,500
7.	Lakshadweep	1,640 - 2,900
(II) State Government's Scales of Pay		
8.	Orissa	I.A.S Scale
9.	Arunachal Pradesh	10,000 - 15,200
10.	Uttar Pradesh	8,550 - 14,600
11.	Gujarat	8,500 - 14,000
12.	Rajasthan	8,000 - 13,500
13.	Meghalaya	5,600 - 10,750
14.	Andaman & Nicobar Islands	5,500 - 9,000
15.	Madhya Pradesh	4,500 - 7,000
16.	Nagaland	4,500 - 5,700
17.	Andhra Pradesh	3,640 - 7,580
18.	Goa	3,000 - 4,500
19.	Kerala	3,000 - 5,000
20.	Tamil Nadu	2,500 - 4,500

21.	Bihar	2,400 - 4,150
22.	Karnataka	2,375 - 4,450
23.	Maharashtra	2,200 - 4,000
24.	Mizoram	2,200 - 4000
25.	West Bengal	2,200 - 4000
26.	Manipur	2,000 - 3,500
27.	Assam	1,375 - 3,375

Finance

Introduction. Public libraries are, by nature, spending institutions and do not have any self-supporting financial base. A public library should have regular and guaranteed sources of income. Finance is required for the essential requirements of purchase of reading materials and modernisation, providing furniture and equipments, payment of staff salary, construction and maintenance of buildings and to meet the emerging contingent expenditures for the day to day functioning of the libraries. Effective functioning of a public library largely depends on availability of adequate financial resources. The motto of public library service "The Best Reading for the Largest number at the Least Cost" cannot be implemented if there is any difficulty in mobilising the finance required for the library.

Budget of SCLs for 5 Years. The budget plays a vital role in the growth and development of State Central Libraries. It is the life-blood for the functioning of the SCLs. Unlike other revenue earning organisation, State Central Libraries are spending institutions. The productivity and the benefits gained by the services provided by the SCLs cannot be measured in terms of money. The budget for the State Central Libraries are normally sanctioned by the State Governments/Central Government or the controlling authority of the respective libraries.

The budget of the SCLs of India for 5 years-beginning from 1993-94 upto 1997-98 is furnished in Table 3.11. The budget figures of SCLs reveal that during the year 1997-98, Nagaland has spent the lowest amount of Rs. 5,18,000 for its SCL whereas Delhi U.T. has utilised Rs. 3,86,31,453 which is roughly 77 times more than what the lowest spending State has allocated. However, considering the geographical area and the population, allocation of Rs. One crore by Andaman and Nicobar Islands Union Territory is highly commendable. It has marched very fast from the 93-94 figure of Rs. 3 lakhs to Rs.1 crores which is an increase of 33 times in four years. In majority of the SCLs one could find only a marginal increase ranging from 10 per cent to 50 per cent. Once again, Nagaland State shows heavy decrease in budget allocation. From the level of Rs. 11,18,004 in 1993-94, it has come down to Rs. 5, 18,000 in 1997-98.

The analysed column of the Table 3.11 on average budget of SCLs for the last 5 years reveals some interesting features. The Delhi U.T. tops the list - with an average budget of Rs. 3,09,14,729 for 5 years, followed by Karnataka (Rs. 65,20,000) and Chandigarh (Rs. 63,60,00). The lowest annual expenditure is incurred by SCL in Madhya Pradesh State with an average budget allotment of Rs. 5,15,064 for the last 5 years. It is surprising to note that two major SCLs at Maharashtra and Tamilnadu which are the designated (National level) libraries to receive books under the Delivery of Books Act, 1954 comes in the position of only 04 and 05 with an average allocation of Rs. 57,68,854 and Rs. 53,74,250 respectively.

Budget in States with Act and Without Act. The Tables 3.12 and 3.13 present the annual average Budget of SCLs in the States with Public Library Acts and in the States without any Act. Interestingly, the top ranking Delhi U.T. and the lowest ranking (24) Madhya Pradesh State comes under the Table 3.14, the States/U.Ts without Public Library Act. The comparative position of Public Library Act substantiates that the enactment of Public Library.

Act alone is not enough to provide adequate budgetary support for the Public Library System considering the situation that among the top 10 spenders for the SCLs both the Tables 3.12 and 3.13 share 5 places each. The States/U.Ts without Act get the top positions of 01,03,08,09 and 10 whereas the States/U.Ts with Act has the ranking of 02, 04, 05, 06 and 07 respectively. The political/administrative will to spend more money for the libraries matter more than the advantage of having an Act passed in the State/U.T.

TABLE 3.11
Budget of SCLs from 1993-94 to 1997-98

Sl. No.	Name of State/U.T.	1993-94	1994-95	1995-96	1996-97	1997-98	Average for 5 Years	Rank
		Rs.	Rs.	Rs.	Rs.	Rs.	Rs.	
1.	Andaman and Nicobar Islands	3,00,000	6,00,000	30,30,000	34,00,000	1,00,00,000	34,66,000	09
2.	Andhra Pradesh	49,28,000	55,82,000	60,60,000	69,34,000	72,66,000	51,54,000	06
3.	Arunachal Pradesh	25,70,000	18,82,716	46,82,178	46,30,312	34,28,442	34,38,737	10
4.	Assam	—	—	—	—	—	—	—
5.	Bihar	12,02,078	12,81,252	14,23,615	14,75,208	18,75,582	14,51,547	18
6.	Chandigarh	53,00,000	50,00,000	70,00,000	72,00,000	73,00,000	63,60,000	03
7.	Delhi	2,30,63,452	2,75,43,495	3,12,04,779	3,41,30,425	3,86,31,45	33,09,14,721	01
8.	Goa	—	—	—	—	—	—	—
9.	Gujarat	14,00,000	13,55,000	12,50,000	13,40,000	15,78,000	13,84,600	19
10.	Haryana	4,90,000	5,02,350	6,07,000	6,65,000	7,18,000	5,96,470	23
11.	Himachal Pradesh	15,67,812	14,68,158	24,36,682	17,79,974	17,07,300	17,94,195	16
12.	Karnataka	40,03,000	68,57,000	50,57,000	86,88,000	79,95,000	65,20,000	02
13.	Kerala	37,15,800	48,14,073	50,04,000	52,00,000	62,00,000	49,86,775	07

Sl. No.	Name of State/U.T.	1993-94	1994-95	1995-96	1996-97	1997-98	Average for 5 Years	Rank
		Rs.	Rs.	Rs.	Rs.	Rs.	Rs.	
14.	Lakshadweep	—	—	—	—	—	—	—
15.	Madhya Pradesh	4,67,379	4,78,204	3,56,332	6,14,036	6,59,368	5,15,064	24
16.	Maharashtra	—	24,28,255	59,79,568	67,39,617	79,27,976	57,68,854	04
17.	Manipur	—	—	27,45,000	27,45,000	27,45,000	27,45,000	12
18.	Meghalaya	—	—	23,00,000	28,00,000	33,00,000	28,00,000	11
19.	Mizoram	21,00,000	—	—	—	—	21,00,000	15
20.	Nagaland	11,18,000	10,68,000	2,68,000	3,08,000	5,18,000	6,56,000	22
21.	Orissa	34,40,000	39,54,000	43,81,000	53,71,000	47,51,000	43,79,200	08
22.	Pondicherry	21,13,997	21,42,764	23,45,266	25,08,074	31,66,900	24,55,400	13
23.	Punjab	14,82,235	16,00,850	17,28,900	17,39,800	18,85,000	16,87,357	17
24.	Rajasthan	6,85,200	7,52,870	8,79,200	9,52,500	9,45,000	8,42,954	21
25.	Tamil Nadu	46,00,000	48,36,000	57,50,000	63,11,000	—	53,74,250	05
26.	Uttar Pradesh	4,66,500	11,31,200	20,76,800	12,43,200	15,96,800	9,42,900	20
27.	West Bengal	14,38,107	13,80,344	14,66,828	39,10,548	23,45,179	21,08,201	14

TABLE 3.12

Average Budget of States/UTs with Library Act

Sl. No.	*State*	*Amount (Rs.)*	*Rank*
1.	Tamil Nadu	5,53,74,250	05
2.	Andhra Pradesh	51,54,000	06
3.	Karnataka	65,20,000	02
4.	Maharashtra	57,68,854	04
5.	West Bengal	21,08,201	14
6.	Haryana	5,96,470	23
7.	Karala	49,86,775	07
8.	Manipur	27,45,000	12
9.	Mizoram	21,00,000	15

TABLE 3.13

Average Budget of States/UTs without Library Act

Sl. No.	*State*	*Amount (Rs.)*	*Rank*
1.	Andaman and Nicobar Islands	34,66,000	09
2.	Arunachal Pradesh	34,38,727	10
3.	Bihar	14,51,547	18
4.	Chandigarh	63,60,000	03
5.	Delhi	3,09,14,721	01
6.	Gujarat	13,84,600	19
7.	Himachal Pradesh	17,91,195	16
8.	Madhya Pradesh	5,15,064	24
9.	Meghalaya	28,00,000	11
10.	Nagaland	6,56,000	22
11.	Orissa	43,79,200	08
12.	Pondicherry	24,55,400	13
13.	Punjab	16,87,357	17
14.	Rajasthan	8,42,954	21
15.	Uttar Pradesh	9,42,900	20

The analysis on the average budget of the State Central Libraries of India in the States with Public Library Acts and in the States/U.Ts without Public Library Acts has also been graphically presented in Chart 8 and Chart 9 respectively.

CHART 3.6
Average Budget of SCLs in India States with Library Act

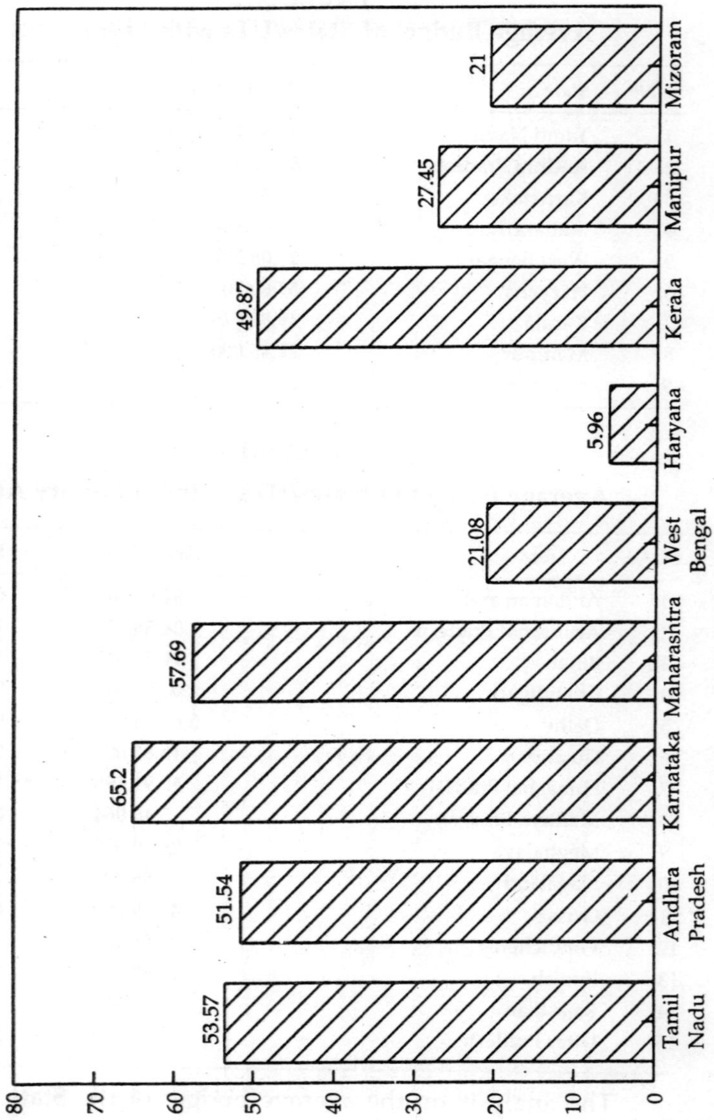

CHART 3.7
Average Budget of SCLs of India States/UTs without Library Act

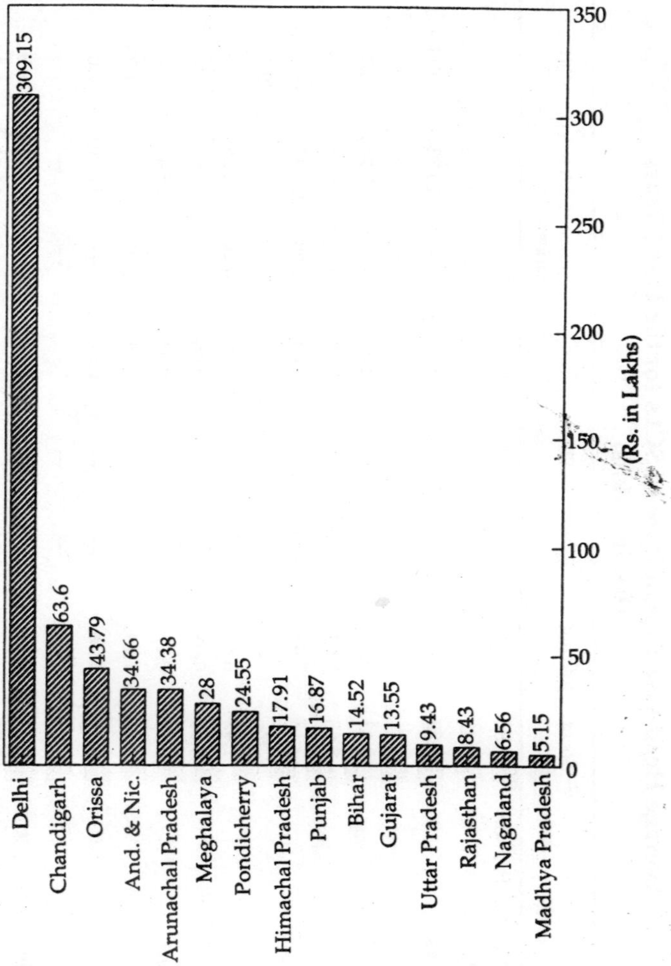

Expenditure on Different Heads. The average headwise expenditures incurred by the SCLs of India for the last 5 years on various heads such as the purchase of books, subscription for current journals, office expenses, purchase of equipment and apparatus, expenditure on modernisation including automation, staff salary and maintenance of building, etc. are summarised in Table 3.14.

TABLE 3.14
Average Headwise Expenditure of SCLs for the Last 5 Years
(Rs. in Lakhs)

Sl. No.	Name of State/U.T.	Books	Journal	Office	Equip	Fur	Auto-mation	Salary	Bldg.	Total
1.	Andaman and Nicobar Islands	7.80	0.51	—	0.74	8.80	—	—	—	34.66
2.	Andhra Pradesh	3.41	1.41	6.45	—	—	—	46.53	—	51.54
3.	Arunachal Pradesh	9.72	0.15	—	0.40	0.97	—	10.33	0.11	34.39
4.	Assam	—	—	—	—	—	—	—	—	—
5.	Bihar	0.43	0.12	0.47	—	0.07	—	3.74	0.06	14.52
6.	Chandigarh	8.63	1.04	15.60	—	0.60	3.30	45.14	—	63.60
7.	Delhi	23.17	7.45	15.59	1.27	1.68	1.90	226.47	19.81	309.15
8.	Goa	—	—	—	1.12	—	—	—	0.13	—
9.	Gujarat	1.45	0.80	0.05	0.30	1.16	0.20	32.29	—	13.85
10.	Haryana	0.04	0.01	—	—	0.06	—	5.96	—	05.96
11.	Himachal Pradesh	0.57	0.25	—	—	0.03	—	15.43	—	17.92
12.	Karnataka	4.14	1.13	—	—	1.28	2.07	—	1.39	65.20
13.	Kerala	6.31	1.24	—	—	0.02	—	17.09	0.07	49.86
14.	Lakshadweep	—	—	—	—	—	—	—	—	—
15.	Madhya Pradesh	0.01	0.14	—	—	—	—	4.95	—	05.15
16.	Maharashtra	12.70	—	3.34	—	—	—	33.13	2.52	57.69

(Contd.)

Sl. No.	Name of State/U.T.	Books	Journal	Office	Equip	Fur	Auto-mation	Salary	Bldg.	Total
17.	Manipur	1.56	0.47	—	—	—	—	10.60	0.30	27.45
18.	Meghalaya	—	—	—	—	—	—	—	—	28.00
19.	Mizoram	—	—	—	—	—	—	—	—	21.00
20.	Nagaland	2.50	0.05	—	—	—	—	—	—	06.56
21.	Orissa	7.12	—	—	0.13	0.04	—	—	0.20	43.79
22.	Pondicherry	3.34	—	—	0.30	—	0.46	20.85	2.51	24.55
23.	Punjab	0.14	0.19	11.00	0.01	0.03	—	15.50	—	16.87
24.	Rajasthan	0.27	0.16	—	—	0.01	—	06.74	—	08.43
25.	Tamilnadu	4.78	3.14	1.93	—	—	1.74	46.08	0.5	53.74
26.	Uttar Pradesh	—	—	0.55	—	—	—	13.02	—	09.43
27.	West Bengal	0.63	1.23	2.12	—	—	0.32	9.50	—	21.08
	Total	98.72	19.51	57.10	4.27	14.76	9.99	563.35	27.15	984.39

The average Membership fee paid by different State Central Libraries for enrolling themselves as Member of various professional bodies like Indian Library Association etc. is as follows : (1) Andaman and Nicobar Islands Rs. 500, (2) Bihar Rs. 641, (3) Himachal Pradesh Rs. 600, (4) Uttar Pradesh Rs. 500 and West Bengal Rs. 1900.

CHART 3.8
Break-up of Budget in SCLs

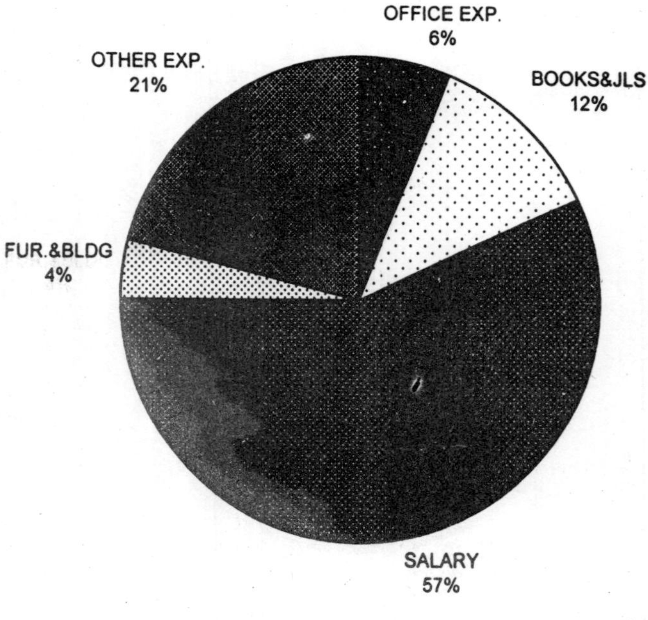

Share of Budget on Different Items. A comparative analysis of the headwise expenditure is provided in the Pie-Chart 10 drawn below which indicates the average annual budget for each of the major expenditure heads. The chart shows that, as expected, the salary of library staff takes a major portion of the budget (57 per cent), followed by 12 per cent for purchase of books and periodicals, 6 per cent for office expenses, 4 per cent for purchase of furniture items and maintenance of building and equipment while the remaining 21 per cent is consumed by other miscellaneous items.

Acquisition. The States/U.Ts spending more money for the acquisition of the latest books for the SCLs are listed below in the following order:

TABLE 3.15
Top States/UTs in Acquisition

Sl. No.	*Name of the States/U.Ts*	*Amount (Rs. in Lakhs)*
1.	Delhi	23.17
2.	Maharashtra	12.70
3.	Arunachal Pradesh	9.72
4.	Chandigarh	8.63
5.	Andaman & Nicobar Islands	7.80
6.	Orissa	7.12
7.	Kerala	6.31
8.	Tamil Nadu	4.78
9.	Karnataka	4.14
10.	Andhra Pradesh	3.04

It is a deplorable condition that 7 States/UTs (26 per cent) (Bihar, Haryana, Himachal Pradesh, Madhya Pradesh, Punjab, Rajasthan and West Bengal) allocate less than one lakh rupees for acquiring new books for the apex library of their respective States.

Current Journals. The current journals provide analysis of the latest development and reflect the cultural trends of the society. It is a common knowledge that in any public library, the section on current journals (which includes newspapers) is the most popular section and receives the maximum patronage by the readers. The information collected from the Questionnaire reveals that, only the following 7 States/U.Ts (26 per cent) spend over Rupees one lakh for paying subscriptions for the current journals.

TABLE 3.16
States/UTs Spending over Rs. 1 Lakhs for Journals

Sl. No.	*Name of the States/U.Ts*	*Amount (Rs.in Lakhs)*
1.	Delhi	7.45
2.	Tamil Nadu	3.14
3.	Andhra Pradesh	1.41
4.	Kerala	1.24
5.	West Bengal	1.23
6.	Karnataka	1.13
7.	Chandigarh	1.04

Automation. The survey further reveals that only 7 SCLs (26 per cent) have incurred an expenditure during the last 5 years for modernisation of their libraries including automation as follows: 1. Chandigarh (Rs. 3.30 lakhs), 2. Kerala (Rs. 2.07 lakhs), 3. Delhi (Rs. 1.90 lakhs), 4. Tamil Nadu (Rs. 1.74 lakhs) 5. Pondicherry (Rs. 0.46 lakhs), 6. West Bengal (Rs. 0.32 lakhs) and 7. Gujarat (Rs. 0.20 lakhs).

The Library authorities of Chandigarh deserve special appreciation for being in the forefront in the country for spending more money for automation of their State Libraries.

The services provided by these 7 libraries through automation include Reference Service, Documentation Service, Bibliographic Service, Inter Library Loan Services, Photoduplication Service and Online Searching Service. In-house operations of the SCLs such as Acquisition, Technical Processing and Circulation Control have also been automated in some of the SCLs.

Revenue from Other Sources. The statistics collected from the SCLs on revenue from other sources during the last 5 years, i.e., 1934-94 to 1997-98 is furnished in Table 3.17.

TABLE 3.17
Average Revenue of SCLs from Other Sources (1993-94 to 1997-98)

Sl. No.	*Name of State/U.T.*	*Membership Fee* Rs.	*Overdue Charges* Rs.	*Fine on Loss of Books* Rs.
1.	Andaman & Nicobar Islands	—	5,288.00	—
2.	Andhra Pradesh	36,339.00	5,681.00	—
3.	Arunachal Pradesh	974.00	1,388.00	38.00
4.	Bihar	26,368.00	—	—
5.	Chandigarh	—	50,465.00	—
6.	Delhi	61,332.00	2,92,773.00	61,938.00
7.	Gujarat	3,400.00	1,096.00	673.00
8.	Haryana	10,240.00	2,600.00	—
9.	Himachal Pradesh	10,986.00	1,763.00	—
10.	Madhya Pradesh	4,503.00	—	181.00

(Contd.)

(Contd.)

Sl. No.	*Name of State/U.T.*	*Membership Fee* Rs.	*Overdue Charges* Rs.	*Fine on Loss of Books* Rs.
11.	Orissa	35,000.00	—	—
12.	Punjab	—	5,223.00	—
13.	Tamil Nadu	—	1,22,000.00	—
14.	Uttar Pradesh	12,500.00	1,486.00	—

Out of 27 States, information on the revenue from other sources is received only from 14 States/U.Ts (52 per cent). The receipts of the library on account of membership fee, overdue charges and loss of books are mentioned in Table 3.17 as revenue.

From the table, it is assessed that by way of membership fee, Delhi has collected the maximum of Rs. 61,332.00 on an average for the past 5 years (1993-94 to 1997-98), followed by Andhra Pradesh (Rs. 36,339.00), Orissa (Rs. 35,000.00), and Bihar (Rs. 26,368.00) while Arunachal Pradesh was able to collect only Rs. 974.00 towards this account. Regarding overdue charges, as usual, Delhi nets the maximum of Rs. 2,92,773.00 on an average and Tamil Nadu comes next by collecting Rs. 1,22,000.00 whereas Gujarat collected the least amount of Rs.1,096.00. As regards to the fine on loss of books, Rs. 61,938.00 collected by Delhi is the maximum average revenue while Rs. 38.00 collected by Arunachal Pradesh is the minimum amount.

The figures indicate that the revenues from other sources is very marginal and insignificant compared to the overall expenditure of the SCLs. The budget allotment of the respective States/U.Ts continues to be the main source of income for the SCLs of India. Owing to the frequent reduction of budget by the authorities, the SCLs can consider innovative methods for collecting revenues to supplement the income of the library. Compiling Bibliographies on p yment, providing Xerox facilities for external materials, offering Internet browsing services and providing consultancy services for library related matters may be considered as so e of the methods to enhance the income of the SCL.

Governance

The governance of libraries is a basic management activity which is concerned not only with the staff and finance management but also with its resources and other relevant functions of the library. A public library exists to serve the reading and information needs of the society. Hence, the objectives of a public library should be the same or similar to those of the society to whom it serves. If one proceeds to analyse the status of State Central Libraries in India, it cannot be done effectively without finding the system of governance or authority so that the objectives and functioning of the SCLs can be seen in the proper perspective.

Administration. The State Central Libraries of India are controlled by different administrative Ministries and various cadres of administrative heads as per the information collected from the questionnaires from the SCLs as depicted under Table 3.18.

TABLE 3.18
Administrative Authorities of SCLs of India

Sl. No.	*State / U.T.*	*Head*	*Ministry*
1.	Andaman and Nicobar Islands	Director of Education	Human Resource Development (HRD)
2.	Andhra Pradesh	Director of Public Libraries	Library Services
3.	Arunachal Pradesh	Secretary	Culture
4.	Assam	Director of Public Libraries	Education
5.	Bihar	Secretary of Library Committee	—
6.	Chandigarh	Director of Public Instruction	Education
7.	Delhi	Director of Delhi Public Library	Human Resource Development
8.	Goa	Director of Art and Culture	Education
9.	Gujarat	Director of Public Libraries	Education and Culture
10.	Haryana	Director of Public Libraries	Education
11.	Himachal Pradesh	Secretary	Education
12.	Karnataka	Director of Public Libraries	Library Services
13.	Kerala	State Librarian	Education

14.	Lakhsadweep	Director of Social Welfare	Education
15.	Madhya Pradesh	Director of Education	Education
16.	Maharashtra	Director of Public Libraries	Higher & Tech. Education
17.	Manipur	Director of Art and Culture	Art & Culture
18.	Meghalaya	Secretary	Culture
19.	Mizoram	Director of Culture	Culture
20.	Nagaland	Director of Culture	Culture
21.	Orissa	Director of State Central Library	Culture
22.	Pondichery	Director of Art & Culture	Education
23.	Punjab	Secretary	
24.	Rajasthan	Director of Education	Education
25.	Tamil Nadu	Director of Public Libraries	School Education
26.	Uttar Pradesh	Division of SCL	Library Service
27.	West Bengal	Director of State Central Library	Library Service

While analysing the status of administrative heads of the SCLs of India, it is observed that the SCLs are headed by the appropriate head of the department, i.e., the Director of Public Libraries only in 7 States (26 per cent)-(1) Andhra Pradesh (2) Assam (3) Gujarat (4) Haryana (5) Karnataka (6) Maharashtra and (7) Tamil Nadu. In another 4 States (15 per cent) viz. 1. Delhi, 2. Kerala, 3. Orissa, 4. Uttar Pradesh and 5. West Bengal, the head of the State Central Library himself has full powers to take decision on matters relating to the SCLs. The Directors of Education/Art and Culture, etc. are the official heads of the SCLs in 11 States/ U.Ts (41 per cent) while the Secretaries at the Ministry level are the deciding authorities for the SCLs of 5 States (18 per cent).

The State governments of the 16 States should see the reason in creating separate Directorate for Public Libraries so that the State Central Library as well as the State Public Library System is put into its rails properly.

It is the official procedure and mechanism that the decisions of the Governments are implemented through the respective Ministries in every State. If there is a separate Ministry for library services, the SCLs/Public Libraries will receive greater attention from their governments in the allocation of funds and uniform development of the public library system in the State. However, the present scenario of the administrative Ministry for SCLs depict a dismal picture.

Among the 27 States, only 4 States (15 per cent) viz., 1. Andhra Pradesh, 2. Karnataka, 3. Uttar Pradesh and 4. West Bengal have separate Ministries exclusively for Library Services. In 11 States (41 per cent), the Education Ministry is looking after the subject of State Central Libraries. The Ministry of Culture/Art and Culture takes care of the functions of the SCLs in 6 States (22 per cent) whereas 2 SCLs (7 per cent) are under the control of Ministry of Human Resources Development.

Library Committee. A Library Committee is an inevitable system of management to devote adequate time and interest for the matters affecting the Library administration. The Library Committee shall serve as an interpreter of the needs and demands of the library for the users as well as for the controlling authority of the library. In brief, a Library Committee can work towards bringing a better understanding of the role of the library among its users and provide necessary support to the librarian for making decisions having immediate implications on the authority and for the users.

In the present analysis, 15 States/U.Ts (56 per cent) have confirmed that there is a separate Library Committee in their SCLs to effectively monitor the functioning of the libraries whereas 19 SCLs (37 per cent) are functioning without any Committee. The librarians of 2 SCLs (7 per cent) have not informed whether any Committee exists for the library or not.

A comparative analysis of the constitution of Library Committee and the powers of such committees functioning in the SCLs of India are enumerated in Table 3.11.

The Secretary of the Library Committee happens to be the Librarian of the SCL in 11 cases (73 per cent), while the President is the representative of the respective Ministry or Head of the Department. The powers of the Committee have also been limited. Among 15 SCLs where the Library Committees are functioning, only 3 SCLs (20 per cent) at (1) Andaman and Nicobar Islands (2) Bihar and (3) Himachal Pradesh have absolute powers to frame rules, make policy decisions, administer the employees and to

TABLE 3.19
Library Committees of SCLs

Sl. No.	State/Union Territories	President	Secretary	Mem	To Frame rules	Make Policy Decision	To Administer Employees	To Award Punishment
1.	Andaman and Nicobar Islands	Chairman, SLPC	Director of Education	14	Yes	Yes	Yes	Yes
2.	Arunachal Pradesh	Secretary	Chief librarian	10	Yes	Yes	No	No
3.	Assam	Commissioner of Education	Director of Public Libraries	11	Yes	Yes	No	No
4.	Bihar	Chief Justice Patna High Court	G.K. Sinha	15	Yes	Yes	Yes	Yes
5.	Chandigarh	Chairman of the Committee	State librarian	15	—	—	—	—
6.	Delhi	Chairperson of Delhi Public Library Board	Director of Delhi Public Librarian	14	Yes	Yes	No	No
7.	Goa	Secretary, Education	Curator of Libraries	09	No	Yes	No	No
8.	Haryana	Deputy Commissioner of the District	State Librarian	—	No	No	No	No

(Contd.)

Sl. No.	State/Union Territories	President	Secretary	Mem	To Frame	Make Policy	To Administer Employees	To Award Punishment
9.	Himachal Pradesh	Secretary, Education	Chief Librarian	12	Yes	Yes	Yes	Yes
10.	Kerala	Secretary, Higher Education	State Librarian	19	Yes	Yes	No	No
11.	Manipur	Secretary, Art and Culture	Chief Librarian	07	Yes	Yes	No	No
12.	Meghalaya	Secretary	Librarian	08	Yes	—	—	—
13.	Nagaland	Director of Art and Culture	Librarian	09	—	—	—	—
14.	Pondicherry	Secretary, Education	Librarian	09	No	No	No	No
15.	Uttar Pradesh	Addl. Director Secondary Education	Librarian - Incharge	—	—	—	—	—
16.	West Bengal	Director of Library Services	Librarian	08	Yes	No	No	No

award punishment wherever necessary. The right to administer employees and award punishment have not been vested with Library Committee in 9 SCLs (60 per cent). No powers are given to the Library Committee on Library Administration in 2 States/U.Ts (13 per cent) viz. Haryana and Pondicherry, while the Library Committee of Goa has power to make only policy decisions. Thus, the powers, functions, states and composition of Library Committee are inconsistent.

Space and Building

The most significant principle among the Five Laws of Library Science, enunciated by the father of library science in India-Prof. S.R. Ranganathan is the fifth law which states 'Library is a growing organism'. He says, "The building of storage library—say a State Central Library or the National Central Library—should be capable of indefinite growth. The site chosen for it should be very large indeed. Its building—particularly the stack room—will have to be extended in a number of successive phases" (Ranganathan; 1988; p. 41).

In order to satisfy the fifth law of library science, the building of every SCL should be planned to accommodate suitable materials required for the readers at present with a provision for the future expansion so as to perform the library services efficiently and effectively to the fullest satisfaction of the readers. The design of the building should be functional rather than monumental providing facilities for open access, scope for future growth, provision of reading rooms around the stock-room and allowing natural light and air to spread the building to the extent possible. It is needless to say that the library should be located in its own building at the central part of the town with sufficient seating capacity to accommodate the ever growing readership. There should be more rooms for offering a variety of services and research cubicles should be provided for serious readers.

The Table 3.20 furnished below provides a glance of the space, building and such other physical conditions of the of SCLs in India. From the table, it is seen that 21 SCLs (78 per cent) are located in their own buildings while 3 at (1) Delhi, (2) Goa and (3) Madhya Pradesh are (11 per cent) situated in government buildings which are not owned by the library authorities. Even after 50 years of independence, 2 State Central Libraries (7 per

TABLE 3.20
Space and Building Condition of SCLs

Sl. No.	Name of State/U.T.	Buildings	Seating Capacity	Carpet Area	Research Cubicles	Total Rooms	Plinth Area
1.	Andaman & Nicobar Islands	Own	175	—	—	10	—
2.	Andhra Pradesh	Own	900	—	12	24	72,247 sq. yards
3.	Arunachal Pradesh	Own	100	100 sq. mt.	—	12	100 sq. mt.
4.	Assam	Own	25	1,592 sq. mt.	—	03	—
5	Bihar	Own	250	—	—	22	28,506 sq. ft.
6.	Chandigarh	Own	—	—	—	—	—
7.	Delhi	Govt. Bldg	—	—	—	—	—
8.	Goa	Govt. Bldg	100	3,657 sq. mt.	6	12	12,000 sq. ft.
9.	Gujarat	Own	1000	24,384 sq. mt.	300	13	13
10.	Haryana	Own	100	1,524 sq. mt.	—	14	4 acres
11.	Himachal Pradesh	Rented	120	—	—	23	—
12.	Karnataka	Own	250	300 sq. mt.	—	09	—
13.	Kerala	Own	350	8,560 sq. mt.	—	13	—
14.	Lakshadweep	Own	25	—	—	05	—

(Contd.)

(Contd.)

Sl. No.	*Name of State/U.T.*	*Buildings*	*Seating Capacity*	*Carpet Area*	*Research Cubicles*	*Total Rooms*	*Plinth Area*
15.	Madhya Pradesh	Govt. Bldg	60	2,134 sq. mt.	—	13	15,000 sq. ft.
16.	Maharashtra	Own	500	9,445 sq. mt.	24	03	31,000 sq. ft.
17.	Manipur	Own	200	—	—	09	—
18.	Meghalaya	Own	200	—	—	15	—
19.	Mizoram	Rented	20	114 sq. mt.	—	05	600 sq. ft.
20.	Nagaland	—	80	—	10	16	—
21.	Orissa	Own	400	—	—	25	—
22.	Pondicherry	Own	250	—	—	10	—
23.	Punjab	Own	200	1,433 sq. mt.	—	20	—
24.	Rajasthan	Own	200	—	—	15	30,000 sq. ft.
25.	Tamil Nadu	Own	350	2,347 sq. mt.	—	12	1,00,000 sq. ft.
26.	Uttar Pradesh	Own	1000	5,354 sq. mt.	—	14	16,688 sq. ft.
27.	West Bengal	Own	200	16,460 sq. mt.	12	09	—
	Total	—	7,055	80,673 sq. mt.	364	306	

cent) at Himachal Pradesh and Mizoram States are surprisingly functioning in the rented buildings, which seems to be an unhealthy trend.

The seating capacity of the apex library of the States/U.Ts vary from a mere 20 seats at Mizoram State to 1,000 seats at Gujarat and Uttar Pradesh. An average of 300 seats (298 to be precise) are available for the readers in the SCLs of India. The statistical figures on carpet area are not filled by 13 respondents out of 27 (48 per cent). The available figures vary from 114 sq.mt at Mizoram State to 24,384 sq. mt. in Gujarat State. Regarding the plinth area, the maximum spaces are mentioned in various units by SCLs such as 72,247 sq. yards by Andhra Pradesh, 4 acres by Haryana and 1,00,000 sq. ft. by Tamil Nadu State. The minimum plinth area is, once again, 600 sq. ft. in Mizoram State.

The numbers of rooms available in SCLs have been analysed. The State Central Library of Orissa State has as many as 25 rooms for providing library services and administration whereas the Assam State accommodates all the stock and offers its services only in 3 rooms. Facilities for research cubicles are offered only in 6 SCLs at Andhra Pradesh, Goa, Gujarat, Maharashtra, Nagaland and West Bengal States respectively. The availability of research cubicles, however, ranges from 6 in Goa to 300 in Gujarat State.

In total, the SCLs of 25 States in India have 7,055 seats at a time in the reading rooms for the users and provides 364 Research Cubicles in 6 SCLs for exclusive study. There are 306 rooms in the SCLs accommodating the bookstocks and other services to the Members of the Libraries. The carpet area of 14 SCLs, from where data were collected, comes to 80,673 sq. mt. From the above statistics, it is ascertained that, on an average, there are 282 seats in the library rooms, 51 research cubicles, 5,762 sq.mt. of carpet area and 13 rooms in each SCL of India.

The year of construction of the library building denotes how long the SCL is offering services to the users from a particular building. As per the data collected through the Questionnaires, the year of construction of the building of SCLs is listed below in chronological order as depicted in Table 3.21. The actual cost of the building at the time of construction is also furnished wherever available.

TABLE 3.21
The Year of Construction and Cost of SCLs

Sl. No.	*Name of State/ U.T.*	*Year of Construction*	*Cost (Rs. in Lakhs)*
1.	Maharashtra	1833	—
2.	Karnataka	1888	—
3.	Tamil Nadu	1896	5.00
4.	Kerala	1900	—
5.	Bihar	1924	—
6.	Andhra Pradesh	1936	5.00
7.	Meghalaya	1954	—
8.	Chandigarh	1955	—
9.	Punjab	1955	12.00
10.	Andaman and Nicobar Islands	1959	10.00
11.	Manipur	1963	—
12.	Orissa	1967	—
13.	Gujarat	1972	50.00
14.	Lakshadweep	1973	—
15.	Pondicherry	1974	—
16.	Uttar Pradesh	1984	45.00
17.	Rajasthan	1990	—
18.	Arunachal Pradesh	1995	127.00
19.	West Bangal	1995	500.00

From the table, it can be assessed that the SCL of Maharashtra, at Mumbai, popularly called as the Town Hall, is functioning from the oldest (166 years old) among the buildings of all SCLs and West Bengal has the latest building constructed just 8 years ago at V.I.P. Road, Kolkata. The cost of the buildings, as per the data available, varies from Rs. 5 lakhs for the old buildings of SCLs at Tamil Nadu and Andhra Pradesh to Rs. 500 lakhs for the recent by constructed building of SCL of West Bengal State.

Physical Conditions

The physical conditions of library, in this context, refers to the furniture, equipments and other facilities available in the State Central Libraries of India. In the survey undertaken by me, the number and categories of furniture and equipments available in 27 SCLs of India have been obtained and listed in Table 3.22.

The table indicates that there are as many as 867 chairs providing seating capacity to the readers at a time in the SCL of Andhra Pradesh whereas only 32 are available in Lakshadweep. The number of tables and desks available in the SCLs vary from 10 in Assam to 350 in Gujarat. While the SCLs of Andaman & Nicobar Islands has 45 bookshelves/racks, the SCL at Delhi has 1,369 of them. The availability of filing trays vary from 1 in Andhra Pradesh State to 40 in Kerala. The Punjab State has only one Dictionary stand to display the dictionaries whereas the SCL of Karnataka has 18 of them in its library. Only one magazine display rack is available in Madhya Pradesh and Maharashtra States while Kerala has 31 of them for the use of the readers.

Newspaper stands are available only in 16 SCLs (60%) ranging from just 2 stands in Himachal Pradesh to 40 in Maharashtra State. Book Display Stands are kept in 16 SCLs (60%) for the perusal of books by the readers—the total number of which is varying from only one each in Haryana, Madhya Pradesh, Nagaland and Tamil Nadu States whereas 18 of them are being used in Gujarat State. Book trolleys, to move the books in bulk from one place to another for rearrangement, are maintained in 12 SCLs ranging from one in Lakshadweep, Punjab and Uttar Pradesh to the maximum of 117 in Delhi. The almirahs are used for keeping books in 23 libraries—the numbers varying from 13 in the State of Karnataka to 293 in Uttar Pradesh State. Being an essential tool for searching of books, catalogue cabinets are maintained to provide subject, author and titles of the books available in the libraries. The number of catalogue cabinets available in SCLs vary from a mere 2 in Madhya Pradesh State to 198 in Maharashtra State. Several SCLs have other categories of furniture and equipments like xerox, codex, cupboards, television, radio and video cassette recorders, etc. which are insignificant in their number.

Thus, among the furniture items available in 27 SCLs of India, there are 7,911 chairs, 2,261 tables/desks, 6,833 bookshelves/racks, 105 filing trays, 42 dictionary stands, 187 magazine display racks, 179 newspaper stands, 152 book trolleys, 1,567 almirahs, 659 catalogue cards, 85 book display stands and other materials.

TABLE 3.22
Number and Categories of Furniture Items in SCLs of India

Sl. No.	Name of State/ UT	Chairs	Tables/ Desks	Book-Shelves	Filling Trays	Dict. Stands	Mag. Display Racks	News-paper Stands	Book Display Stands	Book Trolleys	Almir-ahs	Catalo-gue Cabinets	Any Other Items
(1)	(2)	(3)	(4)	(5)	(6)	(7)	(8)	(9)	(10)	(11)	(12)	(13)	(14)
1.	Andaman and Nicobar Islands	180	45	45	10	05	10	20	15	04	30	32	
2.	Andhra Pradesh	867	210	650	01	—	10	03	10	14	223	57	Xerox
3.	Arunachal Pradesh	150	20	134	—	—	—	—	—	—	19	64	Codex-4
4.	Assam	35	10	52	—	—	—	—	—	—	20	03	—
5.	Bihar	190	78	380	03	—	05	03	06	02	143	07	Photostat
6.	Chandigarh	344	126	105	08	04	10	08	02	02	96	48	—
7.	Delhi	919	223	1369	03	05	05	—	—	117	35	—	—
8.	Goa	—	—	—	—	—	—	—	—	—	—	—	—
9.	Gujarat	400	350	132	08	06	18	28	18	02	60	24	80 Steel Cup boards
10.	Haryana	150	15	175	03	—	02	—	01	—	55	06	—
11.	Himachal Pradesh	320	105	109	04	02	06	02	03	—	162	05	TV, VCR and Radio
12.	Karnataka	136	43	51	10	08	23	06	06	—	13	24	—
13.	Kerala	515	114	426	40	—	31	06	03	—	47	30	—
14.	Lakshadweep	32	12	—	—	03	02	—	—	01	—	—	—

(Contd.)

(Contd.)

(1)	(2)	(3)	(4)	(5)	(6)	(7)	(8)	(9)	(10)	(11)	(12)	(13)	(14)
15.	Madhya Pradesh	60	30	55	—	—	01	—	01	—	83	02	—
16.	Maharashtra	343	149	326	—	—	01	40	08	—	32	198	—
17.	Manipur	200	50	150	—	—	04	10	—	—	50	05	—
18.	Meghalaya	—	—	—	—	—	—	—	—	—	—	—	—
19.	Mizoram	35	15	150	—	—	—	—	—	—	—	30	—
20.	Nagaland	120	50	100	08	—	03	02	01	—	25	03	—
21.	Orissa	452	154	455	02	—	02	06	02	02	31	06	—
22.	Pondicherry	640	48	420	—	—	04	—	—	—	20	15	—
23.	Punjab	200	36	170	01	01	04	07	06	01	60	14	—
24.	Rajasthan	354	98	128	—	—	04	—	02	—	20	09	TV and VCR
25.	Tamil Nadu	425	175	825	—	—	25	12	01	04	20	38	—
26.	Uttar Pradesh	244	47	176	—	04	02	12	—	01	293	29	—
27.	West Bengal	600	60	250	04	04	15	14	—	02	30	10	—
Total		7,911	2,261	6,833	105	42	187	179	85	152	1,567	659	

Automation

Survey on Automation in State Central Libraries. Considering the dire need for application of Information Technology in State Central Libraries, a survey has been conducted to find out the scenario of application of information technology in the State Central Libraries of India, as on 1998.

It is a matter of serious concern that only the following 7 out of 27 States/U.Ts (26 per cent) have applied information technology in the apex library of their respective States:

1. Chandigarh U.T.
2. Delhi U.T.
3. Gujarat State
4. Karnataka State
5. Lakshadweep U.T.
6. Pondicherry U.T., and
7. Tamil Nadu State.

It is ascertained that among the 25 States in India, only 3 States (12 per cent) have adopted information technology whereas 4 out of 7 Union Territories (57 per cent) have utilized the Information Technology for the State Central Library of the respective State/U.T. Thus, it is a matter of satisfaction for the Union Territories that, even though they are smaller in size, population, and fund generation, they are more advanced in going ahead with the time as seen from the adoption of I.T. for their libraries compared to the States with a larger population and fund.

From among the remaining States/U.Ts, the State Central Libraries of 7 States/U.Ts viz. Andaman and Nicobar Islands, Haryana, Himachal Pradesh, Kerala, Maharashtra, Rajasthan and West Bengal have drawn up proposals for the use of computers and communication technology in their libraries as per the information provided by them in their Questionnaires.

All other States/U.T.s viz., Andhra Pradesh, Arunachal Pradesh, Assam, Bihar, Goa, Madhya Pradesh, Manipur, Meghalaya, Mizoram, Nagaland, Orissa, Punjab and Uttar Pradesh do not appear to have any plan or proposal to apply the emerging concept of Information Technology in their libraries, as seen from the Questionnaires.

E-mail and Internet Facility. While surveying the facilities and services of the SCLs of India, it is observed that only 1 State Central Library at Delhi U.T. has E-Mail address and none of them have their own websites or Internet pages to inform the readers and public of the services and resources of the respective library.

Computer Configuration. A comparative statement on the existing computer configuration reported to be available in the SCLs of various States/U.Ts is furnished below in Table 3.23.

TABLE 3.23
Hardware of SCLs of India

Sl. No.	*State/U.T.*	*System*	*Hard Disk*	*RAM*	*Operating Speed*
1.	Chandigarh	586 Pentium	1 GB	32 MB	90 MHz
2.	Delhi	486/386	—	—	—
3.	Gujarat	486	—	2 MB	133 MHz
4.	Karnataka	Pentium	1.2 GB	32 MB	120 MHz
5.	Lakhsadweep	486	—	—	—
6.	Pondicherry	586	2.1 GB	16 MB	166 MHz
7.	Tamilnadu	486	2.1 GB	16 MB	166 MHz

From the above, it can be seen that only two libraries have Pentium-based processors whereas 4 SCLs have 486 based CPUs. Again, in the wake of introducing advanced computer configurations, the SCLs of UTs apparently predominant over the SCLs of States.

Software. If hardware is the body, software is the life/soul of the information technology. The study reveals that the following software tools are used in the 7 State Central Libraries as reflected in Table 3.24.

TABLE 3.24
Softwares Used in SCLs of India

Sl. No.	*State/U.Ts.*	*Application Software*	*System Software*	*Operating System*	*Database Managemment*
1.	Chandigarh	LMIS	Basis Plus	Unix Based	d' Base
2.	Delhi	CDS List	LIBRIS	Windows	Unix
3.	Gujarat	Sanjay Lib	Window'95	—	d'Base
4.	Karnataka	Techlib plus	Dos/Unix	Unix	Foxplus
5.	Lakshadweep	—	—	Ms-Dos/ Win'95	CDS/ISIS
6.	Pondicherry	Foxpro	—	Ms-Dos	—
7.	Tamil Nadu	MS-Word	—	Win'98	d' Base

Windows, Ms-Dos and Unix form the basis of operating systems of SCLs. d'Base, Unix, Foxplus and CDS/ISIS have been used for Database Management. Specialised library softwares such as Sanjay Lib, Techlib plus and LIBRIS are being used by the SCLs for performing the desired functions in the respective libraries.

Services. Information Technology (IT) can be used not only to perform various operations and services at libraries which are repetitive in nature but also for accessing global databases both offline as well as online. Among the types of services which can be provided by the State Central Libraries through information technology, mention should be made of Reference Service, OPAC, Documentation Service, Bibliographic Service, ILL transactions, Photo-duplication Service and Online Searching Service. In-house operations such as acquisition, technical processing and circulation control can also be performed by the libraries more effectively through the application of information technology.

The services of SCLs were grouped under eleven broad categories to which the surveyed Librarians of SCLs were asked to respond. The SCL of Chandigarh UT has applied IT for 9 out of 11 services as reflected in Table 41 except for E-mail and serials control. The services of SCL of Chandigarh UT which are being rendered through IT include acquisition, technical processing, circulation control, reference service, documentation services, bibliographic service, photoduplication activities, online searching

TABLE 3.25
Services Provided by SCLs Through IT

Sl. No.	Name of State/ U.T.	Acqui-sition	Tech Pro-cessing	Circu-lation	Ref. Service	Docume-ntation	Series Control Service	Biblio-graphic cation	Photo Dupli-	Online Searcing	E-mail	In House Operations
		(1)	(2)	(3)	(4)	(5)	(6)	(7)	(8)	(9)	(10)	(11)
1.	Chandigarh	Yes	Yes	Yes	Yes	Yes	No	Yes	Yes	Yes	No	Yes
2.	Delhi Yes	No	No	Yes	No	Yes	Yes	No	Yes	Yes	No	
3.	Gujarat	No	No	No	No	No	No	No	No	No	No	No
4.	Karnataka	Yes	No	No	No	No	No	No	Yes	No	No	No
5.	Lakshadweep	No	No	No	No	No	No	No	No	No	No	No
6.	Pondicherry	No	Yes	No	No	No	No	Yes	No	Yes	No	Yes
7.	Tamilnadu	Yes	No	No	No	No	No	No	No	No	No	No

services and for in-house operations. The SCL of Delhi U.T. utilises automation facilities for acquisition, reference service, serials control, bibliographic service, online searching and for offering E-mail services.

The information technology is adopted for technical processing, bibliographic service, online searching and for in-house operations in the SCL of Pondicherry U.T. while Karnataka State utilises computers primarily for acquisition processes and photoduplication activities, Tamil Nadu State restricts the use of information technology for acquisition alone. It appears that, the SCLs of Gujarat State and Lakshadweep U.T. have just acquired hardware and software for application of information technology. However, they have not yet started exploiting the I.T. for offering library services. The State Central Libraries of Chandigarh and Tamil Nadu have been accessing NICNET Online database while Delhi SCL is hooked to DELENT.

Among the seven State Central Libraries, Chandigarh U.T. has gone well ahead in adoption of information technology to provide public library services. The national official database GISTNIC and international database MEDLARS have been provided online by the State Central Library of Chandigarh U.T. Membership Registration and Catalogue Information System have already been made online and computerisation of Issue-Return service is being implemented in this library. However, application of IT/computerisation is yet to enter into the threshold of the remaining SCLs of 20 surveyed States/UTs.

Problems and Constraints. From the above analysis, it is clear that the overall situation in adopting information technology in the State Central Libraries of India which are the nodal public libraries in the public library system in the country is far from satisfactory. Thus, the use of IT in the public libraries in general and the SCLs in particular is still in a state of infancy.

The delay and backwardness in adopting IT in the State-Central Libraries of India can be attributed to the following reasons :

(i) Lack of adequate funds for acquiring necessary hardware and software;

(ii) Lack of necessary trained manpower in the use of information technology; and

TABLE 3.26
Membership Pattern

Sl. No.	Name of State/U.T.	Free or Fee	Annual Subscription (Rs.)	Overdue Charges per day (Rs.)	Photocopy Charges per page (Rs.)	Orientation Prog.	Membership is Open/ Restricted	User Population
(1)	(2)	(3)	(4)	(5)	(6)	(7)	(8)	(9)
1.	Andaman and Nicobar Islands	Mixed	No	0.50	—	Yes	Restricted for Foreigners	600 per day
2.	Andhra Pradesh	Free	No	0.05	0.50P	No	Open	2,40,435
3.	Arunachal Pradesh	Mixed	2.00	1.00	2.00	No	Open	—
4.	Assam	Free	—	—	—	No	Open	275 per day
5.	Bihar	Mixed	100	0.25	1.50	No	Open	450 per day
6.	Chandigarh	Free	No	0.25	0.50	Yes	Open	5 lakhs per year
7.	Delhi	Free	No	0.50	1.00	Yes	Open to Delhi Residents only	66,231
8.	Goa	Free	No	0.10	1.00	Yes	Open	400 per day
9.	Gujarat	Free	No	0.50	1.00	Yes	Open	17,753

(Contd.)

(1)	(2)	(3)	(4)	(5)	(6)	(7)	(8)	(9)
10.	Haryana	Free	No	1.00	—	Yes	Open	5 lakh
11.	Himachal Pradesh	Free	No	0.50	Nil	Yes	Open	—
12.	Karnataka	Free	No	—	0.75	No	Open	1,636 per day
13.	Kerala	Free	No	—	—	Yes	Open	23,915
14.	Lakshadweep	Free	No	—	—	No	Open	—
15.	Madhya Pradesh	Free	No	—	—	Yes	Open	—
16.	Maharashtra	Free	No	—	—	Yes	Open	800 per day
17.	Manipur	Free	No	—	—	No	Open	28,835
18.	Meghalaya	Fee	5.00	—	—	No	Open	—
19.	Mizoram	Free	No	—	—	Yes	Open	2,500
20.	Nagaland	Fee	50.00	0.50	—	No	Open	1,500
21.	Orissa	Free	5.00 for 3 years	—	0.70	No	Open	10,000
22.	Pondicherry	Free	No	0.05	1.00	No	Open	2,65,500
23.	Punjab	Free	No	—	—	No	Open	—
24.	Rajasthan	Free	No	—	0.50	Yes	Open	200 per day
25.	Tamil Nadu	Fee	25.00	1.00	0.75	Yes	Open	63,000
26.	Uttar Pradesh	Mixed	200.00 for Life	0.20	—	No	Open	—
27.	West Bengal	Free	No	—	—	No	Open	10,000

(iii) Attitude of library staff in resisting the change-over from the traditional practices to the modern applications including I.T.

Membership Pattern

The real strength of a library lies in its usage. The main purpose of functioning of a library is that it should be used by the members—both the registered and the unregistered. The optimum utilisation of the library resources shall also depend upon the organisation of reading materials as well as the efficiency and helpful attitude of the staff members of the library. The basic data required from a library to measure its social significance to the society is the number of volumes circulated or consulted and the number of borrowers served by the library concerned. The number of members registered at a given period of time shall explain the quantitative assessment of the services of the library.

The State Central Library normally enrolls members from the State capital city in which the SCL is located as well as from among the residents of any part of the State/U.T. based on some identifications such as residential certificate, ration card, bank passbook, tax receipt, bonafide certificate of the head of the Institution or a guarantee letter from any responsible person of the locality. However, the modern trend warrants to reduce the guarantee system to a minimum since the library is basically a service institution.

The data on membership pattern obtained from the SCLs of India are presented in Table 3.27. The table clearly demonstrates that, free services are provided to members in 20 SCLs (74 per cent) whereas 7 SCLs (26 per cent) are charging a nominal fee from their members. The details of annual/life fee charged by the seven SCLs are depicted in Table 3.27.

TABLE 3.27
Membership Charges of SCLs

Sl. No.	*Name of the State*	*Charges (Rs.)*
1.	Arunachal Pradesh	2.00 per annum
2.	Bihar	100.00 for Life
3.	Meghalaya	5.00 per annum

(Contd.)

(Contd.)

4.	Nagaland	50.00 for Life
5.	Orissa	5.00 for 3 years
6.	Tamil Nadu	25.00 per annum
7.	Uttar Pradesh	200.00 per annum

The fee collected by the SCLs ranges from Rs.2.00 in Arunachal Pradesh to Rs. 200.00 in Uttar Pradesh State. The fee structure in Bihar and Uttar Pradesh seems to be higher and against the well established canons of a service institution—the public library.

The overdue charges for belated return of books are collected in 12 SCLs (44 %). The overdue charges range from 05 paise per day at Pondicherry U.T. and Andhra Pradesh State to 1 Rupee in the States of Arunachal Pradesh, Haryana and Tamil Nadu. The photocopying facilities are provided in the SCLs of 12 States (44 %) in India where they charge from the users an amount of 0.50 paise per page in Andhra Pradesh, Chandigarh and Rajasthan and upto a maximum of Rs. 2.00 per page in Arunachal Pradesh.

Initiation of freshman and offering orientation to new members on the facilities and services provided by the library shall go a long way in the optimum utilisation of the resources available in SCLs. The survey indicates that only 14 libraries (52 %) are providing some sort of Orientation programme to its members. The remaining 13 SCLs (48 %) do not offer any Orientation programme. Membership is open in 24 SCLs (89 %) allowing any person to enroll as member while 3 SCLs (11 %) still have some restrictions for admitting the members. Since the U.T. of Andaman and Nicobar Islands is situated amidst international sea waters on all sides, it is but natural that the membership of the SCL of Andaman & Nicobar Island is restricted to only Indian citizens. The membership of Delhi SCL is restricted to the citizens residing in Delhi city only. The State Central Library of Tamil Nadu-Connemara Public Library—admits only those who are the residing in Chennai city.

It is strange on the part of the authorities of SCLs of Tamil Nadu and Delhi (the national capital) to restrict their library membership only for the residents of the capital cities as per the information available in the Questionnaires. Readers from any part of the State/U.T. should be allowed to enroll as a member of the apex library without any discrimination. The membership of SCL should be valid for borrowing books in any public library within the State.

User Population

The data furnished by the librarians of the SCLs interestingly reflect myriad patterns of users. The user population is calculated in terms of users per day in the States/U.Ts of Andaman and Nicobar Island (600 per day), Assam (275 per day), Bihar (450 per day), Goa (400 per day), Karnataka (1636 per day), Maharashtra (800 per day), and Rajasthan (250 per day). The SCLs of 4 States have furnished only annual figures—Andhra Pradesh (12,40,435), Chandigarh (5,00,000), Haryana (5,00,000) and Pondicherry (2,65,500).

However, the average number of users using the SCLs have been arrived at by dividing the total number of users per year by the number of holidays notified by the respective library for analysis. As a result, the user population of the four States mentioned above has been estimated as follows : Andhra Pradesh (5,126), Chandigarh (1,667), Haryana (1,667) and Pondicherry (894). The statistical figures furnished for the SCLs of 9 States appear to reflect the registered members of the library—Delhi (66,231), Gujarat (17,853), Kerala (23,915), Manipur (28,835), Mizoram (2,500), Nagaland (1,500) Orissa (10,000), Tamilnadu (63,000) and West Bengal (10,000). The average user population per day has been estimated as 10 per cent of the total registered members which is normally observed in public libraries. The user population for these 9 States has been derived, for the purpose of assessment, as : Delhi (6,623), Gujarat (1,785), Kerala (2,391), Manipur (2,883), Mizoram (250, Nagaland (150), Orissa (1,000), Tamil Nadu (6,300) and West Bengal (1,000).

My efforts to obtain the various categories of user population such as students, children, adult, public, etc. in all SCLs have not succeeded. However, only 4 SCLs—Andaman and Nicobar Island, Arunachal Pradesh and Gujarat have furnished categorywise readers as reflected in Table 3.28.

TABLE 3.28
Categorywise User-Population of 4 SCLs Per Day

Sl. No.	Category	Andaman & Nicobar Islands	Arunachal Pradesh	Gujarat	Rajasthan
1.	Teachers	12	15	15	10
2.	Students	120	106	350	100
3.	Researchers	90	03	18	20
4.	Scientists and Technocrats	12	04	02	10
5.	Government Servants	210	125	180	10
6.	Childran	60	51	120	50
7.	Lawyers	12	02	06	04
8.	Doctors	18	06	10	04
9.	Engineers	24	10	05	06
10.	Artists	30	02	03	10
11.	Others	12	52	1,067	26
	Total	600	376	1,776	250

Dependability on Other Categories of Libraries

No library can efficiently function in isolation. The State Central Library, being the apex library of the State, can have co-ordination or exchange system with National library of India, which is the apex library of the nation and with other categories of libraries such as District Library, Branch Library and Village Library. Any request for hard copy or xerox copy of books/ articles/information available in any part of the country or across the country can be routed through National Library. The resources of State Central Libraries of various States and National Library can be pooled together by the traditional Union Catalogue or common databases and shared for the mutual benefit. This would be an ideal situation for fully exploiting the resources of all SCLs of India, the National Library, and such other categories of libraries to the maximum extent.

However, the information obtained from the librarians of SCLs, through the Questionnaires reveals that, 23 SCLs (85%) do not have any connection or dependence on National Library of India for any of its services. The librarian of Bihar SCL has informed that, on demand, the SCL of Bihar has established contact with National Library for Inter Library Loan purpose. Only 3 SCLs (11%) refer to the National Library for preparation of Indian National Bibliography, especially regarding the books of the State language.

Further, the SCLs do not appear to have any relation or interaction with the District Libraries, Branch Libraries or any other public libraries of the State for networking, guidance or co-ordination as per the information furnished in the Questionnaires. The situation confirms that most of the SCLs of India are currently functioning in isolation, perhaps demanding appropriate and uniform legislative, administrative, financial, and professional support.

Repository Function

The State Central Libraries have a definite role to function as the repository centres of the respective State by stocking all or the maximum number of books printed/published in the State. The statutory provision was also given by the Central government in this direction. The Delivery of Books Act,1954 and Press and Registration of Books Acts,1867 are making provision for the publishers/printers to deposit books to certain designated SCLs.

Delivery of Books Act, 1954. In the year 1954, the Government of India enacted the Delivery of Books (Public Libraries) Act. The Act was later amended in 1956 to include newspapers also in its coverage. As per the Act, the publisher of a book or a newspaper has to deliver a copy of each book/newspaper published by him to National Library at Kolkata; Connemara Public Library, Chennai; Central Library, Mumbai and Delhi Public Library at Delhi. This Act has laid the foundation for the four National Book Depositories in India.

As per the Delivery of Books Act,1954, the 3 SCLs at Delhi, Maharashtra and Tamil Nadu are receiving books in various languages of India. The annual receipt of books under the Act and the total books received by the libraries so far under the provisions of the Act are furnished in Table 3.29.

TABLE 3.29
Collection of Books as per Delivery of Books Act, 1854

Sl. No.	*Name of SCL*	*Annual Receipt of Books*	*Total Books*
1.	Delhi	15,000	1,40,671
2.	Maharashtra	12,000	4,79,475
3.	Tamil Nadu	7,000	3,25,000

The above table clearly shows that the SCL of Delhi U.T. is able to collect 15,000 books per year whereas Maharashtra State has collected 12,000 during the period. Similarly, Tamilnadu was able to get only 7,000 books which is less than half of the number of books received in Delhi Public Library. However, regarding the total number of books collected so far under the Act, Maharashtra has received a maximum of 4,79,475 while Tamilnadu comes second with 3,25,000 books and Delhi is in the last position with only 1,40,671 books in its stock under this provision.

Press and Registration of Books Act, 1867. The Government of India have enacted Press and Registration of Books Act in the year 1867. Under the provisions of the Act, the printer of a book has to deliver a free copy of the book to the respective State Government. If the State Government desires one or two more copies of the book, the printer has to deliver the same to the Government.

The State Government should enter each book with all the necessary details in a 'Catalogue of Books' and the entries thus made in the catalogues in a quarter are to be published at the end of the quarter. The original intention of the Act, passed during the British rule, should have been aimed at checking the publication of any anti-imperialistic or freedom struggle oriented literature in India. However, the Act has been continued in independent India in order to have effective bibliographic control for the benefit of the people.

Among the 27 SCLs covered in the survey, it is ascertained

that only 7 SCLs (26%) have received books under the Registration of Books Act, 1867 as depicted in Table 3.30.

TABLE 3.30
Collection of Books as Per Registration of Books Act, 1867

Sl. No.	*Name of State*	*No. of Books Received annually*	*Total Number of Books*
1	Andhra Pradesh	1,200	47,720
2	Goa	66	—
3	Gujarat	1,315	28,240
4	Karnataka	14,408	87,315
5	Maharashtra	1,200	2,23,856
6	Orissa	300	3,000
7	West Bengal	2,000	25,000

The number of books received per annum varies from 66 in Goa to 14,408 in Karnataka State. Maharashtra State has collected the maximum number of 2,23,856 books as per the Act while Orissa has acquired the lowest number of 3,000 books under the provisions of this Act.

Though the Press and Registration of Books Act, 1867 has a nationwide jurisdiction, it is but strange that only 7 States are getting books under the Act. The remaining State governments should take necessary steps so that the SCLs of their States can function as a real repository centre for the books published/printed in their respective States.

Technical Status

The quantitative strength of collection is not alone sufficient. The resources of the State Central Libraries should be properly classified, catalogued and served to the users so that the maximum utilisation is obtained from the stock of the library. The current position on the technical status of the operations of the SCLs of India is reflected in Table 3.31.

Open Access. Open access system, invariably, increases the use of books. The introduction of open access system requires arranging the books in open book-racks in the library, allowing the users to browse the books without let or hindrance thereby

CHART 3.9
Mode of Access to SCLs of India

TABLE 3.31
Technical Status SCLs

Sl. No.	*Name of State/U.T.*	*Classification System*	*Catalogue Code*	*Subject Headings*	*Access*	*Charging Systems*
1.	Andaman & Nicobar Islands	D.D.C.	AACR-2	Sear's List	Open	Browne
2.	Andhra Pradesh	D.D.C. (16th)	ALA	Sear's List	Open	Browne
3.	Arunachal Pradesh	D.D.C.	AACR-2	Sear's List	Open	SRR's 2 Card System
4.	Assam	D.D.C. (20th)	AACR-2	—	Mixed	— No —
5.	Bihar	D.D.C. (16th)	AACR-1	DDC Based	Closed	Newark
6.	Chardigarh	D.D.C.	AACR-2	Sear's List	Open	Browne
7.	Delhi	D.D.C. (20th)	AACR-2	Subject Heading	Open	Browne
8.	Goa	D.D.C.	AACR-1	Sear's List	Open	Browne
9.	Gujarat	D.D.C. (18th)	CCC	Sear's List	Open	Browne
10.	Haryana	D.D.C. (18th)	ALA	Sear's List	Open	Newark
11.	Himachal Pradesh	D.D.C. (18th)	ALA	Sear's List	Open	Browne
12.	Karnataka	D.D.C. (19th)	CCC	L.C. Subject Heading	Open	— No —
13.	Kerala	C.C.	CCC	No	Open	Browne
14.	Lakshadweep	—	—	—	Open	Browne
15.	Madhya Pradesh	D.D.C.	CCC	—	Mixed	Ledger
16.	Maharashtra	D.D.C.	AACR-2	—	Closed	—

(Contd.)

Sl. No.	*Name of State/U.T.*	*Classification System*	*Catalogue Code*	*Subject Headings*	*Access*	*Charging Systems*
17.	Manipur	D.D.C. (20th)	CCC	—	Mixed	Browne
18.	Meghalaya	D.D.C. (19th)	AACR-1	No	Open	Browne
19.	Mizoram	D.D.C. (18th)	AACR-1	Sear's List	Open	Browne
20.	Nagaland	D.D.C. (18th)	AACR-2	Sear's List	Open	Browne
21.	Orissa	D.D.C. (20th)	AACR-2	Sear's List	Open	- No -
22.	Pondicherry	C.C.	CCC	—	Open	Browne
23.	Punjab	D.D.C. (19th)	AACR-1	Sear's List	Open	Newark
24.	Rajasthan	D.D.C. (18th)	CCC	Subject Heading	Mixed	Browne
25.	Tamil Nadu	D.D.C. (18th)	CCC	Chain Indexing	Mixed	Browne
26.	Uttar Pradesh	D.D.C. (19th)	ALA	—	Open	Browne
27.	West Bengal	D.D.C. (16th)	AACR-1	Sear's List	Mixed	— No —

enabling the users to take away any book from the bookshelves to the reading hall for reference or to circulation counter to borrow the book for home reading. Open access has come to stay in almost all modern public libraries all over the world.

The library stock should be fully accessible to the users. Open access system has been advocated strongly since long by the pioneers of library movement in India like, S.R. Ranganathan who says: "Open access blesseth him who gives and him who takes. The joy of a librarian reaches its maximum in an open access library only when the right reader and the right book choose each other in the Swayamvara set up of open access" (Rangantahn; 1998; p. 55).

From the 27 SCLs taken for analysis, only 19 States (70%) have open access in their apex public libraries. Mixed access by which a part of the stock is closed and part of the remaining stock is open is practised in 6 SCLs (22%). In two SCLs (7%) at Bihar and Maharashtra, the users are not allowed entry into the stock of the library.

Charging Systems. There is a debate on whether the SCLs should be a lending library or a reference library. Each argument has its own merits and pitfalls. Yenawine argues that, "the circulation function in libraries involves every user of library materials and the successful performance of the function is a measure of the effectiveness of all other duties to which all other librarians devote themselves. The best equipped library located in the most modern plant and staffed with most capable librarian would be a mausoleum of recorded knowledge if the circulation function was omitted. The processes and services which result in bringing the users and library materials into productive relationship is the circulation function in libraries" (Yenawine; 1957; p. 3).

The information collected from the respondents of the Questionnaires from the SCLs of India indicate that 22 (81%) out of 27 SCLs covered under the survey, provide lending services. Five SCLs (19%) are serving as Reference Libraries without offering lending services : (1) Assam, (2) Karnataka, (3) Maharashtra, (4) Orissa and (5) West Bengal.

Several Charging Systems are prevalent in the public libraries all over the world which include : (1) Browne System; (2) The Newark System; (3) S.R.R's Two Card System; (4) The Ledger System; (5) Punched Card System; (6) The Indicator System; (7) Shaw's Photocharging System; (8) The Token Charging System; (9) Gaylord System; (10) Plessy Pen System; and (11) The latest computerized OCR Charging System.

Among them, Newark system is popular in American Libraries and Browne Charging System is widely adopted in Indian and British public libraries. The Questionnaires confirm that Browne Charging System is the most dominant in the SCLs of India which is practised in 17 SCLs (63%) out of 27. Newark Charging System, on the other hand, is being followed in 3 SCLs (9%)—Bihar, Haryana and Punjab. The age-old Ledger System is still practised in Madhya Pradesh and S.R. Ranganathan's Two Card System is followed in Himachal Pradesh with national spirit. It was Berelson who said, "Of all library activities, the circulation of books for home use represents by far the major public service provided by the American public library" (Berelson; 1949; p. 51). The prevailing situation proves that the same is absolutely true for the State Central Libraries of India.

Classification System. The technical processing of the accessioned books begins with the classification work followed by cataloguing and preparation for circulation which includes stamping, affixing book packet and due date slips, determining the secret page for stamping, etc. Classification is done by a senior professional staff of the library with enough experience and analytical mind. It is said that "Classification is the highest function of the librarian's work, calling into play every faculty and every attainment of knowledge" (Richardson; 1930; p. 42).

Choosing a suitable classification scheme is vital for arranging the books on the shelves of the library. There are many classification schemes adopted by the public libraries all over the world such as Dewey Decimal Classification, S.R. Ranganathan's Colon Classification, Cutter's Subject Classification, etc.

The classification scheme adopted by almost all the SCLs in India is the universally popular Dewey Decimal Classification Scheme. The survey concurs that, 24 out of 27 SCLs (80%) of India, follow the DDC Scheme. The position of Lakshadweep U.T. is not known. The SCLs of Kerala State and Pondicherry U.T. are following the Indian scheme of Colon Classification. In Karnataka State, Colon Classification is also partly used for some sections along with DDC. Orissa State is utilizing the Area Classification of the senior library expert D.R.Kalia for depth classification.

Among the 24 SCLs using DDC for classification of books, the latest 20th Edition is adopted in 5 States/U.T. (19%) in Assam, Delhi, Maharashtra, Nagaland and Orissa. While 19th Edition is followed in another 5 States(19%)-Karnataka, Manipur, Meghalaya, Punjab and Uttar Pradesh, whereas 18th edition of DDC is still in use in 5 States at Gujarat, Haryana, Mizoram, Rajasthan and Tamil Nadu. Surprisingly, the obsolete 16th Edition of DDC is still continued for the classification of books in Andhra Pradesh, Bihar, Himachal Pradesh and West Bengal States.

Sayers is right when he says, "There is no more important factor in the success or failure of a library than the classification of books and other materials which form its stock. It brings the materials together in subject groups on the shelves and in the catalogues and thus enables both the librarian and the reader to find the books easily. In short, classification is the primary key to the assembling, finding, selecting and rejecting of books" (Sayers; 1949; p. 226).

Cataloguing System. Though classification is helpful in keeping the related subjects in close proximity with one another, the most successful way of ensuring maximum service to the readers is to maintain simple and useful catalogue of reading materials available in the library. A public library without a comprehensive catalogue of its resources is unlikely to help the readers in identifying the complete range of its collection, whatever efficient classification system is followed by the library. Hence, catalogue is an essential and indispensable tool for the readers to have a thorough knowledge of the subject, the names of the authors and titles of the books available in the library. Cataloguing helps the user to locate any document available in the library with whatever criteria followed by the user such as title, author, subject etc.

Among the Catalogue Codes followed by the SCLs of India, Anglo American Cataloguing Rules (AACR) emerges as the most popular one since it is used in 15 SCLs (55%). The American

Library Association Code (ALA) is adopted in 3 States (11%)—Andhra Pradesh, Himachal Pradesh and Uttar Pradesh. The catalogue code evolved by the son of the soil Dr. S.R. Ranganathan is used in 8 SCLs (28%) viz, Haryana, Karnataka, Kerala, Madhya Pradesh, Manipur, Pondicherry, Rajasthan and Tamil Nadu. Among the users of AACR code, AACR-1 version is followed in 9 States and AACR-2 is still continued in 6 States.

Advanced public libraries all over the world and to a certain extent in India have been replacing traditional library catalogues by machine readable catalogues and the computerised OPAC system through automation. However, the SCLs of India have not yet reached this stage due to various reasons.

Subject Headings. There is a long standing controversy over the usefulness and performance of Subject Headings in the catalogue cards. The well known library experts, like Ranganathan and Bliss, have conflicting views on the subject.

"Ranganathan advocated with strong conviction that, the Subject Headings used in the alphabetic subject catalogues or in the dictionary catalogues as well have proved so completely ineffective and illogical that there is little justification for continuing the subject headings operations in cataloguing. A well developed and synthetic scheme of classification can offer as many class numbers as the subjects contained in the books, in addition to specific class number which may well replace the subject headings in alphabetic order" (Viswanathan; 1985; p. 59).

However, Bliss holds the strong view that, "Subject Headings are more complete, more inclusive, more expressive for general concepts, more capable of minute and meaningful sub-division in many cases, and more plastic in showing interrelationships than are any of the classification systems presently known" (Tauber; 1953; p. 150). The view of Bliss is shared by most of the librarians of SCLs. The classification scheme, however, exhaustive it may be cannot entirely substitute the subject headings. The classification and subject headings are complementary to each other in serving the readers to explore the Universe of Knowledge.

There are standing lists of Subject Headings like Sear's List, ALA List, Library of Congress List, etc. The librarians of SCLs in India have preferred, wherever it is adopted, Sear's List in majority of the libraries. There are no indications on the use of subject headings in 9 out of 27 (33%) SCLs of India. From among the 18 SCLs using Subject Heading, 13 States (70%) are adopting Sear's List of Subject Headings for use in their subject entries of the catalogue. Library of Congress List is used in the SCL of Karnataka State.

Chain Indexing is followed in Tamilnadu State whereas DDC classification base was felt sufficient for the subject headings in Bihar State. In Delhi U.T. and Rajasthan State, the SCLs use their own subject headings, as per the information collected from the Questionnaires.

Language Divisions

The State Central Library has a bounden duty to satisfy the document and information needs of the people living in all parts of the State. In every State, many languages are spoken and used by the people for reading and communication. Multi-lingual population is the order of the day in almost all the State capitals due to the cosmopolitan nature of the settlement. Employees of All India Services like Administration, Accounts, Defence, Postal and Telecommunications, Banking and similar fields are serving in different States and are frequently transferred. They shall, naturally, prefer to read literature in their own mother tongues. Hence, there is an imperative need for the State Central Libraries to develop their collections in different languages to cater to the reading needs of multi-lingual population of the State capitals in which the libraries are situated.

The languagewise collection of books acquired in the SCLs of India is reflected in Table 3.32.

The number of language divisions available in a SCL indicates the range of linguistic readers served by the library. The number of language divisions maintained in a library varies from 2 languages in Nagaland State upto 16 languages divisions available in the SCL of the National Capital Territory Delhi. In an average, 4 language divisions are available in SCLs. The top ten libraries having more language divisions can be listed in the following order : (i) Delhi (16); (ii) Maharashtra (15); (iii) Tamil Nadu (15); (iv) Andhra Pradesh (9); (v) Andaman and Nicobar Island (8); (vi) Orissa (8); (vii) Goa (7); (viii) Karnataka (7); (ix) Manipur (6); and, (x) Pondicherry (6).

The SCLs of States/U.Ts of Arunachal Pradesh, Assam,

TABLE 3.32
Languagewise Collection of Books in SCLs

Sl. No.	Name of State/U.T.	English	Hindi	State Languages	Other Languages	Total Collection	No. of Language Division
1.	Andaman and Nicobar Islands	23,885	24,703	—	26,732	75,320	08
2.	Andhra Pradesh	1,28,170	38,093	1,24,305	1,11,045	4,01,613	09
3.	Arunachal Pradesh	18,391	5,791	—	4,546	28,728	05
4.	Assam	42,750	2,500	26,902	7,215	78,367	05
5.	Bihar	82,682	—	45,263	17,509	1,45,454	04
6.	Chandigarh	89,600	30,800	—	19,600	1,40,000	04
7.	Delhi	3,35,463	—	8,26,469	3,18,743	14,80,675	16
8.	Goa	57,000	5,300	1,500	76,200	1,40,000	07
9.	Gujarat	—	—	—	—	79,253	04
10.	Haryana	11,500	—	32,000	14,175	57,675	04
11.	Himachal Pradesh	42,754	—	44,325	4,569	91,648	05
12.	Karnataka	1,20,085	—	96,060	24,027	2,40,172	07
13.	Kerala	1,55,000	10,000	69,000	22,794	2,56,794	05

(Contd.)

Sl. No.	Name of State/U.T.	English	Hindi	State Languages	Other Languages	Total Collection	No. of Language Division
14.	Lakshadweep	15,200	3,530	10,000	1,270	30,000	04
15.	Madhya Pradesh	24,098	—	22,869	15,540	62,507	—
16.	Maharashtra	1,42,338	74,190	55,736	4,37,547	7,09,806	15
17.	Manipur	70,000	5,000	40,000	10,138	1.25,138	06
18.	Meghalaya	—	—	—	—	1,70,000	04
19.	Mizoram	13,000	1,306	2,500	194	17,000	03
20.	Nagaland	—	—	—	—	39,000	02
21.	Orissa	1,00,000	5,000	20,000	75,000	2,00,000	08
22.	Pondicherry	1,00,000	5,000	1,50,000	36,887	2,91,887	06
23.	Punjab	54,070	24,800	33,500	4,517	1,16,887	05
24.	Rajasthan	—	—	—	—	35,488	04
25.	Tamil Nadu	2,75,000	50,000	50,000	1,50,000	5,25,000	15
26.	Uttar Pradesh	29,255	—	22,950	10,445	62,650	05
27.	West Bengal	50,000	500	50,000	4,500	1,05,000	05

Himachal Pradesh, Kerala, Punjab, Uttar Pradesh and West Bengal have 5 language divisions. In another set of 7 SCLs at Bihar, Chandigarh, Gujarat, Haryana, Lakshadweep, Meghalaya and Rajasthan States/U.Ts, books in 4 languages are served to the readers. There are only 3 language divisions in Mizoram State while Nagaland has just 2 language divisions.

While analysing the various language divisions in the State Central Libraries, the languages can be grouped under the following heads : (1) English language, (2) State (Official) languages, (3) Hindi and (4) Other languages. The pie Chart 3.10 shown above indicates the distribution of books in various languages. The chart shows that English language books, forming 37 per cent of total collection, is the most preferred language in all the SCLs followed by the State language of the respective State which takes less than one-third of the collection with 30 per cent of the total books. The books of Hindi language forms a mere 6 per cent in all the SCLs put together whereas other languages contribute 27 per cent of the total collection in the State Central Libraries of India.

CHART 3.10
Languages of Books in SCLs of India

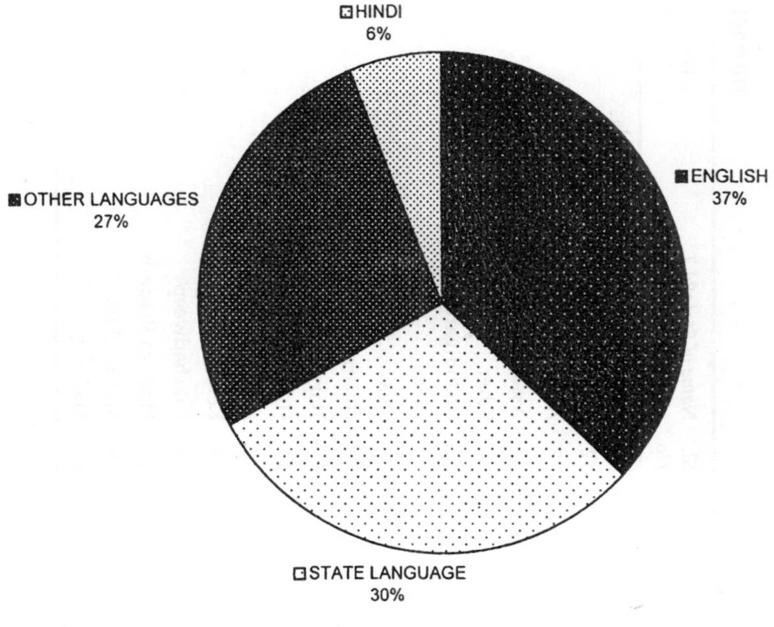

TABLE 3.33
Impact of Library Legislation

Sl. No.	*Name of State/U.T.*	*Whether Act Passed*	*Name and Year of the Act/ Present Position/Year of Amendment*
1.	Andaman and Nicobar Islands	No	Under the consideration of Government
2.	Andhra Pradesh	Yes	Andhra Pradesh Public Library Act, 1960
3.	Arunachal Pradesh	No	No Efforts
4.	Assam	No	Under Consideration
5.	Bihar	No	Under Consideration
6.	Chandigarh	No	No Efforts
7.	Delhi	No	Under Consideration
8.	Goa	Yes	Goa Public Library Act, 1993
9.	Gujarat	No	Gujarat Public Library Act, 2000
10.	Haryana	Yes	Haryana Public Library Act,1989
11.	Himachal Pradesh	No	Under Consideration
12.	Karnataka	Yes	Karnataka Public Library Act, 1965
13.	Kerala	Yes	Kerala Public Library Act, 1989
14.	Lakshadweep	No	No Efforts
15.	Madhya Pradesh	No	Under Consideration
16.	Maharashtra	Yes	Maharashtra Public Library Act, 1967
17.	Manipur	Yes	Manipur Public Library Act, 1993

(Contd.)

Sl. No.	*Name of State/U.T.*	*Whether Act Passed*	*Name and Year of the Act/ Present Position/Year of Amendment*
18.	Meghalaya	No	No Efforts
19.	Mizoram	Yes	Mizoram Public Library Act, 1993
20.	Nagaland	No	No Efforts
21.	Orissa	No	Orissa Public Library Act, 2000
22.	Pondicherry	No	No Efforts
23.	Punjab	No	No Efforts
24.	Rajasthan	No	Under Consideration
25.	Tamil Nadu	Yes	Tamil Nadu Public Library Act, 1948
26.	Uttar Pradesh	No	Under Consideration
27.	West Bengal	Yes	West Bengal Public Library Act, 1979

MAP 3.1
States/UTs with/without Public Library Act

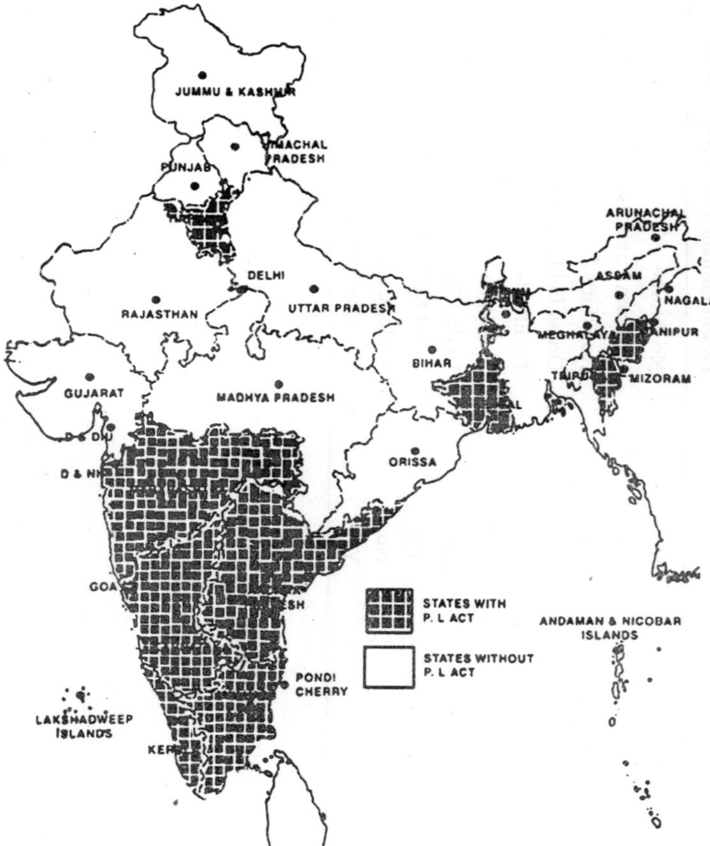

MAP 3.2
Position of Public Library Act in India

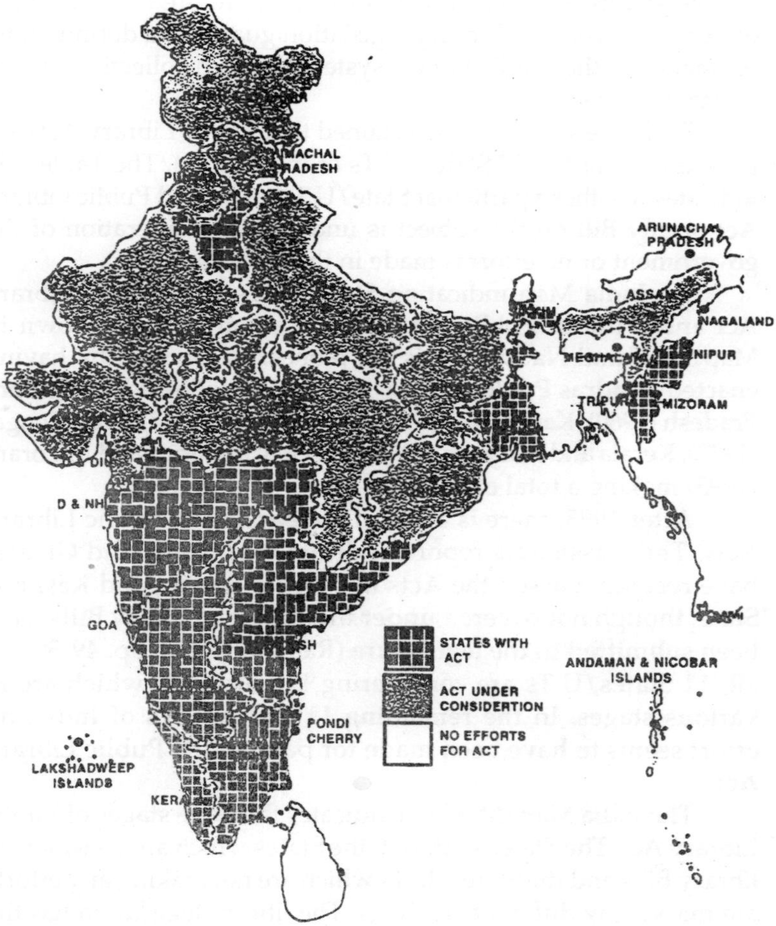

Impact of Library Legislation

Library legislation is essential to provide comprehensive public library services in the States. Network of public libraries can be established, maintained as well as monitored with the help of library legislation. Library legislation guarantees definite flow of finance in the public library system through collection of cess or other means.

From the study, it is ascertained that Public Library Acts are passed in 10 out of 27 States/U.Ts of India (30%). The Table 3.33 indicates whether a particular State/U.T. has passed Public Library Act or any Bill on the subject is under the consideration of the government or no effort is made in the direction.

An India Map indicating States/U.Ts with Public Library Act and without Public Library Act, as on 1998, is shown in Map 3.1. Tamil Nadu State is the pioneer in the field by having enacted Madras Public Library Act in 1948 followed by Andhra Pradesh (1960), Karnataka (1965), Maharashtra (1967), West Bengal (1979), Kerala and Haryana (1989) and Goa, Manipur and Mizoram (1993) making a total of 10 States.

After 1993, there is a lull in the passing of Public Library Acts. The massmedia reports indicate that Orissa and Gujarat have recently passed the Acts in 2000. In Jammu and Kashmir State, though not covered under this survey, Library Bills have been submitted to the legislature (Ramaiah;1998; pp. 49-50). In all, 11 States/U.Ts are considering Library Bills which are in various stages. In the remaining 11 States/U.Ts of India, no effort seems to have been made for passing the Public Library Act.

The India Map (Map 3.2) indicates the three stages of Public Library Act. The States with Act, the States which are considering library Bills and the States/U.Ts which are not making any efforts are marked by different shadings. The library legislation has the following impact on the State Central Libraries.

(1) The Act shall identify or elevate/recognise any established public library in the State capital as State Central Library of the State as per the terms of the Act. The State Central Libraries of Andhra Pradesh, Goa, Haryana, Karnataka, Kerala and Tamil Nadu owe their status to the Public Library Act of the State.

(2) New State Central Libraries can be established under the provisions of the Act, wherever any library of standing is not functioning in the State capital. The State Central Libraries of Maharastra and West Bengal have been established under the provisions of the Act.

(3) The Public Library Act ensures the establishment of a State Library Authority and regular flow of funds to the State Central Library either through Library Cess or through budget allocation of the State Library Authorities/ Directorate of Public Libraries.

However, an analysis of the Public Library Acts of India reflects certain deficiencies in providing a sound State Central Library of the State which is very well pointed out by Balekar as :

"The Maharashtra Public Library Act, 1967 prescribed for the establishment of a State Central Library, but does not stipulate the functions and its expected role in the system. The Tamil Nadu Act (1948) omits to specify the establishment and functions of State Central Library, but designates the Connemara Public Library, Madras (now Chennai) as State Central Library. The Andhra Pradesh Act (1960) provides for State Central Library and through Rules designate the Asafia Library, Hyderabad as State Central Library. The West Bengal, Kerala and Manipur Acts also stipulate for State Central Libraries. But, the provision of Karnataka and Haryana are more specific and stipulate various sections and functions of its units" (Balekar; 1996; p. 119).

Future Trend

From the survey seen above, it can be stated that the State Central Libraries are making steady progress in various activities and functions, especially in the areas of collection development, manpower requirements, providing adequate finance and budgetary support for its myriad activities, membership drive, efficient governance, having adequate space, building and physical conditions, adoption of modern technology and automation, technical status and overall development. Hence, there should be no doubt that the State Central Libraries are poised towards achieving a spectacular progress in the future. The existing trend of slanting towards the implementation of information technology shall lead the SCLs to be the pioneering public libraries of 21st century.

Conclusion

The present status of the State Central Libraries, though not up to the mark, indicate that they have a greater role to play in serving as an apex library of the State and in providing adequate library facilities for its users. What they need at this crucial juncture is a bit administrative, financial, political, and technological support so as to prove themselves as the most effective disseminator of information on a wide spectrum of subjects in the next millennium.

After analysing the existing status of the SCLs, the next chapter surveys the myriad activities and services of the SCLs such as lending service, current awareness services, SDI, Bibliographic Service, Reference and Referral Services, Inter Library Loan Service, Online Searching Services, the Indexing and Abstracting services and the various extension activities at length.

Bibliography

1. American Library Association (ALA). Committee on Post-war Planning. Post-war Standards for Public Libraries, 1942. A.L.A; Chicago, p. 7.
2. Balekar, R.S. Role of State Central, Divisional and District Libraries in the National Development. *In* Kumar, R.P. and others, ed. *Role of Libraries in National Development Papers of the 42nd All India Library Conference held at Calicut during Dec. 21-24, 1996.* Indian Library Association; Delhi, pp. 119-24.
3. Carnousky, L. Measurement of Public Library Book Collection. 1953. Library Trends, Vol. 2 (1); p. 463.
4. Ramaiah, L.S. Public Library Legislation. *In* Jain, M.K., ed. *50 years Library and Information Services in India,* 1998. Shipra Publications; Delhi, pp. 49-50.
5. Mookerjee (Subodh Kumar) and Sengupta (Benoyendra). Library Organisation and Administration, 1977. The World Press; Calcutta, p. 408.
6. Ranganathan, S.R. *Library Manual: For Library Authorities, Librarians and Library Workers,* 1988. Sarada Ranganathan Endowment for Library Science; Bangalore, p. 414.

7. Richardson, E.C. *Classification: Theoretical and Practical*, 1930. H.W. Wilson; New York, p. 42.
8. Sayers, Berwick, W.C., ed. *J.D. Brown's Manual of Library Economy*, 1949. London; Grafton, p. 226.
9. Tauber, M.F. Technical Services in Libraries, 1953. Columbia University Press; New York, p. 150.
10. Viswanathan, C.G. Public Library Operations and Services : A short manual, 1985. Print House (India); Lucknow, p. 59.
11. Yenawine, Warfue S. *Introduction-Current Trends in Circulation Services*, 1957. Illinois; University of Illinois Press, p. 3.

4

Activities and Services of State Central Libraries

Introduction

After analysing the existing status of State Central Libraries in terms of their collection development, manpower, finance, governance, space, building and physical facilities, areas of automation, membership composition pattern, degree of their dependability upon the national, district, branch and other libraries, repository function, technical status, language divisions, impact of library legislation and the future trends, the present chapter deals with the myriad activities of and services provided in the State Central Libraries of India such as lending documents for home reading, current awareness service, selective dissemination of information service, bibliographic service, reference service, referral service, inter library loan service, online searching through computerised networks, indexing service, abstracting service and other extension activities.

Survey on Rating of Various Services of SCLs. Through the Questionnaires, I have requested the Librarians of various State Central Libraries of India to rate how frequently and with what varying degree of priority that several services provided by the SCLs are availed by the users. Keeping in view the traditional and embryonic state of most of the public libraries in India, the services that are considered rudimentary to any public library system are grouped under ten broad categories to which the respondents were asked to determine their priorities. The ratings are graded as 1-Regularly, 2-Frequently, 3-Rarely and 4-Not Used. The ratings of the Librarians are tabulated in Table 4.1.

TABLE 4.1

Rating of Usage of Services of SCLs by the Users

Sl. No.	Name of State/ U.T.	Lending for Home	Lending within the Library	Reference Services	Referral Services	CAS	SDI	Biblio-graphic Services	Inter Library Loan	Online Sear-ching	Any Other
(1)	(2)	(3)	(4)	(5)	(6)	(7)	(8)	(9)	(10)	(11)	(12)
1.	Andaman & Nicobar Islands	1	1	1	1	4	4	4	2	2	4
2.	Andhra Pradesh	1	1	1	2	4	4	4	3	4	4
3.	Arunachal Pradesh	1	4	1	2	1	4	4	4	4	4
4.	Assam	4	2	1	3	3	4	3	4	4	4
5.	Bihar	1	1	1	4	4	4	4	3	4	4
6.	Chandigarh	1	2	1	1	3	4	2	3	1	1
7.	Delhi	1	2	1	1	4	4	3	3	4	4
8.	Goa	1	1	1	3	3	3	2	2	4	4
9.	Gujarat	1	1	1	4	4	4	3	2	4	4
10.	Haryana	1	1	1	4	4	4	4	4	4	4
11.	Himachal Pradesh	1	1	1	1	2	4	3	3	4	4
12.	Karnataka	4	1	2	2	4	4	3	3	4	4
13.	Kerala	1	2	1	2	4	4	4	4	4	4

(Contd.)

(1)	(2)	(3)	(4)	(5)	(6)	(7)	(8)	(9)	(10)	(11)	(12)
14.	Lakshadweep	1	1	1	1	4	3	3	3	4	4
15.	Madhya Pradesh	1	1	1	4	4	4	4	4	4	4
16.	Maharashtra	4	1	1	2	2	2	2	2	4	4
17.	Manipur	1	2	2	3	3	4	3	3	4	4
18.	Meghalaya	1	4	1	1	4	4	4	3	4	4
19.	Mizoram	1	2	3	3	4	4	4	4	4	4
20.	Nagaland	1	1	4	4	4	4	4	4	4	4
21.	Orissa	4	1	2	2	2	3	3	4	4	4
22.	Pondicherry	1	2	2	4	2	4	4	3	4	4
23.	Punjab	1	2	2	2	4	4	4	3	4	4
24.	Rajasthan	1	1	2	2	1	1	3	4	4	4
25.	Tamil Nadu	1	1	2	3	3	3	3	3	4	4
26.	Uttar Pradesh	1	1	1	4	4	4	4	4	4	4
27.	West Bengal	4	1	2	2	4	4	3	3	4	4

1 = Regularly 3 = Rarely

2 = Frequently 4 = Not Used

Analysis of the ratings are furnished in the succeeding paragraphs while discussing the various services offered by the State Central Libraries of India.

Lending Services

Traditionally, lending of books and other documents for home reading constitutes to be the most popular and the most sought after service in public libraries of all categories all over the world. In this service, books are loaned to the registered borrowers and records are maintained of the books lent by the libraries. In public libraries, membership is open to all without any restriction. For providing lending service, a variety of data such as the profiles of readers, the number of books borrowed, the extent of use of the library collection, the number of books issued and returned by the library everyday have to be maintained. In recent times, many public libraries have automated the lending services by adopting Bar Code System and Optical Character Recognition (OCR) Charging System.

The State Central Libraries of India have always been in the forefront in offering this core service. The survey undertaken by reveals that 23 SCLs (85%) are offering lending service and the remaining 4 libraries (15%) are not providing this service in the States of Assam, Karnataka, Maharashtra and West Bengal. These four State Central Libraries have been declared as State Central Reference Libraries and hence do not provide Lending Services for home reading. Lending of documents within the library premises is another kind of service offered by the public libraries. This service may also be called as 'Consultation Service'. The temporary lending of documents within the library premises is provided in the apex libraries of 25 States (93%) while the SCLs of Arunachal Pradesh and Meghalaya States are not allowing the readers to temporarily borrow books for reading within the library premises.

The details of availability of lending services for home reading, temporary lending within the library premises, number of volumes charged per day, number of volumes discharged per day and the number of volumes consulted per day within the library premises in various State Central Libraries of India are furnished in Table 4.2.

TABLE 4.2
Lending Services in SCLs of India

		Lending for Home			*Temporary Lending within the Library*		
Sl. No.	*Name of State/U.T.*	*Home Lending Services*	*Volumes Charged per day*	*Volumes Discharged per day*	*Temporary Lending Service*	*Volumes Consulted per day*	*Total Vols. Transacted*
(1)	*(2)*	*(3)*	*(4)*	*(5)*	*(6)*	*(7)*	*(8)*
1.	Andaman & Nicobar Islands	Yes	275	270	Yes	125	670
2.	Andhra Pradesh	Yes	90	120	Yes	350	560
3.	Arunachal Pradesh	Yes	30	30	No	12	72
4.	Assam	No	Nil	Nil	Yes	—	—
5.	Bihar	Yes	50	40	Yes	60	150
6.	Chandigarh	Yes	500	500	Yes	1,000	2,000
7.	Delhi	Yes	6,000	—	Yes	—	6,000
8.	Goa	Yes	170	170	Yes	250	590
9.	Gujarat	Yes	650	575	Yes	80	1,305
10.	Haryana	Yes	250	200	Yes	105	555
11.	Himachal Pradesh	Yes	200	200	Yes	150	550
12.	Karnataka	No	Nil	Nil	Yes	1,600	1,600

(Contd.)

(1)	(2)	(3)	(4)	(5)	(6)	(7)	(8)
13.	Kerala	Yes	965	1,120	Yes	375	2,460
14.	Lakshadweep	Yes	70	60	Yes	150	280
15.	Madhya Pradesh	Yes	—	—	Yes	—	—
16.	Maharashtra	No	Nil	Nil	Yes	—	—
17.	Manipur	Yes	200	200	Yes	150	550
18.	Meghalaya	Yes	80	72	No	—	152
19.	Mizoram	Yes	20	10	Yes	05	35
20.	Nagaland	Yes	60	70	Yes	120	250
21.	Orissa	No	Nil	Nil	Yes	5,000	5,000
22.	Pondicherry	Yes	290	300	Yes	75	665
23.	Punjab	Yes	150	125	Yes	600	875
24.	Rajasthan	Yes	50	50	Yes	70	170
25.	Tamil Nadu	Yes	580	450	Yes	4,500	5,530
26.	Uttar Pradesh	Yes	150	150	Yes	190	490
27.	West Bengal	No	Nil	Nil	Yes	200	200
	Total	—	10,830	4,712	—	15,167	30,709

[—] = data not available.

The analysis shows that the State Central Library of Delhi U.T. lends 6,000 volumes per day as the maximum among the SCLs included in the survey while Mizoram Library issues only 20 documents per day. The rate of volumes discharged per day is as low as 10 in Mizoram whereas Kerala receives the maximum of 1,120 volumes per day. Regarding the number of books consulted or temporarily lent within the premises of the library, Orissa State tops the list with 5,000 volumes per day while Mizoram is at the bottom of the table by lending only 5 volumes within the library premises a day.

On the whole, the total number of volumes transacted per day ranges from a mere 35 in Mizoram State to the maximum of 6,000 in Delhi Union Territory. The higher figures of transactions as reflected in Delhi (6,000) and Tamilnadu (5,530) rely on the fact that these two libraries are situated in metropolis towns and they get large number of books under the Delivery of Books Act, 1954. The lower transaction figures of Mizoram (35) and Arunachal Pradesh (72) can be attributed to the less number of books available in the respective State Central Libraries.

When the Librarians of SCLs were requested to rate the usage of lending service for home lending by grading as 'Regularly', 'Frequently', 'Rarely' and 'Not Used', it was ascertained that, 23 Librarians (85%) have placed the usage of lending services for home reading under the category of 'Regularly'. Regarding the temporary lending of documents within the library premises, the users of 18 SCLs (67%) are 'Regularly' availing this service and in 7 SCLs (26%) this service is used 'Frequently' and in 2 Libraries (07%) this service is 'Not Used' at all.

Reference Service

Reference Service has since long been considered as the second most important service, next only to the lending service, provided by the public libraries to their users. This service is rendered to assist the users in their search for information on various subjects. According to S.R. Rangathan, Reference Service is "the process of establishing right contact between the right reader and the right books at the right time and in the right personal way. It is a personal service to each reader in helping him to find the documents answering his interest at the moment, pin-pointedly, exhaustively and expeditiously" (*Ranganathan;* 1988; p. 105).

It is that part of personalised library service rendered by the librarian or any library staff, either directly or indirectly, to the users of the library in locating a required book or a piece of information with reference to their study or research. Sharma says, "the basic object of any reference service is to assist readers at all levels to obtain literature or information they require by serving as guide, interpreter and information agency" (Sharma; 1983; p. 163).

In every public library there is a separate section for offering reference service. Specially prepared reading materials such as encyclopaedias, year books, directories, handbooks, dictionaries, standards, manuals, etc. are being regularly consulted by the reference librarian for providing this service on demand. The survey reports that 26 State Central libraries (96 per cent) are offering reference service which is apparently a healthy sign. Only one Librarian of Nagaland State (04%) has informed that reference service is not provided in the library. On rating the frequency of utilisation of reference service by the users of the State Central Libraries of India, it is ascertained that, in 7 libraries (26%), this service is availed 'Regularly', in 8 libraries (30%)-'Frequently', in 3 libraries (11%)- 'Rarely' and in 1 library (04%) at Nagaland it is 'Not Used'.

Referral Service

Referral Service, different from Reference Service, is defined as "a service directing the researcher for information and data to appropriate sources such as libraries, agencies, documentation centres and individuals" (Prytherch; 1995 p. 542). When a particular book or information required by the user is not available in the library, the librarian directs the user to refer another library or information centre or institution where the reading material or information could be obtained. This is the essence of referral service. For providing this service, the librarian of the public library should be well-equipped with standard reference tools, bibliographic sources, union catalogues, directories, handbooks and other similar documents.

The librarians of 21 SCLs (78%) have informed that they are providing Referral Service to their readers while 6 states (22%) do not provide this service in their apex libraries. Referral Service is utilised by the readers 'Regularly' in 6 SCLs (22%), 'Frequently' in 9 SCLs (33%), 'Rarely in 5 SCLs (19%) and 'Not Used' in 7 State Central Libraries of India (26%).

Current Awareness Service (CAS)

Current Awareness Service is a sophisticated service offered by the libraries to enable the users to cope up with the flood of information originating in every field of knowledge. The concept of 'Current Awareness' can be elaborated as the knowledge of recent development. It refers, specially, to those pieces of information which are of particular interest to the individual users. It denotes the knowledge of the contents of nascent publication of an information in any given field. Kemp defines Current Awarements Service as a "System for reviewing the newly available documents, selecting items relevant to the needs of an individual or group, and recording them so that notifications may be sent to those individuals or groups to whose needs they are related" (Kemp; 1979; p. 12).

Three stages are involved in providing current awareness service to the users. They are :

(i) The review or scanning of documents;
(ii) The selection of articles, items, passages or relevant texts by comparing them with the needs of those to whom the service is to be provided; and
(iii) The notification or passing the information of those selected items of interest to the appropriate users.

Prashar rightly elaborates : "A current awareness service is a device of the information system through which the users of information can be informed promptly as soon as possible after publication, but before absorption into the comprehensive secondary sources of current literature, on a subject field or an area in which a group of persons are interested, and presented in a manner, volume and rhythm intended to facilitate or cultivate current approach to information. In the context of a library, the time limit should be after the receipt of publications but well before the receipt of the secondary publications containing them " (Prashar; 1993; p. 65).

The survey on rendering Current Awareness Service to the users of State Central Libraries confirms that only 17 SCLs of India (63%) provide Current Awareness Service for its users and the remaining 10 libraries (37%) are not offering this service, perhaps owing to the paucity of professional manpower and funds.

When the librarians of various State Central Libraries were requested to grade the levels of usage of this service by the users of their respective libraries, it came to light that in 2 SCLs (07%) of Arunachal Pradesh and Rajasthan, this service is being utilised 'Regularly', while the CAS is frequently used in 4 SCLs (15%) at Himachal Pradesh, Maharashtra, Orissa and Pondicherry whereas the users of 5 SCLs (19%) of Assam, Chandigarh, Goa, Manipur and Tamil Nadu are 'Rarely' using this service. In the remaining 16 SCLs (59%), the Current Awareness Services are 'Not Used' by the users of the libraries, obviously due to the fact that this service is not provided by the apex libraries concerned.

The lack of appreciation of this useful service in the State Central Libraries of India is a matter of serious concern. By not providing this service in 16 SCLs, the Authority of the SCLs concerned appear to be losing a good chance of publicity of themselves and the opportunity to reach a large number of the existing as well as potential users in the cross section of the society to which the SCLs are meant to serve and have a greater role to play.

Selective Dissemination of Information (SDI)

The service of Selected Dissemination of Information, popularly called as SDI, is an advanced form of Current Awareness Service, but mostly provided through computers. According to Murison, *"SDI is no more than a way of saying that once a day, once a week or once a month, librarian searches the available new literature and prepares a bibliography of materials likely to be of interest to an individual"* (Murison; 1988; p. 23).

The SDI service requires that for each member of the library, a description of his areas of interest known as, 'User's Profile' is prepared. Simultaneously, a 'Document Record' is prepared for each and every document added to the library. If a document record matches an 'Users Profile', it is considered as a "hit" for the particular user's profile. The list of all hits related to a particular User Profile is then compiled and the list is typed/printed and delivered to the member (user) of the library. This service is provided through computers effectively in most of the libraries. The Librarian's Glossary sums up the functioning of SDI service as a "System, usually automated, whereby literature items are matched against the interest profiles of the individual or corporate users of an information service and relevant documents or abstracts are supplied to the users immediately" (Prytherch; 1995; p. 575).

The objective behind the SDI service is to provide a personalised Current Awareness Service for the users of a library through automation and to save the time of the users by selecting the relevant information from the flood of information which enables them to manage the information explosion problem. Describing how a typical SDI service would function, Housman aptly explains : "A typical SDI Service provides each subscriber with a periodic, tailored listing of new documents that have been entered into the file and that are likely to apply to his work or be of interest to him as a professional. In such a system, each subscriber gets a different set of references, depending on his personal interest, as defined in his interest profiles" (Housman; 1973; p. 222).

The survey reveals that 21 SCLs (78%) are not offering this sophisticated SDI service. The SCLs of Goa, Lakshadweep, Maharashtra, Orissa, Rajasthan and Tamil Nadu (22%) are providing this service, as per the information furnished in the Questionnaires. The librarians of 4 SCLs (15%) at Goa, Lakhsadweep, Orissa and Tamilnadu States/U.Ts have informed that their users are soliciting SDI service only 'Rarely'. In Maharashtra, the SDI service is availed 'Frequently' whereas in the SCL of Rajasthan, the users are 'Regularly' utilising this service. Since automation is not available in some of the libraries stated to be providing this service, as per the information collected, it is presumed that the librarians are providing SDI service by manual process in these libraries.

Bibliographic Service

The term 'Bibliography' was coined for the first time by Louis Jacob de Saint Charles in his book *Bibliographic Partisiana* (1645) and has become popular in the 18th Century. The word is derived from two Greek terms "Biblion" and "Graphein" which means "Books" and "To Write" respectively. Thus, etymologically, bibliography denotes the "writing of books", as per the original meaning given in Oxford English Dictionary during the 17th

Century. The German Bibliographer F. Ebert defines Bibliography as "in the broadest sense, the science that deals with literary productions" (Bowers; 1959; p. 495). Hence, Bibliography means the science of books. The word, however, by pace of time has undergone many changes. The metamorphosis of the term has led to the modern meaning in which the term "Bibliography" denotes a list of documents relating to a particular subject or written by a particular author which may be either comprehensive or selective.

The Bibliography is compiled to inform the user of the availability of a group of documents pertaining to a subject or an author. The bibliographies can be arranged alphabetically according to the author or by title or subject headings. The Bibliographic Service is defined as "the facilities, procedures and devices which are employed to produce a bibliography consisting of a continuing series of publications or bibliographic information as requested" (Prytherch; 1995; p. 16). Bibliography is considered as the most effective aid for a researcher in leading to a scientific path of searching.

Bibliographic services are offered in 15 SCLs (56%) of India and the remaining 12 libraries have not yet started this service as per the information collected from the Questionnaires. The Bibliographic Services are 'Not Used' by the users of 13 SCLs (48%), 'Rarely' used by the members of 11 SCLs (41%) and 'Frequently' used in 3 SCLs at Chandigarh, Goa and Maharashtra respectively. Surprisingly, the Bibliographic Service is not being 'Regularly' used in any State Central Library in India.

State Bibliography

Bibliography is a technique of systematically producing description lists of written or published records. Bibliographies can be prepared according to the author, title or subject. Place of origin of publication can also be used as the basis to compile Bibliographies. Under this category, one can include Regional Bibliography, District Bibliography, State Bibliography, National Bibliography and International Bibliography.

State Bibliography may be defined as a Bibliography of all books published in the State/Union Territory or the books published in the official language of the State. In practice, the State Bibliography is actually a list of books received by the State Central

Library from the publishers/printers under the Press and Registration of Books Act, 1867 or the Delivery of Books Act, 1954. State Bibliographies are compiled only in 8 State Central Libraries (30%) of India in the States of Goa, Gujarat, Karnataka, Madhya Pradesh, Maharashtra, Orissa, Tamil Nadu and West Bengal States respectively. The authorities of the remaining 19 State Central Libraries (70%) should consider bringing out State Bibliographies so that effective bibliographic control can be exercised.

Inter Library Loan

Owing to the regular increase in the cost of books and sharp increase in the annual subscription to periodicals, it is inevitable that the public libraries, which are already in shortage of funds, should explore the possibility of sharing the resources of one library with another in order to serve the needs of the users of the library efficiently. In this connection, Inter Library Loan (ILL) System among the public libraries is a very important step in resource sharing.

Further, no library, however larger and wide ranging its collection may be, can claim to be exhaustive in its collection. This rule applies to even the National Libraries and Library of Congress which are considered as the largest libraries. Since the public libraries exist primarily to satisfy the needs of the users, they have a moral obligation to provide any document or information required by the users irrespective of its location or availability in any part of the globe. Naturally, Inter Library Loan is the obvious and natural choice to completely quench the thirst of the users for information. Khanna says, "Inter Library Loan has two complimentary purposes. First, to aid the researcher in acquiring specialised material of whatever origin and of whatever location; second, to assist the general reader to borrow material to which the reader does not have any access, owing to the lack of proper library facilities" (Khanna; 1989; p. 236).

In order to provide Inter Library Loan Services, a library has to negotiate with the user and identify the document required by the user as well as to ascertain that the document is essentially required for the user who comes up with a request for a particular document. Then, the librarian has to find out, from the bibliographical sources such as Union Catalogues, Directories, or any other sources, that the documents required by the user is available in a particular library at a different location. In the next stage, a request has to be sent to the particular library by surface mail or E-Mail for supplying the document. Finally, on receipt of the document from the requested library, the document shall be issued to the user.

Among the State Central Libraries of India, 17 libraries (63%) are providing Inter Library Loan Services to the users and the remaining 10 libraries are not operating this service. From among the 17 libraries, this service is 'Frequently' availed by the users of 4 libraries (15%) in the States / Union Territories of Andaman and Nicobar Islands, Goa, Gujarat and Maharashtra respectively. In the remaining 13 libraries (48%), however, the Inter Library loan service is 'Rarely' used.

Online Searching

We are in the midst of a global revolution in the field of Information and Communication Technology. Everyday large number of documents and articles are published all over the world. It is impossible for any library to acquire all the documents published due to the shortage of funds, storage space and the demand from the users. Hence, sharing of resources among the libraries becomes essential. A network is usually developed when a group of libraries providing computerised library services decide to exchange information and share their resources. In any computerised networking, online searching is a key function for information interchange.

Online searching can be explained as the computer assisted retrieval of bibliographic citations from the innumerable databases floating in the computerised networks around the globe. It denotes the searching process wherein the computerised search is processing while the user is connected to the computer thereby allowing the user to interact with the computer and alter the search according to the computer's responses and the specific requirements of the user.

Among the existing SCLs of India, only 2 libraries (7%) are offering this service, while the remaining 25 SCLs (93%) are not providing online searching facility. In SCL of Chandigarh U.T., this service is 'Regularly' used while the users of the Library of Andaman and Nicobar Islands are 'Frequently' availing this facility.

Indexing and Abstracting Service

It will be difficult for the users of the public libraries to keep themselves apprised of the latest developments in different fields of knowledge due to information explosion almost in every field of knowledge. In order to assist the users in selecting the relevant information, indexing and abstracting services are provided by public libraries. "Indexing is an assignment of index terms to documents or objects with the aim to be able to later on retrieve the documents or objects according to the selected concepts designated by the index terms. Abstracting refers to a form of bibliography in which sometimes books, but mainly contributions to periodicals are summarised" (Dilli; 1997; p. 133).

The process of preparing the indexes and abstracts, depending on the specific needs and requirements of the users, may be referred to as the Indexing and Abstracting Services. "The indexing service is described as a periodical publication which regularly and systematically indexes the contents of periodicals and sometimes other forms of publication, either of general nature or within a specified subject field" (Prythrech; 1995; p. 316). If the Indexing service is supported with an abstract in each of the entry, it is called as Abstracting service. The librarians of SCLs of India have informed that only 4 apex libraries (15%) of Bihar, Chandigarh, Goa and Orissa States/U.Ts are offering Indexing and Abstracting Services to their users.

Extension Services

If a library offers non-conventional services, other than traditional library services, with a view to attract the general public outside its membership, such services are called Extension Services. Ranganathan has defined and elaborated on the following extension services in his 'Library Manual'. "The object of extension service may be said to be to turn the library into a social centre with the encouragement of reading as its ultimate objective. Its aim is to create an ultimate desire for good reading and to bring the reader and the book together" (Ranganathan; 1988; p. 75-78).

1. Reading to illiterates;
2. Reading of manuscripts;
3. Reading circle;
4. Intellectual centre;
5. Library talk;

6. Story hours;
7. Lantern talks;
8. Kalakshapam or Katha; and
9. Festivals and Fairs

Venkateswara Rao further explains the objective of extension services as: "The objective of an extension service is to convert a library into cultural and intellectual centre which provides an insight into the stream of knowledge. The library can be an effective facilitator of self learning through its extension service activities" (Venkateswara Rao; 1994; p. 371).

Among the State Central Libraries of India surveyed for this project, 17 SCLs (63%) are providing extension services in addition to their normal library activities. While the librarians were requested to state whether they are providing certain extension services, it is ascertained that Mobile Library Services are offered by only 8 libraries (30%), Seminars, Talks and Group Discussions are provided in 17 libraries (63%), Adult Education Services are rendered in 7 libraries (26%), Cultural Meetings are organised in 16 SCLs (59%) and various other extension services are offered in 13 apex libraries (48%) of the States/Union Territories of India.

Among the other extension services provided, it is ascertained that Book Exhibitions are conducted in 4 SCLs (15%) at Chandigarh, Gujarat, Kerala and Maharashtra States. In addition, Chandigarh SCL is offering Braille Service to its users. The following Table 52 specifies the various extension services offered by different State Central Libraries of India.

Working Hours and Holidays

The State Central Library, being the apex public library of the State, should function for the maximum number of hours to serve the users of the Library. The Table 53 furnished below lists out the working hours of the SCLs of India and the holidays on which the libraries are closed.

Analysis of the data on working hours indicates that, on an average, State Central Libraries in India are open for 09 hours and 20 minutes a day. The Textbook Section of State Central Library of Andhra Pradesh is kept open for the maximum of 16 hours (08.00 hours to 12.00 Midnight). Gujarat State Central Library functions for the maximum of 14 hours a day starting from 08.00 a.m. in the morning to 10.00 a.m. in the night. The State

TABLE 4.3
Extension Services Offered by SCLs

Sl. No.	*Name of State/ U.T.*	*Mobile Library Service*	*Seminar/ Talk/Group Discussion*	*Adult Educ- ation*	*Cultural Meeting*	*Any Other Service*
1.	Andaman & Nicobar Islands	No	Yes	Yes	Yes	No
2.	Andhra Pradesh	No	Yes	Yes	Yes	Yes
3.	Arunachal Pradesh	No	No	No	No	No
4.	Assam	No	Yes	No	No	Yes
5.	Bihar	No	No	No	Yes	Yes
6.	Chandigarh	Yes	Yes	No	Yes	Yes
7.	Delhi	Yes	Yes	No	Yes	Yes
8.	Goa	Yes	No	No	No	No
9.	Gujarat	Yes	Yes	Yes	Yes	Yes
10.	Haryana	No	No	No	No	No
11.	Himachal Pradesh	No	Yes	Yes	Yes	Yes
12.	Karnataka	No	No	No	No	No
13.	Kerala	No	Yes	No	Yes	Yes
14.	Lakshadweep	No	Yes	Yes	Yes	No
15.	Madhya Pradesh	Yes	Yes	Yes	Yes	No
16.	Maharashtra	No	Yes	No	Yes	Yes
17.	Manipur	No	Yes	No	Yes	No
18.	Meghalaya	No	No	No	No	No
19.	Mizoram	No	Yes	No	Yes	No
20.	Nagaland	No	No	No	No	No
21.	Orissa	No	Yes	No	Yes	Yes
22.	Pondicherry	Yes	No	No	No	Yes
23.	Punjab	Yes	Yes	Yes	Yes	Yes
24.	Rajasthan	Yes	No	No	No	No
25.	Tamil Nadu	No	Yes	No	No	Yes
26.	Uttar Pradesh	No	No	No	No	No
27.	West Bengal	No	Yes	No	Yes	No
	Total	Yes = 08 No = 19	Yes = 17 No = 12	Yes = 07 No = 20	Yes = 16 No = 11	Yes = 13 No = 14

TABLE 4.4
Working Hours and Holidays of SCLs

Sl. No.	*Name of State/U.T.*	*Total Working Hours*	*Working Hours*	*No. of Holidays*	*Weekly Holiday*
01.	Andaman & Nicobar Islands	08.00	—	—	Sundays
02.	Andhra Pradesh	12.00	08.00 A.M. to 08.00 P.M. (Text Book Section upto 12.00 Midnight)	83	Thursday
03.	Arunachal Pradesh	07.00	—	68	—
04.	Assam	07.00	10.00 A.M. to 05.00 P.M.	109	—
05.	Bihar	08.00	10.00 A.M. to 05.00 P.M.	84	Saturday
06.	Chandigarh	07.30	—	D.N.A	Sunday
07.	Delhi	11.30	08.30 A.M. to 08.00 P.M.	70	—
08.	Goa	09.15	09.00 A.M. to 01.15 P.M.	—	Sunday
09.	Gujarat	14.00	02.00 to 7.00 P.M.	07	Nil
10.	Haryana	07.00	08.00 A.M. to 10.00 P.M.	—	Sunday
11.	Himachal Pradesh	07.00	10.00 A.M. to 05.00 P.M.	02	Nil
12.	Karnataka	10.00	11.00 A.M. to 06.00 P.M.	81	Monday
13.	Kerala	12.00	80.00 A.M. to 08.00 P.M.	45	—
14.	Lakshadweep	06.00	10.00 A.M. to 01.00 P.M.	—	Sunday
15.	Madhya Pradesh	06.00	05.00 A.M. to 08.00 P.M.	—	Sunday

(Contd.)

Sl. No.	Name of State/U.T.	Total Working Hours	Working Hours	No. of Holidays	Weekly Holiday
16.	Maharashtra	08.15	09.45 A.M. to 06.00 P.M.	—	Sunday
17.	Manipur	06.30	11.00 A.M. to 05.30 P.M.	75	—
18.	Meghalaya	06.00	—	24	—
19.	Mizoram	08.00	09.00 A.M. to 05.00 P.M.	120	—
20.	Nagaland	06.00	11.00 A.M. to 05.00 P.M.	100	—
21.	Orissa	12.00	08.00 A.M. to 08.00 P.M.	—	Govt. Holidays
22.	Pondicherry	12.00	07.25 A.M. to 08.35 P.M.	68	Monday
23.	Punjab	09.30	08.30 A.M to 06.00 P.M.	—	Sunday
24.	Rajasthan	12.00	07.00 A.M. to 07.00 P.M.	—	—
25.	Tamil Nadu	10.30	09.00 A.M. to 07.30 P.M.	09	Nil
26.	Uttar Pradesh	09.00	D.N.A.	94	D.N.A.
27.	West Bengal	07.00	12 Noon to 07.00 P.M.	80	Sunday

[—] = Data not available

Central Libraries of Lakshadweep, Meghalaya and Nagaland States are working for only 6 hours in a day which is the minimum working hours compared to the other State Central Libraries in India. While all State Central Libraries are working both in the forenoon and afternoon on various timings, the SCL of West Bengal State functions only in the afternoon from 12 noon to 7.00 P.M. Thus, there is no consistency and uniformity among the State Central Libraries in India with regard to working hours—each State Central Library has an unique time structure depending on the local conditions.

The holidays of State Central Libraries range from only 02 days in the State of Himachal Pradesh to the maximum of 120 days in Mizoram State. The weekly holidays are not uniform in State Central Libraries wherever they are closed for one day in a week. The last day of the week Sunday appears to be the most favoured holiday since 9 SCLs (33%) are closed on Sundays, followed by 02 each on Mondays and Saturdays (07%) while the State Central Library of Andhra Pradesh is closed on every Thursday.

Conclusion

There is a general perception that public libraries are no more than mere book lending centres. The public libraries offer different kinds of services depending on the resources available, demands of the users and the technical know-how of the manpower available in the libraries concerned. The State Central Libraries are, in reality, offering a wide range of services to the public ranging from home lending to the online searching, but in a limited way.

From the survey undertaken by me in 27 SCLs of India (90%) out of a total number of 30 SCLs functioning in the country, on the services provided by the State Central Libraries, it is observed that the Lending of documents for home reading is provided in 23 SCLs (85%), Temporary lending of documents within the library premises is available in 25 SCL (93%), Reference Service is available in 26 SCLs (93%), Referral Service is being offered in 21 SCLs (78%), the sophisticated service of Current Awareness Service is extended in 17 SCLs (63%), computerised/manual Selective Dissemination of Information (SDI) service is utilised in 21 SCLs (78%), Bibliographies are compiled for the users in 15 SCLs (56%), State

CHART 4.1
Services Offered by Various SCLs

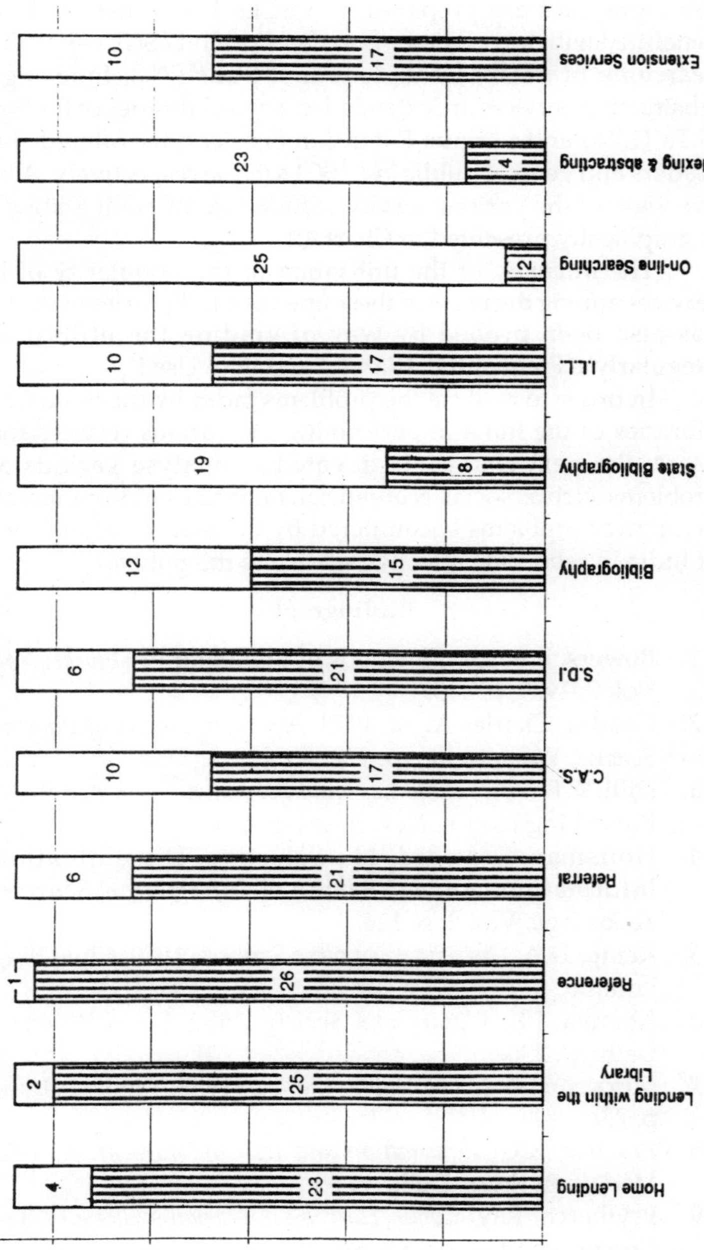

Bibliographies are prepared in 8 SCLs (30%), the readers are benefitted with Inter Library Loan Services in 17 SCL (63%), Online Searching of databases is done in 2 SCLs (7%), Indexing and Abstracting Services are extended in 4 apex Libraries of the States/ U.Ts (15%) and various Extension Services are offered for the readers and general public in 17 SCLs (63%) respectively. A bird's eye view of the various services offered in different States/U.Ts is graphically presented in Chart 4.1.

The intensity of the utilisation or the popularity of these services among the users of these apex public libraries of the States has also been probed by way of grading the utilisation as 'Regularly', 'Frequently', 'Rarely' and 'Not Used'.

In order to analyse the problems faced by the State Central Libraries of the India in performing the various services for the users, the next chapter is devoted to analyse various other problems such as social, economical, financial, environmental and manpower problems encountered by the State Central Libraries of India in rendering effective service to the public.

Bibliography

1. Bowers, Fredsor. Functions of Bibliography. *Library Trends.* Vol. 7, 1959, p. 495.
2. Cuadra, Charles A., *ed.* 1973. *American Society of Information Science,* Washington, p. 222.
3. Dilli, K.T. *Basics of Library and Information Science,* 1997, Vikas Publishing House; New Delhi, p. 133.
4. Housman, Edward M. Selective Dissemination of Information. *Annual Review of Information Science and Technology,* Vol. 8, p. 126.
5. Kemp, D.A. *Current Awareness Services,* 1979, Clive Bingley; London, p. 12.
6. Khanna, J.K. *Library and Society,* 1989, Esses Publication; Delhi, p. 236.
7. Murrison, W.J. *The Public Library,* 1988, Bingley; London, p. 23.
8. Prashar, R.G. *Information and Its Communication,* 1993, A Medallion Press; Delhi, p. 65.
9. Prytherch, Ray, *Comp. Harrod's Librarian's Glossary.* Hant's Gower; London, pp. 61, 595.

10. Ranganathan, S.R. *Library Manual : For Library Authorities, Librarians and Library Workers,* 1988, Sarada Ranganathan Endowment for Library Science; Bangalore, p. 414.
11. Sharma, C.D. *Use of Libraries : Guide to Better Use of Libraries and Their Resources,* 1983, Printwell; Jaipur, p. 163.
12. Ventakateswara, Rao, L. Opening of School and College Libraries to Public. *In* Vashisth, C.P. et. al., *ed. New Horizons in Library and Information Science,* 1974, T.R. Publications; Madras, p. 371.

5

Problems of State Central Libraries

Introduction

Every institution, irrespective of its size and kind, has its own problems. State Central Libraries, being one of the vital service institutions, are not an exception to this dictum. In performing the role of the apex public libraries of the States/U.Ts, the State Central Libraries are providing myriad services—both conventional and sophisticated—such as lending of books within the library premises and for home reading, reference service, referral service, current awareness service, selective dissemination of information, bibliographic service, inter library loan, online searching through computerised networks, indexing and abstracting services as well as the multi-faceted extension services to satisfy the information needs of the users and in fulfilling the obligations and duties as State Central Libraries.

While discharging the designated duties and functions, the State Central Libraries encounter a number of problems in their activities that hamper not only their present services but also their future expansion and growth. The comprehensive picture of State Central Libraries cannot be obtained without analysing the various problems faced by them. As State Central Libraries are non-profit motive organisations, the problems are varied and multi-faceted. Hence, this chapter is devoted to analyse the various problems affecting the function and growth of State Central Libraries in India.

Problems of SCLs

The multifarious problems of State Central Libraries have been broadly grouped under the following five headings :

(i) Social and Economic Problems;
(ii) Financial Problems;

(iii) Environmental Problems;
(iv) Technical Problems; and
(v) Manpower Problems.

Under the above five headings, the following 12 problems are selectively taken up for detailed analysis in this study:

1. Lack of understanding the value of education by illiterates;
2. The education and economic conditions of the State is below expectations;
3. Paucity of funds;
4. Lack of proper administrative support;
5. Lack of space to introduce new services;
6. Lack of a compatible environment to work;
7. Lack of library awareness among the clientele of the SCLs;
8. Lack of library modernisation/automation;
9. Lack of proper co-ordination and networking;
10. Lack of attitude of library staff/work culture;
11. Shortage of professional staff; and
12. Staff are not fully aware of technical know-how of modern library system.

The major social and economic problems which are obstacles for the proper growth and developments of State Central Libraries are identified as the lack of understanding of education by the illiterates and the situation in which the educational and economic conditions of the State/Union Territory is below the normal expectations. The financial problem, as every one is aware, is primarily the paucity of funds that shall seriously affect the allocation of sufficient resources for providing various services to the users of State Central Libraries.

The environmental problems are taken up next in this study. The environmental problem, in this context, does not denote the common and natural environmental problems such as atmospheric pollution, global warming, ecological balance, etc. The environment of the State Central Libraries may be further subdivided as internal and external environment. Lack of administrative support for the State Central Library may be considered as the external environment problem. The internal environmental problems are listed as the lack of space to introduce new services, lack of amiable environment to work for the staff coupled with a compatible and user-friendly atmosphere for study and research; and the lack of awareness of the facilities and services by the users of the State Central Libraries.

Technical problems include the lack of modernisation of State Central Libraries and lack of co-ordination and networking among the various categories of libraries functioning in the State/Union Territory as well as outside the boundaries of the State. Lastly, Manpower problems are analysed in terms of shortage of professional staff, the situation of staff members being unaware of the latest technical know-how in library and information field and, last but not the least, the lack of work culture among the staff of State Central Libraries.

Survey of Problems of SCLs

While analysing the different problems of State Central Libraries with reference to the available resources and status of the State Central Libraries, an attempt has been made to solicit the learned opinions of the librarians of the State Central Libraries on the problems faced by them in their day-to-day routine activities as well as the long standing and recurring issues based on their personal experiences and knowledge. The librarians of various State Central Libraries have been requested to express the degree of the intensity of the problems by grading them as :

1. Extreme Problem
2. Considerable Problem
3. A Little Problem, and
4. No Problem At All

The opinions of the Chief Librarians of the State Central Libraries grading the intensity of the problems in the light of their supervisory and administrative experiences are furnished in Table 5.1.

Social and Economic Problems

Public libraries have become an integral part of our social life for the development of educational, social and cultural activities. It is rightly said that, "no society can advance beyond a certain point without effective access to its collective memory of records, or, conversely, an advanced society that loses control of the record will regress" (Swank; 1971; p. 20). Hence, the problems of SCL cannot be analysed in isolation because the public library and society are linked together.

On reorienting the slogan of democracy, one can say that public libraries are for the people, by the people and, of course, of

TABLE 5.1
Problems of SCLs

Sl. No.	State U.T.	Social & Economic Problems		Financial Problems	Environmental Problems				Technical Problems		Manpower Problems		
(1)	(2)	(3)	(4)	(5)	(6)	(7)	(8)	(9)	(10)	(11)	(12)	(13)	(14)
1.	Andaman and Nicobar Islands	4	4	4	4	3	4	3	3	3	4	3	4
2.	Andhra Pradesh	4	2	1	4	3	4	3	1	1	4	3	2
3.	Arunachal Pradesh	1	1	1	2	4	1	3	1	1	3	1	2
4.	Assam	4	3	1	2	1	3	3	1	3	3	1	4
5.	Bihar	2	3	1	4	2	3	3	1	2	3	2	2
6.	Chandigarh	4	4	3	3	2	4	4	3	3	3	3	3
7.	Delhi	3	3	1	3	2	2	3	1	2	2	3	2
8.	Goa	3	1	2	2	1	3	3	2	1	2	2	4
9.	Gujarat	2	3	2	3	4	4	3	2	3	3	1	3
10.	Haryana	4	3	1	4	2	3	3	2	2	4	2	3
11.	Himachal Pradesh	2	3	1	2	1	3	2	1	1	3	2	1
12.	Karnataka	3	4	1	3	1	4	4	4	1	3	1	2
13.	Kerala	4	4	2	2	2	3	3	1	1	3	3	3

(Contd.)

(1)	(2)	(3)	(4)	(5)	(6)	(7)	(8)	(9)	(10)	(11)	(12)	(13)	(14)
14.	Lakshadweep	3	4	2	2	2	3	3	1	4	3	4	3
15.	Madhya Pradesh	1	1	1	3	1	3	3	1	1	3	2	2
16.	Maharashtra	1	4	2	1	1	3	4	1	2	2	1	4
17.	Manipur	3	2	1	1	1	2	4	1	3	2	1	3
18.	Meghalaya	4	3	3	3	4	3	3	2	3	4	3	3
19.	Mizoram	2	3	1	2	2	2	2	1	2	2	1	2
20.	Nagaland	2	2	2	2	4	3	2	1	2	1	1	1
21.	Orissa	3	3	1	3	1	4	3	2	2	3	3	3
22.	Pondicherry	4	4	4	4	4	4	3	1	3	3	1	3
23.	Punjab	3	2	2	2	4	4	3	2	1	4	1	2
24.	Rajasthan	3	1	1	1	2	2	2	1	1	2	3	1
25.	Tamil Nadu	2	3	1	3	1	3	3	1	1	2	1	2
26.	Uttar Pradesh	4	4	1	4	4	4	4	4	4	4	4	4
27.	West Bengal	2	2	2	3	2	2	2	1	1	2	1	2

1 = Extreme Problem 3 = A Little Problem.
2 = Considerable Problem 4 = No Problem at all.

the (professional) people. Whatever be the efforts and initiatives taken by the library authorities of State Central Libraries in providing excellent services, such services cannot reach the targetted people due to the social and economic problems prevailing in the society. The optimum utilisation of SCLs necessitate higher literacy rate. If the people of a State, especially, illiterates are not willing to understand the value of education, it will be a problem for the SCL to serve the society of the State effectively. If more illiterates understand the value of education, they will aspire to be literates which shall lead to higher literacy and shall ultimately lead the State/U.T. in the maximum utilisation of State Central Libraries.

Hence, the lack of understanding of the value of education by illiterates has been taken up as the first social problem. The Librarians of 3 SCLs (11%) at Arunachal Pradesh, Madhya Pradesh and Maharashtra States consider this problem as 'Extreme Problem'. In this context, it has to be remembered that among the three States mentioned above, Arunachal Pradesh State, with 41.59 per cent literacy and Madhya Pradesh State with 44.20 per cent literacy rate are at the bottom of the literacy level among the States/U.Ts of India. Further, in the SCLs of 7 States/U.Ts (26%), this problem is graded as 'Considerable Problem'. In 8 States (30%), this problem is just 'A Little Problem'.

In the States/U.Ts which have higher literacy rates such as Kerala (90.92%), Chandigarh (81.76%), Pondicherry (81.76%) and Andaman and Nicobar Islands (81.18%), the literates understand the value of education and are gradually transforming themselves as 'educated' leading to the better utilisation of resources and services of State Central Libraries. Hence, it is obvious that in 9 SCLs (33%) this problem seems to be 'No Problem at All'. (*India;* 2002; p. 13).

Further, if a State/U.T. is economically and educationally backward it is but natural that the people living in the State/U.T. shall not be in a position to give priority for using the State Central Libraries. In fact, 'The New Educational Policy' adopted by the Indian Parliament in 1986 clearly underlines this situation by interlinking the development of education and libraries. In Section 8.9, the policy proclaims that, "Together with the development of books, a nationwide movement for the improvement of existing libraries and the establishment of new ones will be taken up.

Provision will be made in educational institutions for library facilities and the status of Librarians improved" (Mangla; 1998; p. 5)

Hence, the situation of 'the educational and economic conditions of the State is below expectations' is taken up as the next social problem tormenting the State Central Libraries of India. In the opinions of the Librarians of State Central Libraries, this problem is classified as 'Extreme Problem' in 4 States (15%) viz., Arunachal Pradesh, Goa, Madhya Pradesh and Rajasthan; 'Considerable Problem' in 5 States (19%); 'A Little Problem' in 10 States (37%) and 'No Problem at All' in 8 States/U.T.s (30%) of Andaman and Nicobar Islands, Chandigarh, Karnataka, Kerala, Lakshadweep, Maharashtra, Pondicherry and Uttar Pradesh respectively.

Financial Problem

The factor of finance, as has always been the case, is of critical importance. The Librarian of a State Central Library is most unlikely to be in a position to decide how much fund he could spend for the library. The money is allocated/sanctioned by the Government/management or Library Committee based on the resources, priorities and the previous year's expenditure.

If more funds are allotted, the librarian could spend as per the needs and requirements of the users and the planning of the librarian. If there is a reduction in allotment or if the budget proposal of the librarian is not considered or only partly approved, the situation shall lead to depression in the mind of the librarian.

Then, the librarian should decide which expenditure has to be reduced or modified. Whether the number of periodicals has to be reduced ? Whether the recruitment of vacancy caused by retirement or resignation of the staff should be postponed? Whether the purchase of new books can be limited? Whether the new services proposed to be initiated or expansion plans of the library on the anvil has to be postponed? Perhaps, these are some of the crucial questions that the Librarian is often confronted with. Paucity of funds has always been a universal problem for any category of library anywhere in the world. The same situation applies to the librarians of State Central Libraries also.

It is, therefore, essential to examine whether the State Central Libraries of India have been adequately financed to meet the requirements and demands of the users. Hence, the question of 'Paucity of funds' has been taken up as the major financial problem for analysis. The librarians of State Central Libraries expressed their assessments on the pinch they experience due to the paucity of funds by way of grading the financial situation in four grades. It is a rare occasion to note that the librarians of 2 Union Territories (7%) of Andaman and Nicobar Islands and Pondicherry are satisfied about the financial allocation. They express cheerfully that 'Paucity of funds' is 'No Problem at All' for their libraries. This is perhaps because of liberal funding allocated by the Central Government for various schemes in Union Territories.

The analysis on the state of budget of these two Union Territories support their opinions. The Budget of the State Central Library of Andaman and Nicobar Islands has increased from a mere Rs. 3,00,000 in the year 1993-94 to Rs. 1,00,00,000 (Rupees one crore) in 1997-98. The percentage of increase is as follows :

TABLE 5.2

Budget of Andaman & Nicobar Islands U.T. for 5 Years

Sl. No.	*Year*	*Amount Rs.*	*Percentage of budget over the previous year*
1.	1993 - 94	3,00,000	—
2.	1994 - 95	6,00,000	200%
3.	1995 - 96	30,30,000	505%
4.	1996 - 97	34,00,000	112%
5.	1997 - 98	1,00,00,000	294%

If the total allocation is compared over the five years from the year 1993-94 to 1997-98, as seen in Table 5.2, the percentage of increase is a whooping figure of 3,333 per cent. Definitely, the administrative authority of Andaman and Nicobar Islands should be more liberal in sanctioning enormous funds to the State Central Library of the Union Territory.

The Pondicherry Union Territory has also shown a substantial increase in allocation of funds to the State Central Library of the Union Territory. The budget of Pondicherry SCL has increased from Rs. 21,31,997.00 (1993-94) to Rs. 31,66,900.00 (1997-98) over a period of 5 years which is roughly 150% of the previous budget.

The apex library of Chandigarh Union Territory has shown an increase of 73% in budget allotment over the last 5 years. Meghalaya State has increased the budget of its State Central Library by 70% in three years from 1995-96 to 1997-98. Hence, it is not a surprise that the paucity of fund does not seem to be a bigger problem in the State Central Libraries of Chandigarh Union Territory and Meghalaya State as the librarians of these libraries consider financial problem as 'A Little Problem' for them.

However, as is observed in the libraries of all over the world, the paucity of funds is felt in the functioning of the majority of 23 SCLs (85%) in which financial crunch is seen as either 'Extreme Problem' in 8 SCLs (30%) or 'Considerable Problem' in 15 SCLs (56%). The budget position and the annual increase/decrease of the budget of the apex libraries of these States substantiate the assessments. The financial problem has been termed as 'Considerable Problem' by the librarians of the State Central Libraries of Goa, Gujarat, Kerala, Lakshadweep, Maharashtra, Nagaland, Punjab and West Bengal States and Union Territories. Their opinions can be properly understood by taking up the case study of Gujarat and Nagaland States.

In Gujarat State, the State Central Library has received a budget allocation of Rs. 14,00,000 in the year 1993 - 94. However, the allotment was reduced to Rs.13,55,000 in the next year, which shows a decrease of 3.2 per cent over the previous year. Further, in the year 1995-96, the budget was further reduced to Rs. 12,50,000 per cent which is a deduction of 7.75 per cent over the previous year and a total reduction of 10.71 per cent compared to the budget allotment of 1993 - 94. In the days of ever increasing cost of reading materials, staff salary and inflation, the reduction in budget shall naturally result in curtailment of certain services and resources.

The situation is worse in Nagaland State. The comparative figures of the budget allotment of the State Central Library of Nagaland State for five years' are as follows in Table 5.3:

TABLE 5.3
Budget of Nagaland State for 5 Years

Sl. No.	*Year*	*Budget Rs.*	*Percentage of Budget over the previous year*	*Percentage of Increase/Decrease*
1.	1993 - 94	11,18,000	—	—
2.	1994 - 95	10,68,000	95.53%	– 4.47%
3.	1995 - 96	2,68,000	25.09%	– 74.07%
4.	1996 - 97	3,08,000	114.93%	+ 14.93%
5.	1997 - 98	5,18,000	168.18%	+ 68.18%

The budget allotment has been reduced by 4.47 per cent in the financial year 1994-95 and 74.09 per cent in the subsequent year for the State Central Library of Nagaland. Hence, it is but natural that the Librarians of these two SCLs feel the financial problem as a'Considerable Problem'. In the same way, the librarians of 15 SCLs in the States/U.Ts at Andhra Pradesh, Arunachal Pradesh, Assam, Bihar, Delhi, Haryana, Himachal Pradesh, Karnataka, Madhya Pradesh, Manipur, Mizoram, Orissa, Rajasthan, Tamil Nadu and Uttar Pradesh have reported that the paucity of fund threatens them as the 'Extreme Problem' in their State Central Libraries. Among these States, the case studies of Manipur, Orissa and Uttar Pradesh States can be analysed to substantiate the financial difficulties faced by the librarians for the SCLs.

In Manipur State, the budget allotment has been a stagnant figure of Rs. 27,45,000 for 3 consecutive years from 1995-96, 1996-97 and 1997-98. The State Central Library of Orissa State was allocated Rs.53,71,000 in 1996-97 which was reduced to Rs. 47,51,000 in 1997-98 (a reduction of 11.54 per cent over the previous year).

The situation is still worse in the State Central Library of Uttar Pradesh State, the largest populated State in India. From the allotment of Rs. 20,76,800 for the year 1995-96, the SCL got lesser allotment of Rs. 12,43,200 in 1996-97 which witnessed a reduction of 40.14 per cent over the previous year. Though there was a marginal increase of budget amounting to Rs. 15,96,800 in

1997-98, still the net allotment of 1997-98 is less than 23.11 per cent compared to the allotment of 1995-96. Hence, it is clear that the paucity of funds continues to be a major problem for the State Central Libraries of India.

Environmental Problems

Environmental problem can be considered as the most crucial among all other problems. Problems like proper administrative support, adequate space for future expansion, conducive work-environment, effective awareness among the clientele, ability of the staff to understand user needs, proper and accessible location, flexible building, compatible climate, effective work culture are some of the vital issues that have an important bearing on the effective and meaningful functioning of any service library. However, the four major issues that are directly related to library environment of SCLs are discussed in the succeeding paragraphs.

Lack of Administrative Support

The environment in and around the State Central Library should be conducive and encouraging for the efficient functioning of the library. The external environment may be viewed as the financial and administrative support for the librarian with regard to supervision and management of the library. The lack of proper administrative support from the controlling authority of the States/U.Ts is viewed as the first environmental problem.

In the opinions of the librarians, the problem of 'Lack of administrative support' is considered as 'Extreme Problem' in 3 States (11%) at Maharashtra, Manipur and Rajasthan, 'Considerable Problem' in 9 States (33%), 'A Little Problem' in yet another 9 States, but 'No problem at All' in 6 States / U.Ts (22%) of Andaman and Nicobar Islands, Andhra Pradesh, Bihar, Haryana, Pondicherry and Uttar Pradesh respectively.

Lack of Space to Introduce New Services

The State Central Libraries have to provide a number of services to fulfill their mandate to satisfy the information and document requirements of the people of the respective States and Union Territories. Sufficient space is required for providing the mandatory services. In-house operations such as technical processing, administration and extension activities shall also take a lion's share in the available space of the State Central Libraries.

Above all, new services have to be initiated in order to harness the emerging technological developments such as Internet, multimedia and such other computer network oriented IR activities. Provision should be made at the planning and lay-out stage of the library building for adequate space to provide new services in future depending on the resources of the library and the requirements of the users.

The problem of 'Lack of space to introduce new services' is viewed as 'No Problem at All' by the librarians of 7 States/U.Ts (26%) at Arunachal Pradesh, Gujarat, Meghalaya, Nagaland, Pondicherry, Punjab and Uttar Pradesh; 'A Little Problem' by Andhra Pradesh State and Union Territory of Andaman and Nicobar Islands; 'Considerable Problem' by 9 States (33%) and 'Extreme Problem' by the remaining 9 States / U.Ts (33%) of Assam, Goa, Himachal Pradesh, Karnataka, Madhya Pradesh, Maharashtra, Manipur, Orissa and Tamil Nadu respectively.

Lack of a Compatible Environment to Work

Effective and user-friendly work-environment may make or mar the library service to a greater deal. However, larger resources are allotted and whatever be the space and technical staff position of a State Central Library, if the atmosphere or the environment is not smoother and conducive for the staff, the productivity and the efficiency of the services are bound to suffer. Adequate promotional opportunities, reasonable compensation in terms of salary and allowances, encouragement and appreciation of sincere and honest service and management with humanitarian considerations - all these, and many other similar factors contribute to provide a compatible environment to library work.

Hence, 'Lack of a compatible environment to work' is the next problem coming under the probe. It is satisfying to note from the opinions of the librarians of SCLs that in a majority of 21 SCLs (78%), this problem is either 'No Problem at All' in 9 SCLs or 'A Little Problem' in 12 SCLs. Only 5 librarians (19%) feel this as 'Considerably Problem' and only one librarian (4%) at Arunachal Pradesh treat this as 'Extreme Problem'. One may feel satisfied that in majority of the State Central Libraries of India, the staff are working in compatible environments, thereby promoting higher productivity and excellent services for the users of the SCLs which seem to be a healthy sign.

Lack of Library Awareness Among the Clienteles

The users of the library should be library conscious people. They should be aware of the importance of visiting the State Central Libraries at the first instance and once become users of the libraries, they should know the myriad services offered by the library. They should be able to locate the required documents as well as to assess the information potential of the libraries.

On having clear knowledge and thorough understanding of the resources of the libraries, the users shall be able to make the optimum utilisation of the services and resources of the libraries. If there is no utilisation or understanding of the services provided by the library among the users, there is no purpose in providing a variety of services at enormous cost in the apex libraries of the States/Union Territories.

It is interesting to know that none of the librarians have expressed that this is an 'Extreme Problem' when they are asked to state their opinion on the environmental problem of 'Lack of Library Awareness among the Clienteles' of the State Central Libraries. Only 5 librarians (19%) at the State Central Libraries of Himachal Pradesh, Mizoram, Nagaland, Rajasthan and West Bengal States—all from northern and eastern parts of the country feel this is a 'Considerable Problem'. More than three-fourth of the respondents, i.e., 21 librarians (81%) of SCLs of India feel that this is 'A Little Problem' (17 States) or 'No Problem at All' (5 States).

Technical Problems

Lack of Modernisation/Automation. Technological revolution is sweep in all the spheres of everyday's life. State Central Libraries being an essential and integral part of the society and service institutions cannot be exceptions to this trend. The existing tools and facilities available in the libraries and the emerging technological advancements in the field can be compared to the fighting of a battle with swords and spears against an enemy having AK-47 guns and long range missiles. Thus, lack of modernisation/automation, creates serious impediments on the growth and expansion of any service institution—the library. In the present era of Internet, the use of ITs and Super Computers makes the library a virtual and electronic global village ensuring free flow of information world wide.

It has thus been rightly said that, "Basically what we are seeing is an accelerating process of technological innovation. Its message is : innovate, automate or evaporate. No country can survive in a global economy with obsolescent facilities" (Merrifield;1986; p. 39). The State Central Libraries, therefore, should take advantage of the present technological revolution and provide sophisticated services to their users. The concept of modernization in library environment has been explained as follows : "By modernization of libraries, we mean : (a) better systems of organisation and management ; (b) introduction of new technologies for fast and efficient service ; (c) better bibliographic control ; and (d) standardization of systems and services" (Kumar; 1988; p. 158). The technological revolution and modernisation has resulted in automation of the activities of libraries through the use of computers and communication facilities.

The problem of lack of modernisation / automation has been identified as the first technical problem affecting the development of State Central Libraries. In the opinions of the librarians of SCLs, this problem appears to be the 'Extreme Problem' in 17 libraries (63%), 'Considerable Problem' in 6 SCLs (22%), 'A Little Problem' in the SCLs of 2 Union Territories of Andaman and Nicobar Islands and Chandigarh, whereas it is 'No Problem at All' in 2 State Central Libraries of Karnataka and Uttar Pradesh States respectively.

It is assessed from the survey of State Central Libraries of India that, only 7 States/U.Ts (26%) out of 27 units surveyed for this project have applied information technology of some kind in their apex libraries in the States/Union Territories of Chandigarh, Delhi, Gujarat, Karnataka, Lakshadweep and Pondicherry. Hence, it is but natural to expect from 23 librarians of SCLs (85%) that 'Lack of Modernisation/Automation' continues to be a serious technical problem for the State Central Libraries of India.

Lack of Proper Co-ordination and Networking. Cooperation and co-ordination are some of the refined social activities of the human beings which are as old as human civilisation. The object of co-ordination is to achieve what the individual members of the group cannot achieve individually and to pool the resources at one place so that any one can take anything from the common pool depending on the needs and requirements of the individuals at any time.

Co-ordination and Resource Sharing in State Central Libraries are aimed to extend the abundant resources and myriad services of the member libraries to a wider range of all the State/ U.Ts of India and outside India. This endeavour brings together the libraries which are otherwise remaining as isolated institutions without any channels of communication and interaction. Coordination and networking shall be helpful for the technical activities of libraries such as Inter Library Loan, Union Catalogue. Centralised Acquisition and Technical Processing.

Networking is the emerging area of coordination and resource sharing which shall provide comprehensive access to the documents and information in multimode linkages between libraries of various kinds and other institutions of relevance. Networking concept can be explained as coming together of inter-related information systems connected with data communication facilities which have agreed to coordinate by way of regular arrangements to jointly exchange information in order to pool their resources with an ultimate object of serving the users on a common platform.

The beginning of library networks can be traced from the evaluation of Library of Congress card production and distribution for the documents accessioned in the Library of Congress. In 1969 Library of Congress started the distribution of machine readable cataloguing data. In U.S.A. alone, important library networks like OCLC, SOLINET, AMIGOS, WLN, RLG, CLASS, BALLOTS, NELINET, MEDLARS and several others have started networking. At the international scene, several networks like DIALOG, UTLAS, BLAISE, AGRICOLA, INFOTERRA, ICDET, IRRD, EURYDICE, ERIC, APINMAP, ORBIT, ESANET, EURONET, SCANNET, TELENET, TYMNET and a host of others are delivering information by interchanging their resources through their computerised networks.

In the Indian scenario too, NICNET, INDONET, INFLIBNET, VIDYANET and similar networks are functioning at national level. In the regional level, DELNET, MALIBNET, CALIBNET, etc. are functioning by interchanging information from among the libraries and information providing institutions.

A question on whether the State Central Libraries are facing the problem of 'Lack of Proper Co-ordination and Networking', was posed to the libraries concerned. For this question, 18 libraries

(67%) have expressed this as an 'Extreme Problem' (11 libraries) and 'Considerable Problem' (7 libraries). In another 7 libraries (26%), this is felt as 'A Little Problem'. Only 2 Librarians of SCLs (7%) in the States of Uttar Pradesh and Lakshadweep consider this as 'No Problem at All'.

In the context of the automation of libraries done at only 7 SCLs of this country and due to the fact that there has been no computerised network among the State Central Libraries or among the various categories of public libraries of any State/Union Territory of India, this problem should be viewed as a very serious problem for all State Central Libraries of India.

Manpower Problems

The successful performance of the services of State Central Libraries would to a larger extent depend on the competence, calibre, number and the quality of library manpower. Manpower is a term which usually denotes the entire staff of an organisation—both the professional, and the non-professional.

Deshmukh outlines the objectives of manpower policy: "The objectives of an information manpower policy would be:

To interpret the implications of national development in terms of information requirements;

To develop appropriate mechanisms for effective information handling and transfer;

To meet these requirements, and to relate these mechanisms to those in current use" (Deshmukh; 1994; p. 219).

The major difference between the professional and non-professional staff is that it requires several years of relevant higher education, training and experience for the professional staff whereas the non-professional staff are required to have only a minimum general education and age restriction as prescribed in the Service Rules of the Library.

The largest collection of a public library does not guarantee effective service if the manpower of the library is not efficient, enthusiastic and encouraging for the users of the library. Hence, it has been proposed to discuss the manpower problems faced by the State Central Libraries of India. Under this heading, the problems of lack of attitude of library staff/work culture, shortage of professional staff and the situation in which the staff are not fully aware of technical know-how of modern library system, are analysed.

Lack of Attitude of Library Staff/Work Culture. Irrespective of selecting the best staff with higher qualifications and longer experience, if the attitude of the library staff is not helpful and encouraging for the users of the State Central Libraries, the services of the SCLs will be seriously affected. Work culture should be imbibed among the staff. Ranganathan emphasizes the need for the proper attitude and work culture among the library staff as follows : "The stuff of which the staff is made, the relation among the staff and the atmosphere will affect very intimately the service of the library. If these relations are bad, neither good buildings, nor good collections, nor efficient methods will be of any use. The members of the staff should be on the most cordial terms among themselves. There should not be the least trace of jealous or envy. Self should be suppressed to such a degree that every member is prepared to pass off all work as anonymous. Materlink's picture of work in the beehive contains the most vivid and accurate description of the spirit that should come over a library staff, if it is to function with maximum efficiency" (Ranganathan; 1988; p. 346). It is needless to emphasise that the manpower of the State Central Libraries should be properly oriented towards helping the users of the libraries in whatever way they can. This attitude is required more among the professional staff.

Kesavan says that, "the objectives of professional training are to assure ourselves that the persons so trained will fit into the context of this society, in such a manner, as to assure the members of the society of his competence in serving his fellowmen in his particular discipline" (Sharma; 1990; p. 74).

Hence, the first problem taken up under the heading, 'Manpower Problem' is the problem of 'Lack of attitude of Library Staff/Work Culture' among the staff of State Central Libraries of India. The survey reveals that the 'Lack of attitude among the staff of the State Central Libraries' is graded as 'No Problem at All' in 6 SCLs (22%) of Andaman and Nicobar Islands, Andhra Pradesh, Haryana, Meghalaya, Punjab and Uttar Pradesh; 'A Little Problem' in 12 libraries (44%); 'Considerable Problem' in 8 libraries (30%) and 'Extreme Problem' in the SCL of Nagaland State.

Shortage of Professional Staff. The term 'Professional Staff', in the field of libraries, has been defined by UNESCO as *"Staff who have a qualification in librarianship or information work. The* *qualification will normally have been obtained as a result of education at postgraduate or undergraduate level*" (Nick Moore; 1992; p. 204). It will not be sufficient if the State Central Libraries are provided with adequate staff but it is essential that the number and categories of professional staff should be adequate and as per the requirements of the collection of the library, services provided by the library, and the user population the library serves so that various conventional and sophisticated services can be undertaken by the State Central Libraries.

The professional staff should have a sound general education, required professional education and training at an accredited school of librarianship and the possession of a certificate issued by a statutory authority. Just as a qualified doctor is allowed to practice as a physician in a hospital or a lawyer, engineer, or chartered accountant is practising in the relevant professional fields, the professional staff of a library with proper technical education, training and certificates alone should be allowed to be employed for performing technical and supervisory functions in the State Central Libraries.

The necessity of professional staff in librarianship is advocated by Danton as, "Librarianship today is a highly complex profession requiring specific and detailed knowledge of many kinds—personal, financial, bibliographical and bibliothecal. The complicated services which a modern library renders do not organise and run themselves but must be organised and operated; they must be modified, improved and extended in the light of changing conditions. This can be done only by one who knows the objectives and potentialities of the library, the techniques, tools and means of achieving them, and the purposes and limitations of the means" (Danton; 1949; p. 6). The professional staff alone can handle several specialised services such as Circulation, Reference, Referral, Current Awareness, Bibliography, Selective Discrimination of Information, Online Searching, Inter Library Loan and such other services as discussed in the previous chapters.

If there is a shortage in the number and level of professional staff, it will affect the services, activities and performances of the State Central Libraries. How to decide the ratio of professional and non-professional staff? "The IFLA Standards recommend that between 33% and 40% of the staff should be professionally qualified" (Nick Moore; 1992; p. 189). The survey of 27 State

Central Libraries of India reveals that there are 779 professional and semi-professional staff (56%) out of the total number of 1,387 staff members serving in these Libraries. Hence, the overall situation appears to be satisfactory for the availability of professional staff compared to the non-professional staff. But, the problem of shortage of professional staff prevails in several State Central Libraries. As per the assessments of the Librarians of State Central Libraries of India, the problem of 'Shortage of Professional Staff' is considered as 'Extreme Problem' in 12 SCLs (44%), 'Considerable Problem' in 5 libraries (19%), 'A Little Problem' in 8 Libraries (30%) and 'No Problem at All' in the SCLs of Lakshadweep U.T. and Uttar Pradesh State.

Awareness of Modern Technical Knowhow. Despite of having large number of highly qualified professional staff with appropriate attitude/work culture, if they are not uptodate in technical knowledge and modern systems and techniques, the State Central Libraries shall not be in a position to perform their duties as pioneering apex libraries of the States/U.T.s and offer various services in the emerging areas of Universe of Knowledge. The on-going technological revolution, in fact, has posed a challenge to change the mindset of technophobic professionals. Computer and IT literacy will soon be an essential qualifiction for all LIS professionals.

The library staff, therefore, should be fully aware of technical knowhow and modern library systems due to the impact of information technology, demand for specialised services in the emerging areas of information, growing knowledge explosion, increasing number of users, proliferation of published literature and for effective bibliographic control. Further, they have to satisfy the specific needs of the users in the newer areas, upgrade and update their knowledge and skill in order to overcome the deficiencies in job performance so as to ensure qualitative library services. Any professional problems encountered in their service by the library staff can be solved/cleared only through experts/resource persons who are well versed with the latest technical know-how. From the survey undertaken by the investigator in the SCLs of India, it is ascertained that only in the following 6 SCLs (22%), the library staff were deputed for training programmes/seminars in the last 5 years, as per Table 5.4.

It can be seen that only 29 Staff Members (02%) out of a total number of 1,387 working in various SCLs of India have been deputed for training programmes. This sombre state of updating the knowledge of the in-service LIS professionals is not at all conducive to the qualitative and need-based services.

TABLE 5.4
Staff Deputed for Training in SCLs

Sl. No.	*Name of State/U.T.*	*No. of Staff Deputed for Training*
1.	Andhra Pradesh	2
2.	Gujarat	3
3.	Himachal Pradesh	2
4.	Lakshadweep	2
5.	Punjab	1
6.	Rajasthan	19
	Total	29

In a survey undertaken in Tamil Nadu State from the professional staff working in State Central Library and other public libraries of Chennai city, the library staff were asked to state on the attitude of library staff towards application of Information Technology. As per the results of the survey, it is reported that 68 per cent of the staff agree that the lack of adequate trained staff in IT applications is the reason for poor application of Information Technology in public libraries (Ramesh Babu and Parameswaram; 1999; p. 117). In the opinion of the Librarians of SCLs of India, the problem that the 'Staff are not fully aware of technical know-how of modern library system' is treated as 'No Problem at All' in 4 States/U.Ts (15%) of Andaman and Nicobar Islands, Assam, Goa, Maharashtra and Uttar Pradesh; 'A Little, Problem' in 10 SCLs (37%); 'Considerable Problem' in another 10 SCLs whereas this problem is treated as an 'Extreme Problem' in 3 States of Himachal Pradesh, Nagaland and Rajasthan States respectively.

Conclusion

An in-dpeth analysis of various problems faced by the State Central Libraries of India, namely, social and economic problems, financial problems, environmental problems, technical problems and manpower problems has been undertaken in this chapter.

The analysis indicates that unless the social and economic conditions of the people living in the States/U.Ts of India are improved, the problems of State Central Libraries shall persist. The financial problem continues to be a major problem in most of the State Central Libraries in this country. Though the environmental problems such as, the lack of proper administrative support, lack of space to introduce new services, lack of a compatible environment to work and lack of library awareness among the library clientele of the SCLs are some of the major problems felt by the librarians, these problems are in a manageable situation and they do not seriously hamper the services of the States Central Libraries in larger proportions.

Technical problems such as the lack of library modernisation/automation and lack of proper co-ordination and networking constitute major impediments in providing latest techniques and modern tools for the benefit of the users of the State Central Libraries. The State Central Libraries are, in fact, far behind in harnessing the advantages of information and communication technology. Among the manpower problems, lack of attitude of library staff/work culture and the shortage of professional staff are manageable problems whereas the situation that the staff are not fully aware of technical know-how of modern library system constitute an urgent problem to be attended immediately failing which the staff members of the SCLs will not be able to cope up with the modern library system and shall be treated as obsolete.

In the next chapter, the prospects of the State Central Libraries in the areas of increased productivity, extension of library activities, participation in networking, promotion of reading habits and restoring the social order and peace are discussed. If the present chapter depicts a gloomy picture of the State Central Libraries, the next chapter shall show a luminous path for a bright future for the State Central Libraries of India.

Bibliography

1. Danton, J.P. Education for Librarianship. 1949. UNESCO; Paris, p. 6.

2. Deshmukh, P.P. Manpower Needs for Agricultural Information Management in India. *In* Prashar, R.G., *ed. Personnel Problems in Indian Libraries*. 1994. Madallion Press; New Delhi, p. 219.
3. Kumar, P.S.G. Modernisation Vis-a-vis Library and Information Science Education in India. *In* Vashisth, C.P. *ed. Modernisation in Libraries*, 1988, Indian Library Association; Delhi, p. 158.
4. Mangla, P.B. National Policies on Libraries, Information Systems and Services in India : An Overview. *In* Neelameghan, A. and Prasad, K.N. *ed. Information Systems, Networks and Trends*, 1998. Ranganathan Centre for Information Studies; Bangalore, p. 5.
5. India. Research, Reference and Training Division, India 2002; *A Reference Annual, 2002*, Ministry of Education, New Delhi, p. 13.
6. Merrifield, Bruce. Innovate, Automate or Evaporate. *Span*, 1986, Oct., p. 39.
7. Nick Moore. Measuring the Performance of Public Libaries; A Draft Manual (UNESCO). *Granthana-Indian Journal of Library Studies*. 1992 July, Vol. 3, No. 2, pp. 160-206.
8. Ramesh Babu, B. and Parameshwaran, R. Attitude of the Public Library Staff Towards Automation of Public Libraries in Chennai. *In* Kannan, R. and Ramasamy, R., *ed. Proceedings of the National Seminar on Library Movement in India After Independence-Problems and Prospects* held on 5-6, April 1999. Department of Public Libraries; Government of Tamil Nadu; Chennai, p. 117
9. Sharma, C.K. Modern Library Systems. 1990. Y.K. Publishers; Agra, p. 74.
10. Swank, R.C. Inter Library Co-operation, Inter-Library Communications and Information Networks : Explanation and Definition. *In* Proceedings of the Conference on Interlibrary Communications and Information Networks. 1971. American Library Association; Chicago, p. 204.

6

Future Prospects of SCLs

Introduction

The State Central Library is a service institution providing various services to the users of the library and the general public living in any part of State. It serves as a leader for all public libraries functioning in the State. The role of State Central Library is crucial in networking and the establishment of uniform library procedures in the State. However, the apex library of the State faces several problems in performing its functions such as social and economic problems, environmental problems, financial problems, technical problems and manpower problems. Inspite of the seriousness and gravity of the above problems encountered by the State Central Libraries, the future prospects of the SCLs are very bright and promising. The future prospects of the SCLs may be listed as increased productivity, extension of library activities, participation in networking, promotion of reading habits and restoring the social order and peace among others.

Propositions on the Future Prospects of SCLs

In order to analyse the future prospects of the State Central Libraries of India, I have made the following propositions under five broad headings which are indicative and suggestive of the nature of prospects :

I. Increased Productivity

1. The SCL will witness a spectacular increase in document use.
2. The SCL can improve the quality of its services.
3. The SCL can save the time of its clientele by resorting to measures to transfer information at a much faster rate than before.
4. Optimum use of library materials can be ensured.
5. The more the library is advanced, the greater would be its economy and efficiency in the long run/days to come.

II. Extension of Library Activities

6. In the emerging era of Internet, the Information superhighway will help to increase the work efficiency of the library staff (through www).
7. Optical technology with computer and other electronic devices will help to store vast ocean of information in least space.

III. Participation in Networking

8. It can play the role of a leader in guiding the District Central Libraries, Branch Libraries, Rural libraries and such other public libraries of the State to serve the population effectively.
9. The SCL can participate effectively through library networking.
10. I.T. revolution will ease Inter Library Loan traffic better than expectation.

IV. Promotion of Reading Habits

11. It will help to eradicate illiteracy and poverty through adult and continuing education.

V. Restoring Social Order and Peace

12. It can help its citizens to inculcate reading habits, inject competitive spirit and to remove blind beliefs and superstitions.
13. It can promote social order and peace.

The propositions so devised have been placed before the Librarians of the State Central Libraries. They have been requested to state which of the propositions mentioned above shall bring in bright future prospects to overcome the myriad problems being faced by the State Central Libraries, as discussed in the previous chapter. The librarians were requested to state, in their opinions, which of the propositions are (1) Quite True, (2) True, (3) Doubtful and (4) False depending on the appropriateness of the prospect pertaining to their individual State Central Libraries. The opinions of the librarians on the appropriateness of each of the proposition are enumerated in Table 6.1. The opinions of the librarians on the propositions proposed by me are analysed and incorporated in the succeeding paragraphs of this chapter.

TABLE 6.1
Prospects of SCLs of India

Sl. No.	*State/U.T.*	*Increased Productivity*					*Extension of Library Activities*		*Participation in Networking*			*Promotion of Reading Habits*	*Resorting Social Order and Peace*	
(1)	(2)	(3)	(4)	(5)	(6)	(7)	(8)	(9)	(10)	(11)	(12)	(13)	(14)	(15)
1.	Andaman and Nicobar Islands	2	2	1	1	2	2	3	2	1	2	2	2	2
2.	Andhra Pradesh	2	1	3	2	1	4	4	1	4	4	1	1	1
3.	Arunachal Pradesh	3	3	3	1	2	1	1	2	2	1	2	2	2
4.	Assam	2	2	3	1	1	3	3	1	3	4	1	1	1
5.	Bihar	1	1	1	1	2	4	1	2	1	4	1	1	3
6.	Chandigarh	1	1	1	3	3	3	3	3	1	3	3	3	3
7.	Delhi	1	2	1	2	2	2	1	1	2	2	3	2	2
8.	Goa	2	2	2	2	2	2	2	2	2	2	2	2	2
9.	Gujarat	1	1	2	2	1	2	1	1	2	1	1	1	1
10.	Haryana	2	2	2	2	2	2	2	2	2	2	2	2	2
11.	Himachal Pradesh	1	1	1	1	1	1	1	1	1	1	1	1	1
12.	Karnataka	1	1	2	2	1	1	2	1	1	1	3	2	2
13.	Kerala	1	2	3	2	1	3	3	1	3	3	1	1	1

(Contd.)

(1)	(2)	(3)	(4)	(5)	(6)	(7)	(8)	(9)	(10)	(11)	(12)	(13)	(14)	(15)
14.	Lakshadweep	1	1	2	1	1	1	2	1	1	1	1	1	1
15.	Madhya Pradesh	1	1	2	1	1	3	2	1	2	3	1	1	1
16.	Maharashtra	1	1	2	1	1	3	3	2	3	2	2	1	1
17.	Manipur	1	1	2	1	1	3	1	1	1	3	1	1	1
18.	Meghalaya	2	1	3	1	1	2	3	1	3	2	1	1	1
19.	Mizoram	1	2	4	2	1	4	4	1	4	4	1	1	1
20.	Nagaland	2	1	2	1	2	2	2	2	2	3	2	1	3
21.	Orissa	1	1	2	2	2	2	1	2	1	2	3	3	3
22.	Pondicherry	1	1	1	1	1	3	3	1	1	3	1	1	1
23.	Punjab	1	2	2	2	2	2	2	2	2	2	2	2	2
24.	Rajasthan	1	1	2	2	1	1	1	1	1	2	2	1	1
25.	Tamil Nadu	1	1	1	1	2	1	1	1	1	1	2	2	1
26.	Uttar Pradesh	2	2	4	4	3	3	4	2	1	3	2	2	2
27.	West Bengal	2	2	2	2	2	2	2	2	2	2	3	3	3

1 = Quite True 3 = Doubtful
2 = True 4 = False.

Increased Productivity

The concept of productivity is not the prerogative of industries alone; its meaning can be extended to other areas of human activity including 'Library Services'. Extension of this concept in the field of library service is very much significant considering the fact that the field of library service is increasingly known, at present, as information industry where the 'information' provided by the libraries are considered as 'goods' which are consumed/utilised by the clientele of the information industry who is also often described as information consumer. Hence, the State Central Libraries can also be grouped within the information industry. The goods produced by the SCLs are the 'information service and book lending service' and the consumers are the 'users' of SCLs.

In order to assess the productivity of SCLs, the following five propositions, have been evolved as the prospects of SCLs :

1. The SCL will witness a spectacular increase in document use;
2. The SCL can improve the quality of its services;
3. The SCL can save the time of the clientele (user) by resorting to measures to transfer information at much faster rate than before;
4. Optimum use of library materials can be ensured; and
5. The more the library is advanced, the greater would be its economy and efficiency in the long run / days to come.

Spectacular Increase in Document Use

The first proposition under the aspect 'increased productivity' expects that 'the SCL will witness a spectacular increase in document use'. This proposition is seen under the light of the status of SCLs as already discussed. As per the status report, 23 SCLs (85%) out of 27 are offering the service of lending of documents for home reading which is reported as 'Regularly' in 18 libraries (67%). The service of 'Temporary lending of documents within the library premises' is also available in 25 SCLs (93%) which has been reported as 'Regularly' and 'Frequently' in 25 SCLs (93%) put together. Only in 2 SCLs this service was not used.

When the growth rate of collection development is analysed, it is found that there is an overall growth rate of 3.12 per cent of the total collection in all SCLs. The growth rate has been as higher 6.89 per cent in Karnataka State and 5.07 per cent in Delhi U.T.

The States/Union Territories of Mizoram (3.82%), Orissa (3.65%), Gujarat (3.46%), Lakshadweep (3.37%) and Andaman and Nicobar Islands (3.32%) have shown a higher rate of growth than the all India average growth rate of 3.12 per cent in collection development. In the budget front, several States/Union Territories have been showing spectacular increase in budget allotment for their SCLs. For example, the Union Territory of Andaman and Nicobar Island has been increasing its annual budget for its SCL by an average rate of 278 per cent for 4 years continuously from the year 1994-95 to 1997-98. The gross increase of the budget of the SCL of this U.T. is an astonishing figure of 3,333 per cent from the year of 1993-94 to 1997-98 within a gap of four years. The Union Territory of Pondicherry has also shown an aggregate increase of 150 per cent in the budget of its SCL from the year 1993-94 to 1997-98.

If more funds are flowing, followed by considerable growth in collection development and the increasing availability of documents to the users of SCLs by way of lending documents for home reading and temporary lending within the library premises, the ultimate result would naturally be the spectacular increase in document use. When the librarians of SCLs were requested to offer their opinions on the first proposition,'The SCLs will witness a spectacular increase in document use' the answer is a strong 'Quite True' in 17 cases and 'True' in 9 libraries. In all, 26 librarians (96%) are highly optimistic that the SCLs will witness a spectacular increase in document use and only 1 librarian (4%) at Arunachal Pradesh State feels that this proposition is 'Doubtful'. Interestingly, no librarian has mentioned this proposition as 'False'.

Further, when the librarians of SCLs were asked to offer their suggestions on the improvement of SCLs, the librarian of the SCL of Himachal Pradesh has suggested that 'Books are to be purchased as per the demand' of the readers. The suggestion of this librarian shall also be useful in showing a clear trend of witnessing a spectacular increase in document use.

SCL can Improve the Quality of its Services

In the next proposition, the prospect of improving the quality of services of SCLs is taken up. The SCLs are offering a number of services such as lending of documents for home reading, temporary lending within the library services, reference service, referral service, current awareness service, selective dissemination of information, bibliographic service, state bibliography, inter library loan, online searching, indexing and abstracting, and extension services.

The term, 'Quality', here implies value added services irrespective of the number and categories of services offered by the institutions. If the quality of service is higher, the satisfaction level of the readers will be appreciable. The quality of service will also attract large number of users to the State Central Libraries. Quality service of a SCL would also result the increase of readers, increase of circulation transactions, optimal use of library resources, increase in ILL traffic, and would witness a track record of reference queries of the reference desk.

When the librarians of SCLs were asked to confirm or reject the proposition 'SCL can improve the quality of its services' an overwhelming number of 26 librarians have confirmed that the SCL can improve the quality of its services. Among the 27 librarians, 26 librarians (96%) have concurred with this proposition by confirming this proportion as 'Quite True' in 16 States and 'True' in 10 States respectively. Again, the librarian of Arunachal Pradesh State alone hesitates to accept this proposition and considers this as 'Doubtful' proposition. However, none is of the opinion that this is a 'False' proposition.

SCL Can Save the Time of its Clientele in Transfer of Information Very Fast

The third proposition under the prospect of SCL 'Increased Productivity' declares that 'the SCL can save the time of its clientele by resorting to measures to transfer information at a much faster rate than before'. The fourth law of library science enunciated by S.R.Ranganathan legislates to 'Save the time of the Reader'. Hence, saving the time of its clientele is a fundamental canon of library science. Due to the emerging trends of information technology, multimedia, Internet and World Wide Web, the SCL shall naturally move forward in transferring the information to its users at a much faster rate than before thereby saving the time of its users.

When the librarians were contacted to offer their opinions on the prospect of transferring the information at a much faster rate than before, 2 librarians at Uttar Pradesh and Mizoram State Central Libraries have termed this prospect as 'False' and in the opinions of librarians of 5 SCLs of Andhra Pradesh, Arunachal Pradesh, Assam and Maghalaya States, the prospect of the possibility of this proposition is considered as 'Doubtful'. Thus, 7 librarians (26%) are not sure about their State Central Libraries taking measures to transfer information at a much faster rate than before. Their views indicate that they are facing difficulties in introducing modern technologies in their libraries either due to paucity of funds or due to the attitudes of the controlling authorities. However, 20 librarians (74%) assert that this proposition is 'True' or 'Quite True'.

Optimum use of Library Materials can be Ensured

The term 'Library Materials' shall include books, journals, audio, video and digital materials. Being the apex library of the State, the SCL acquires enormous book and non-book materials. Mere acquisition of materials alone will not be sufficient. Available materials should be put to maximum use. The more the materials are utilised, the maximum would be the benefit derived out of the materials in terms of readers satisfaction. Adequate resource materials, availability of technical staff and awareness of the resources by the users - are the three basic requirements for better utilisation of the resources of SCLs.

Hence, the next proposition placed before the librarians of SCLs is, 'Optimum use of library materials can be ensured'. For this proposition, 25 librarians (93%) of SCLs of various States/ Union Territories have replied in affirmative stating as 'Quite True' (13 States), and 'True' (12 States) respectively. The librarian of Chandigarh, however, feels this is 'Doubtful' and the librarian of SCL of Uttar Pradesh State has not agreed with this proposition and rejects this as 'False', probably due to the constraints being experienced by the librarian.

Greater Economy and Efficiency

The next proposition under the prospect 'Increased Productivity' placed before the librarians of SCLs of India is as follows: 'The more the library is advanced, the greater would be its economy and efficiency in the long run/days to come'. The advancement/development/improvement in the resources and services of the SCL shall lead the library to economy and efficiency in its functioning. The SCLs are advancing in terms of collection development, manpower, finance, governance, space, building, physical conditions, and automation, as already discussed in Chapter 3. The services such as lending, current awareness, SDI, bibliographic service, reference and referral, inter library loan, online searching, indexing and abstracting services and extension activities provided by the SCLs are also showing considerable advancements as analysed in Chapter 4. As a result of these advancements, it is expected that in the longer run the SCLs will have the benefit of greater economy and efficiency in their functioning. The librarians of SCLs of India have overwhelmingly expressed that this proposition will become a definite reality. Among the librarians of all SCLs, 25 librarians (93%) are of the opinion that this proposition is 'Quite True' or 'True'.

Only 2 librarians (7%) at Chandigarh Union Territory and Uttar Pradesh State consider it as 'Doubtful'. However, no one denies this proposition as 'False'.

Extension of Library Activities

In addition to the conventional extension activities carried out by the SCLs, there has been a spurt in the extension of library activities in the SCLs of India, especially in the emerging areas of global advancements in Information Technology. By utilising this technology, SCLs can not only expand the existing services but also introduce new services through different information networks, subscribe different online data bases, obtain online reprints of research articles and can increase Inter Library Loan traffic effectively. By information technology is meant the present day convergence of technologies that are useful and profitable in their own right to form together a powerful new approach to information storage, transfer and retrieval. These are the technologies of computers, telecommunications and micrographics with the micro electronics as the facilitator (Teague; 1985; p. 96).

In order to analyse the extension of library activities in the field of information technology in SCLs of India, the following two propositions have been devised :

1. In the emerging era of Internet, the Information Superhighway will help to increase the work efficiency of the staff through World Wide Web; and
2. Optical technology with computer devices will help to store vast ocean of information in least space.

Information Superhighway will Increase Work Efficiency of the Staff

The professionals of library and information services are in the midst of Internet revolution happening around the world. The term, 'Internet' comes from the concept 'Inter networking' which denotes the interaction between different networks of computers. It is a vast collection of large and small inter connected computer networks extending all the way across the globe. 'Information Superhighway, is making phenomenal progress by linking computerised networks in all corners of the world. The technological advancement of Internet can be very much helpful for increasing the work efficiency of the staff.

Hence, the next proposition addressed to the librarians of SCLs states: 'In the emerging era of Internet, the information Superhighway will help to increase the work efficiency of the staff (through World Wide Web)'. Since the introduction of information technology has been very slow in the SCLs of India, librarians of 10 SCLs (37%) do not feel that this proposition will become true by expressing as 'False' by 3 librarians of Andhra Pradesh, Bihar and Mizoram States and as 'Doubtful' by 7 librarians. However, the remaining 17 librarians (73%) of SCLs of India have the confidence in implementation of information technology and Internet in their respective libraries and assert that this proposition is 'Quite True' or 'True'.

Optical Technology to Store Information

Optical technology seems to have opened its account as a viable storage medium in the library circle in 1985 with the introduction of its first CD-PACs by Brodart (Bills and Helgerson; 1988; p. 67).

Optical technology involves the use of lasers. Through optical technology, information can be directly entered into a computer without the necessity of entering through keyboards. Optical disks, generally known as compact discs, are encoded with information through a laser beam burning microscopic 'Pits' into disc surface through a metallised reflective film surface beneath. Optical disks are available as CD-ROM, CD-WORM and CD-EOD. Optical technology has created different types of secondary storage media for computers ensuring faster information transfer and retrieval. This technology has made a revolution in storing vast amount of information in the least space thereby saving the space of the library and simultaneously ensuring speedy information retrieval.

'Optical technology with computer devices will help to store vast ocean of information in least space'- a proposition proposed to the librarians of SCLs has evoked a mixed response similar to the previous proposition. In the opinions of the librarians of 3 State Central Libraries of Andhra Pradesh, Mizoram and Uttar Pradesh States, this proposition is considered as 'False' and 7 librarians consider this as 'Doubtful'. While 17 librarians (63%) are confident of this proposition becoming a reality by expressing as 'Quite True' or 'True', the remaining 10 librarians (37%) do not think in favour of this proposition.

Participation in Networking

The SCLs can share their resources among themselves for providing efficient services to their users. The process of resource sharing shall be more effective and result-oriented, if a planned and well developed network is established among the SCLs. There are different kinds of networks like, star network, hierarchical network, distributed network and ring network.

The SCL can take part in any kind of network. The network involving State Central Libraries can be extended at the higher level by linking with National Library of India and the National Libraries of other nations as well. The same network can also penetrate down below by incorporating Regional Libraries, Divisional Libraries, District Central libraries, Taluk/Tehsil Libraries, Block Libraries, Village Libraries Delivery Stations and other categories of academic and public libraries.

Martin defines network as "a group of individuals or organisations that are connected through some communication mechanisms" (Martin; 1981; p. 1) Networking allows more than one user to share common resources. The term, 'networking' has been increasingly used in the context of computer and communication technology. In this connection, the Dictionary of Computers defines the term 'network' as "the system of inter connected computer based installations or telecommunication systems and terminals so as to derive the maximum transmission efficiency" (Jain and Hazarika; 1994; p. 245).

The prospects of State Central Libraries participating in networking have been further probed through the following propositions:

1. The SCL can play the role of leader in guiding District Central Libraries and other public libraries of the State to serve the population effectively;
2. The SCL can participate more effectively through library networking; and
3. Information Technology revolution will ease Inter Library Loan traffic better than expectation.

The SCL can Play the Role of a Leader in Guiding Public Libraries

The State Central Library, by its nature, is the apex public library of the State. Hence, the expectations from the SCL on guiding the other public libraries of the State/Union Territory are enormous. The networking contemplated in this connection is 'hierarchical networking' in which SCL is to be at the top of the pyramid of hierarchical networking. Hence, a proposition stating that 'the SCL can play the role of the leader in guiding the District Central Libraries and other public libraries of the State to serve the population effectively' is placed before the librarians of SCLs for their opinions.

As many as 26 librarians (96%) have emphatically recorded that this proposition is 'Quite True' or 'True'. Only one librarian at Chandigarh Union Territory feels it is 'Doubtful'. From their opinions, it is clear that there is a bright prospect of the State Central Library playing the role of a leader in guiding the District Central Libraries and other public libraries to serve the population more effectively. The SCL can play the role of a leader in the areas of centralised acquisition, classification, cataloguing and technical control - to name a few areas.

SCL Can Participate More Effectively through Library Networking

The SCL has already been performing myriad activities and services. If the library networking has been implemented by the SCL, either computerised or otherwise, there is a tremendous scope for its effective participation in providing lending services to the people of the State/Union Territory more effectively.

Since the inter connectivity among the homogeneous and heterogeneous computers located anywhere has already become a reality through Wide Area Network (WAN) due to the advent of advanced networking hardware and software system, the State

Central Library can participate more effectively in the services offered by other public libraries of the State/Union Territory.

Having this in mind, the librarians of SCLs were requested to offer their views on the proposition 'State Central Library can participate more effectively through library networking' for which 21 librarians (78%) comment as 'Quite True' or 'True' while 4 librarians consider this as 'Doubtful' and 2 librarians of the SCLs of Andhra Pradesh and Mizoram States consider the above proposition as 'False'.

IT Revolution will Ease Inter Library Loan Traffic

The information technology (IT) revolution is sweeping the universe. In several fronts of library activity, the information technology is making distinct impacts. The Inter Library Loan services are offered in the State Central Libraries by borrowing books and other documents from other libraries and supplying them to their users on specific requests from the users. In the advent of IT revolution, the SCLs will be in a better position to collect the documents from other libraries, irrespective of their location, by sending its request through E-Mail and lending the documents to the users without any lapse in time. The IT will ultimately reduce the Inter library loan traffic since the information and the contents of the documents can be obtained in digital form and transferred to the users immediately through computerised library networking.

The next proposition placed before the librarians of SCLs is 'Information Technology revolution will ease Inter Library Loan traffic better than expectation'. The librarians responded by saying 'Quite True' or 'True' in the case of 16 SCLs (59%), 'Doubtful' in 7 SCLs (26%) and 'False' in 4 libraries (15%) of Andhra Pradesh, Assam, Bihar and Mizoram States. The prospect of IT revolution easing Inter Library Loan traffic appears to be less than expectations as only 41 per cent of the librarians surprisingly consider this proposition as 'Doubtful' or 'False'.

Promotion of Reading Habits

One of the objectives of public library service is to improve and promote reading habits among the people whom it serves through different services and facilities. India is a developing country with an average literacy of 65.38 per cent (*Manorama;* 2002; p. 272). Even among the literate people, many of them cannot read and write fluently. Most of the so called educated people, including the graduates, do not normally read more general books except the text-books prescribed for their academic courses. Hence, the reading habits should be developed among the population of the State. In the given circumstance, promotion of reading habits should be one of the primary aims and objectives of the SCLs so that the readership will increase and optimum utilisation of SCLs can be ensured.

SCL will help to Eradicate Illiteracy through Education

The illiteracy and poverty are the two main causes for the social and economic backwardness of the people. It is a vicious circle that illiteracy is the result of poverty and poverty is an outcome of illiteracy. Hence, SCL has a bright prospect of playing its role to cut the knot of this vicious circle through adult and continuing education as well as through its myriad extension activities.

The next proposition is evolved as 'SCL will help to eradicate illiteracy and poverty through adult and continuing education and through its myriad extension activities'. This proposition has received positive verdict from 22 librarians of SCLs (81%) as 'Quite True' or 'True', whereas 5 librarians (19%) of Chandigarh, Delhi, Kerala, Orissa and West Bengal States/Union Territories consider this as 'Doubtful'. Interestingly, no one has negatived it by saying 'False'.

Restoring Social Order and Peace

Public libraries are part and parcel of the society. Further, they have a moral role to evolve a social order and establish a peaceful society. If the society is divided and agitated over social problems, the SCL, as the apex public library of the State can play a positive role in bringing social order. With this in mind, the following two propositions have been enunciated to solicit the opinions of the Librarians of SCLs of India :

(i) The SCL can help its citizens to inculcate reading habits, inject competitive spirit and to remove blind beliefs and superstitions; and
(ii) The SCL can promote social order and peace by educating them.

SCL can Help its Citizens to Inculcate Reading Habits

The State Central Library has a moral responsibility to develop the people living in the State/Union Territory as a better citizen in several ways. As has been already discussed, inculcating the reading habit is a basic activity of SCL. The people of a State should have a competitive spirit so that they can outshine the people of other States in different fields.

Even among themselves, the people of a State should try to outsmart one another through competitive spirit. If the competitive spirit is not sufficient enough, the SCL can inject the competitive spirit in the minds of the people of the State/Union Territory by conducting competitions in various subjects of interest and awarding prizes. By generation after generation, the blind beliefs and superstitions are not only continuing but also aggravating and increasing. The blind beliefs and superstitions are obstacles to the progress and development of the society. Under the given situation, the SCL can play its part in removing the blind beliefs and superstitions of the society so that the citizens living in the State/Union Territory can move forward progressively.

When the librarians of SCLs have been asked to comment on the prospect of SCL in terms of the proposition 'The SCL can help its citizens to inculcate reading habits, inject competitive spirit and to remove blind beliefs and superstitions', 24 of them (89%) have optimistically responded by saying it is 'Quite True' or 'True'. Only 3 librarians (11%) of the States/Union Territories of Chandigarh, Orissa and West Bengal have expressed the prospect of this proposition as 'Doubtful'. However, no librarian considers it as 'False'.

SCL Can Promote Social Order and Peace

In the days of social disorders, political anarchy and economic stagnation, the SCL can play a crucial role in neutralising the ill-effects of the society by effective extension activities and efficient information services. If the SCL conducts social awareness programmes, exhibitions, seminars and similar information providing activities on the burning social problems, the people of the State/Union Territory can be properly educated, informed and awakened positively leading to the establishment of social order and peace. The SCL can promote social order and peace by converting the State Central Library into a social information centre through its various extension activities and information services.

For the proposition, 'SCL can promote social order and peace', an overwhelming number of 22 librarians of SCLs (81%) have positive opinions stating this as 'Quite True' or 'True'. However, the librarians of 5 SCLs (19%) of Bihar State, Chandigarh Union Territory, Nagaland State, Orissa State, and West Bengal State have some reservations, as in their opinion, the prospect of this proposition is 'Doubtful'. No librarian, however, comments this proposition as 'False'.

Prospects of SCLs

It is assessed from the collective opinions of the librarians of State Central Libraries on the suggested propositions that, the prospects of State Central Libraries are brighter in the following areas:

TABLE 6.2
Percentage of Prospects of SCLs

	% of Prospect
I. Increased Productivity	
1. The SCL will witness a specular increase in document use	96%
2. The SCL can improve the quality of its services	96%
3. The SCL can save the time of its readers in transfer of information	74%
4. Optimum use of materials can be ensured	93%
5. Greater economy and efficiency can be ensured due to advancement of the library	93%
II. Extension of Library Activities	
6. Internet will increase the work efficiency of the staff	63%
7. Optical technology will help to store vast information in least space.	63%
III. Participatin in Networking	
8. SCL can play the role of a leader in guiding other public libraries	96%
9. SCL can participate in networking	78%
10. IT revolution will ease ILL traffic	59%
IV. Promotion of Reading Habits	
11. SCL will help to eradicate illiteracy and poverty	81%

(Contd.)

(Contd.)

V. Restoring Social Order and Peace	
12. SCL can help its citizens to live in social harmony by educating their responsibility towards society.	96%
13. SCL can promote social order and peace	81%

From the above analysis, it is seen that wherever the IT is involved, the percentage of the prospects of the proposition is less and in other aspects the percentage of prospects is comparatively more.Hence, it can be said that though the prospects of SCLs are bright in many areas, the improvements in terms of implementation of information technology seem to be very much slower than expected.

Conclusion

The State Central Libraries of India have bright prospects in future in terms of increased productivity, extension of library activities, participation in networking, promotion of reading habits and restoring social order and peace. The opinions of the librarians of the State Central Libraries have also been overwhelmingly in favour of these prospects. Some prospects appear to be dim due to the lack of implementation of information technology in State Central Libraries. In order to achieve economy and efficiency in providing optimum services to the users of the SCLs, the authorities of SCLs should seriously engage themselves in computerisation of the SCLs. They must also actively participate in library networking by becoming a part of any network and by subscribing to the Internet and other national and international networks and online databases.

In the next and concluding chapter, the data collected from the SCLs will be analysed, the hypotheses evolved for this project will be tested and suitable measures for the improvement of the services of the State Central Libraries will be suggested. Scope for further research in this field will also be dealt with.

Bibliography

1. Bills, Linda, G. and Helgerson, Linda W. CD-ROM Public Access Catalogues: Database Selection and Maintenance. Lib Hitech; Vol. 16; No. 1;1988; pp. 67-88. *In* Panda, K.C. and

Karisiddappa, C.R., *ed. New Dimensions in Information Science and Technology*. 1993. Parimal Pub; Delhi, pp. 89-90.

2. Jain, V.K. and Hazarika, S. *Dictionary of Computer 1994.* Academic (India) Publications; New Delhi, p. 245.
3. *Manorma Year Book.* 2002. Malayala Manorama; Kottayam, p. 272.
4. Martin, Susns. *Library Networks,* 1981. Knowledge and Industry Publication; New York, p. 1.
5. Teague, S. John. Microform, Video and Electronic Media Librarianship. 1985. Butterworth; London, p. 96.

7

Testing of Hypothesis and Analysis of Data

Introduction

The study on the status of State Central Libraries has brought out interesting and useful data on various aspects of the resources, services, problems and future prospects of the SCLs of India. In this concluding chapter, certain recognised statistical tests are applied to prove and confirm the hypotheses arrived at in the course of study. The findings under different heads of the study are also summarised for drawing the immediate attention of the concerned authorities for arriving at proper solutions, while taking into account the constraints faced by the State Central Libraries in matters such as manpower collection, finance, service, and in general the usefulness of the State Central Libraries for the society.

Expected Role of SCLs

State Central Library of a State/U.T. acts as the apex public library of a State and provides leadership to all public libraries of the concerned State. It functions as a conservation centre for reading materials concerned with the culture of the particular State/U.T. and offers documents highlighting the composite culture of the nation. The State Central Library is the main source for reference materials for research workers and scholars. It promotes inter library co-operation by resorting to inter library loan among other categories of public libraries as well as academic and research libraries in the region. It serves as the prime agency for inter regional and inter State loaning and exchange of documents.

It acts as a clearing house of information on all State and national subjects of importance. It organises book exhibitions and professional conferences. Centralised acquisition, classification and cataloguing are undertaken by the State Central Libraries and catalogue cards are distributed to the individual libraries. As the apex public library, it supervises Regional/Divisional, District and other public libraries of the State. It promotes reading habits, social order and peace and eradicates illiteracy and poverty through myriad extension activities and awareness programmes.

Evaluation of SCLs

Some of the activities and functions expected to be performed by a State Central Library are enumerated above. However, whether the existing State Central Libraries are performing the expected functions is a vital question. In order to assess the performance and functions of the SCLs, I have taken up a project on "Status of State Central Libraries of India:An analytical study" which is a topic of great importance to the library professionals as well as to the State and Central Governments.

Methodology

For this project, a pre-ordained structured questionnaires was prepared and mailed to the Chief Librarians of all SCLs who are geographically scattered. However, for 10 State Central Libraries, I have personally visited and followed the questionnaires to assess the prevailing situation. Among the 30 SCLs functioning in India, 27 (90%) Chief Librarians have responded with filled-in questionnaires. Since the topic of the study is very wide, 7 vital hypotheses were evolved. The hypotheses are tested by applying X^2 (Chi-square) Test, Wilcoxon Signed Ranks Test, Linear Regression Model, Arithmetic Mean, etc. in order to make the resulting analysis statistically sound and meaningful.

Testing of Hypothesis

Hypothesis 1

Poor Allocation of Funds. The hypothesis-1 evolved for this project is as follows: "The State Central Libraries being the apex of the Public Library Systems of the respective State are in a state of sombre owing to the poor allocation of funds by their authorities".

For testing this hypothesis, the annual budget of 21 States/ U.T. for the period of 5 years ranging from 1993-94 to 1997-98 have been taken up as the basic source as already furnished in Table 3.11 in Chapter 3. Due to incomplete figures on certain years, the budget figures of 6 States/U.Ts could not be included in this analysis. Since the objective of this hypothesis is to study the growth pattern of fund allocation for every State Central Library and the combined growth of all State Central Libraries, a simple linear model has been fitted for 5 year annual budget figures of each library.

The statistical formula applied to test this hypothesis can be explained as: "Fitting of a Straight Line in Linear Equation is $Y = a + bX$ to a set of n points $(x_t, y_t); i = 2, \ldots n$. Equation represents a family of straight lines for different values of the arbitrary constant a and b. The problem is to determine a and b so that line $Y = a + bX$ is the line of 'best fit'. The term, 'best fit' is interpreted in accordance with Legender's Principle of least square which consists in minimising the sum of the squares of the deviations of the actual value y from its estimated values as given by the lines of best fit" (Gupta and Kapoor; 1994 ; p. 566).

The fitted equation is of the form of $y = a + bt$ where y = Annual Budget, a and b are parameters and t = years. The results are summarised in Table 7.1. The statistical presentation of the table can be explained with an example of figures of a particular State.

For example, the fitted linear equation for the State of Orissa is given as: Annual Budget = 3167700 + 403900 × year. Hence, for the State of Orissa, the budget allocation increases by an average amount of Rs. 4,03,900 per year. The analysis indicates that R^2 value is found to be high and the fitted equation is marginally significant. Further, the fitted equation for the average budget of all SCLs is given as:

Average Annual Budget = 25074 287 + 597064 × year.

The yearly increment in average budget allocation of all SCLs comes to a mere Rs. 5,97,064 which is a very poor allocation.

In order to properly understand the percentage of growth in budget allocation to each SCL, an index of growth has been worked out as follows :

The percentage of growth for each SCL is also given in the Table 7.1. It is observed from the table that, the growth percentage (3,333%) is phenomenally higher in Union Territory of Andaman and Nicobar Islands. Nagaland State has recorded a negative

TABLE 7.1
Growth Percentage of Budget of SCLs

Sl. No.	Name of State/U.T.	R^2 Value	d.f.	F.	P. Value	A	B	% of Budget Growth
1.	Andaman & Nicobar Islands	.806	3	12.49	.039	- 3.E+06	2220000	3333.33%
2.	Andhra Pradesh	.986	3	216.46	.001	4345600	602800	47.44%
3.	Arunachal Pradesh	.325	3	1.44	.316	2099386	446448	33.40%
4.	Assam	—	—	—	—	—	—	—
5.	Bihar	.872	3	20.40	.020	989258	154096	56.03%
6.	Chandigarh	.773	3	10.22	.049	4500000	620000	37.74%
7.	Delhi	.995	3	629.22	.000	2.0Ex 07	3772293	67.50%
8.	Goa	—	—	—	—	—		—
9.	Gujarat	.198	3	.74	.452	1282300	34100.0	12.71%
10.	Haryana	.962	3	76.63	.003	410875	61865.0	46.53%
11.	Himachal Pradesh	.060	3	.19	.690	164748	59079.2	08.90%
12.	Karnataka	.623	3	4.96	.112	3575500	981500	99.73%
13.	Kerala	.906	3	29.06	.013	3380476	535433	66.86%
14.	Lakshadweep	—	—	—	—	—	—	—
15.	Madhya Pradesh	.455	3	2.50	.212	359121	51981.0	41.00%
16.	Maharashtra	.886	2	15.56	.059	- 271870	1725921	226.49%

(Contd.)

Sl. No.	Name of State/U.T.	R^2 Value	d.f.	F.	P. Value	A	B	% of Budget Growth
17.	Manipur	—	—	—	—	—	—	—
18.	Meghalaya	—	—	—	—	—	—	—
19.	Mizoram	—	—	—	—	—	—	—
20.	Nagaland	.570	3	3.98	.140	1244000	- 19600	-53.67%
21.	Orissa	.747	3	8.84	.059	3167700	403900	38.11%
22.	Pondicherry	.830	3	14.68	.031	1714065	247112	49.81%
23.	Punjab	.958	3	68.74	.004	1404013	9448.0	27.17%
24.	Rajashan	.912	3	31.04	.011	627185	71923.0	37.92%
25.	Tamil Nadu	.958	3	45.96	.021	3862500	604700	37.20%
26.	Uttar Pradesh	.397	3	1.98	.255	591120	437260	242.29%
27.	West Bengal	.402	3	2.02	.251	804897	434435	63.07%
	Average growth/year - 6268231.5							
	Average	.994	3	462.33	.000	2574287	597064	210.46%

growth rate of 53.67 per cent. If the average growth is considered by leaving Andaman and Nicobar Islands U.T., the increase comes to a mere 59.06 per cent for a period of 5 years which is very poor compared to the annual growth of any other field considering the inflationary trend of the last five years.

Hence, the hypothesis, i.e., the SCLs being the apex of the public library systems of the respective States are perhaps in a state of sombre owing to the poor allocation of funds by their authorities, is proved.

Hypothesis 2

SCLs have Wide Cross Sectional User Population. The second hypothesis states : "The SCLs, owing to their undiscreminating and open membership policy, are having a wide range of cross sectional user population at their credit than any other library system has."

Since the survey has been undertaken for only one category of public libraries, i.e., State Central Libraries, the data on other categories of public libraries have not been collected for comparison. The hypothesis is tested only on the basis of the collected data on SCLs.

Further, even among the 27 SCLs from which data has been collected, the section on the various categories of user population is filled by only 4 SCLs of Andaman and Nicobar Islands, Arunachal Pradesh, Gujarat and Rajasthan State/U.Ts. The user population of 4 SCLs is listed in the following table:

TABLE 7.2

Wide Cross Sectional User Population of SCLs

Sl. No.	*Category of Users*	*A. & N. U.T.*	*Arunachal Pradesh*	*Gujarat State*	*Rajasthan State*	*Total*
(1)	*(2)*	*(3)*	*(4)*	*(5)*	*(6)*	*(7)*
1.	Teachers	12	15	15	10	52
2.	Students	120	106	350	100	676
3.	Researchers	90	03	18	20	131
4.	Scientists and Technocrats	12	04	02	10	28
5.	Government Servants	210	125	180	10	525
6.	Children	60	51	120	50	281

(Contd.)

(Contd.)

(1) (2)	(3)	(4)	(5)	(6)	(7)
7. Lawyers	12	02	06	04	24
8. Doctors	18	06	10	04	38
9. Engineers	24	10	05	06	45
10. Artists	30	02	03	10	45
11. Other Public	12	52	1067	26	1157
Total	600	376	1776	250	3.257
X_c^2 value	730.56	237.92	3408.42	260.19	4961.32
d f	10	6	6	8	10
X_t^2 v alue	18.31	12.59	12.59	15.59 -	18.31
$X_c^2 > X_t^2$ – Significant					

Table 7.2 reveals the wide cross sectional users of the State Central Libraries concerned in the categories of teachers, students, researchers, scientists and technocrats, government servants, childrens, lawyers, doctors, engineers, artists and other categories of public using the SCLs.

This hypothesis is analysed by applying 'Chi-square Test of Goodness of fit'. Chi-square Test is "a very powerful test for testing the significance of the discrepancy between theory and experiment given by Prof. Karl Pearson in 1900. It enables one to find out if the deviation of the experiment from the theory is just by chance or is it really due to the inadequacy of the theory to fit the observed data. If O_i, $(i = 1, 2 \ldots, n)$ is a set of observed (experiemental) frequencies and E_i, $(i = 1, 2 \ldots, n)$ is the corresponding set of expected (theoretical or hypothetical) frequencies, then Karl Pearson's Chi-square, given by

$$\left[\chi^2 = \sum_{i=1} n \frac{(O_i - E_i)^2}{E_i} ; \left(\sum_{i=1}^{n} O_i = \sum_{i=2}^{n} E_i \right) \right]$$

follows the Chi-square distribution with *(n-1) d.f.*" (Gupta and Kapoor ; 1994; p. 797). From the statistical analysis of Table 7.3, it is evident that the calculated value of χ^2 at 5 per cent level of significance is greater than the tabulated value for all 4 SCLs. Hence, there is significant difference between the proportion of various categories of user population in each SCL. Thus, the hypothesis-the State Central Libraries, owing to their undiscriminating and open membership policy, are having a wide range of cross sectional user population at their credit—is proved.

Hypothesis 3

Imbalance in Collection Development. "Owing to the repository character of the SCLs under the provision of Press and Registration of Books Act, 1867, there is an imbalance in collection development between the respective regional languages and the books of other languages", says the Hypothesis No. 3. For testing this hypothesis, the collection of books in regional languages, i.e., official languages of the respective State/U.T. and the total collection of books in all other languages available in SCLs are tabulated, compared and tested. The comparative figures are furnished below :

TABLE 7.3
Imbalance in Collection Development

Sl. No.	*Name of State/U.T.*	*Collection in Regional Language*	*Collection in Other Languages*	*Total Books*
(1)	*(2)*	*(3)*	*(4)*	*(5)*
1.	Andaman and Nicobar Islands	51,435	23,885	75,320
2.	Andhra Pradesh	1,24,305	2,77,308	4,01,613
3.	Arunachal Pradesh	—	28,728	28,728
4.	Assam	26,902	51,465	78,367
5.	Bihar	45,263	1,00,191	1,45,454
6.	Chandigarh	43,400	96,600	1,40,000
7.	Delhi	8,26,469	6,54,206	14,80,675
8.	Goa	1,500	1,38,500	1,40,000
9.	Gujarat	—	—	79,253
10.	Haryana	32,000	25,675	57,675
11.	Himachal Pradesh	44,335	47,323	91,648
12.	Karnataka	96,060	1,44,112	2,40,172

(Contd.)

(Contd.)

(1)	*(2)*	*(3)*	*(4)*	*(5)*
13.	Kerala	69,000	1,87,794	2,56,794
14.	Lakshadweep	10,000	20,000	30,000
15.	Madhya Pradesh	22,869	39,638	62,507
16.	Maharashtra	55,736	6,54,070	7,09,806
17.	Manipur	40,000	85,138	1,25,138
18.	Meghalaya	—	—	39,000
19.	Mizoram	2,500	14,500	17,000
20.	Nagaland	—	—	39,000
21.	Orissa	20,000	1,80,000	2,00,000
22.	Pondicherry	1,50,000	1,41,887	2,91,887
23.	Punjab	33,500	83,387	1,16,887
24.	Rajashan	—	—	35,488
25.	Tamil Nadu	50,000	4,75,000	5,25,400
26.	Uttar Pradesh	22,950	37,700	62,650
27.	West Bengal	50,000	55,000	1,05,000
Total		18,18,214	35,64,107	57,06,062
	Mean	82,646.094	1,54,961.17	
	Std. Dev.	1,70,070.047	1,88,422.39	

Mean Rank	**Cases**	
9.25	4 - Ranks	(Other languages lesser than Regional language)
12.00	18-Ranks	(Other languages greater than Regional language)

$Z = 2.9057$

The hypothesis is tested by applying non-parametric Wilcoxon Signed Ranks test. "The Wilcoxon signed ranks test is a very useful test for the behaviourial scientist. With behavioural data, the researcher can (1) tell which member of a pair is "greater than,", i.e., tell the sign of the difference between any pair, and (2) rank the differences in order of absolute size. That is, the researcher can make the judgement of "greater than" between any pair's two values as well as between any two difference scores arising from any two pairs. With such information the experimenter may use the Wilcoxon signed ranks test" (Siegel and Castella ; 1988 ; p. 87). The results are given below :

Mean Rank Cases

Mean Rank	Cases
9.25	04 (Other languages lesser than Regional languages)
12.00	18 (Other languages greater than Regional languages)

The calculated Z value is 2.9057. The normal tabulated value for 5 per cent level of significance is 1.96. Since the calculated value is greater than the tabulated value, the hypothesis (There is an imbalance in collection development between the books of the respective regional languages and the books of other languages) is proved.

Hence, it can be concluded that, there is a significant difference between the average number of books in regional languages and other languages in SCLs of India.

Hypothesis 4

Adequate Professional Staff. The survey on manpower of State Central Libraries of India has indicated that there are 1,387 staff in 27 SCLs of India out of which 719 are professional and semi-professional staff. It is needless to emphasise that adequate professional manpower should be available. In this connection "IFLA standards recommend that between 33 per cent and 40 per cent of the staff should be professionally qualified" (Nick Moore; 1992; p. 188). The guidelines evolved by Raja Rammohun Roy Library Foundation (RRRLF) stipulate that "in case of (State) Central Libraries, the proportion of professional staff to the total staff should be 40 percent against 33 percent in other public libraries" (Kalia, et. al; 1991; p. 62). RRRLF guidelines may be taken as the standard for the required professional staff in SCLs of India.

In this connection, a hypothesis (No. 4) has been evolved as: "The SCLs being the leaders of public library system are having a human force of reasonable size to take care of their technical processing of the acquired documents in order to ensure the scientific and helpful organisation of the documents on the shelves for their effective use".

For testing this hypothesis, the manpower scenario of SCLs by indicating the actual professional staff working in each SCL and the professional staff required as per the standard mentioned above is furnished in Table 7.4. The hypothesis is tested by application of Wilcoxon Signed Ranks Test between the standard staff and actual staff available in SCLs.

TABLE 7.4
Adequate Professional Staff

Sl. No.	*Name of State/U.T.*	*Std. Prof. Staff*	*Actual Prof. Staff*	*Non-Prof. Staff*	*Total Staff*
1.	Andaman and Nicobar Islands	08	05	07	12
2.	Andhra Pradesh	53	33	100	133
3.	Arunachal Pradesh	06	12	04	16
4.	Assam	03	03	05	08
5.	Bihar	10	05	20	25
6.	Chandigarh	38	48	46	94
7.	Delhi	160	298	103	401
8.	Goa	14	14	20	34
9.	Gujarat	10	16	08	24
10.	Haryana	06	05	09	14
11.	Himachal Pradesh	12	10	20	30
12.	Karnataka	10	14	12	26
13.	Kerala	26	35	29	64
14.	Lakshadweep	03	04	04	68
15.	Madhya Pradesh	03	05	02	07
16.	Maharashtra	30	20	56	76
17.	Manipur	14	15	20	35
18.	Meghalaya	13	11	22	33
19.	Mizoram	05	05	07	12
20.	Nagaland	06	04	10	14
21.	Orissa	25	44	18	62
22.	Pondicherry	08	06	15	21
23.	Punjab	15	15	22	37
24.	Rajasthan	08	07	12	19
25.	Tamil Nadu	48	57	62	119
26.	Uttar Pradesh	11	12	15	27
27.	West Bengal	14	16	20	36
	Total	559	719	668	1,387
Mean		20.59259	30.86479		
Std. dev		26.74074	56.10882		

A cursory glance of the Table 7.4 reveals further that the number of actual professional staff is greater than standard requirement of professional staff in 13 SCLs of the States/U.Ts. of Arunachal Pradesh, Chandigarh, Delhi, Gujarat, Karnataka, Kerala, Lakshadweep, Madhya Pradesh, Manipur, Orissa, Tamil Nadu, Utttar Pradesh and West Bengal. In the States of Assam, Goa, Mizoram and Punjab, the number of actual professional staff is the same as the number of standard staff required for undertaking professional work in SCLs. In the remaining 10 SCLs there is a dearth of professional staff compared to the standard requirement of professional staff.

The hypothesis is tested by Wilcoxon Signed Ranks Test. The results are given below:

Mean Rank	**Cases**	
10.61	10	(Actual staff lesser than standard staff)
12.89	13	(Actual staff greater than standard staff)
	4	(Actual staff are equal to standard staff)
		Z = 1.2926

The calculated Z value is 1.2926. The null hypothesis that there is no significant difference between the average number of professional staff requirement (40 per cent of the total staff) and the actual staff in SCLs is accepted at 5 per cent level of significance. Hence, the hypothesis (SCLs are having a human force of reasonable size to take care of their technical processing of the acquired documents in order to ensure the scientific and helpful organisation of the documents on shelves for effective use) is proved. Thus, it is concluded that there is no significant difference between the average number of required professional staff and the actual professional staff available in SCLs.

Hypothesis 5

Low Budget for Automation in SCLs. Automation is the order of the day. Information Technology is applied in every field of human activity. Public libraries are no exception to this trend all over the world. "The Internet is used by the staff of various (public) library authorities of United Kingdom for the following functions : 1. Reference enquiry work; 2. Professional awareness; 3. Communication (E-mail); 4. Exploration/experiment; 5. Online databases; 6. Systems support; and 7. Cataloguing and acquisition.

There is already evidence that UK public library managers recognize the future potential of the Internet as a means of creating and shading new resources. EARL (Electronic Access to Resources in Library. www.earl.org.uk) is a co-operative venture with a paying membership of over 130 UK local Public library authorities across U.K." (Batt; 1998 ; pp. 19-20). Having this global I.T. phenomena in mind, the study on SCLs has made a special survey on the application of IT in SCLs of India.

"The State Central Libraries being the non-profit organisations hardly receive any attention of the State authorities in the matter of automation/computerisation of their information retrieval related activities and due to their low budget profile, the SCLs are at the threshold of the beginning of automation" is the next hypothesis (No. 5) evolved to assess the impact of IT in SCLs of various State/U.Ts. The hypothesis can be seen in 2 parts :

(i) SCLs hardly receive any attention of State authorities for automation; and

(ii) Due to low budget profile, the SCLs are at the threshold of automation.

For the first part of this hypothesis, it is assessed from the survey that SCLs of only 07 State/U.Ts. (26%) - Chandigarh, Delhi, Gujarat, Karnataka, Lakshadweep, Pondicherry and Tamil Nadu have applied information technology in the apex library of their respective States/U.T.s and the remaining 20 States (74%) have not received any attention of the State Library Authorities for automation. Hence, the first part of the hypothesis came true.

Regarding the second part of the hypothesis,'Low budget profile for automation', the budget provisions of these 7 SCLs for automation is furnished below in Table 7.5.

TABLE 7.5
Budget on Automation

Sl. No.	*Name of State/U.T.*	*Total Budget (Rs. in Lakhs)*	*Budget on Automation (Rs. in Lakhs)*	*% of Total Budget*
1.	Chandigarh U.T.	63.60	3.30	05.00%
2.	Delhi U.T.	309.15	1.90	00.61%
3.	Gujarat	13.85	0.20	01.44%

4.	Kerala	49.87	2.07	04.15%
5.	Pondicherry	24.55	0.46	01.87%
6.	Tamilnadu	53.74	1.47	02.74%
7.	West Bengal	21.08	0.32	01.52%
	Total	535.84	9.72	1.81%
	Mean Value	76.5485	1.3885	

In view of the fact that the budget of automation is very meagre compared to the total budget of the respective State/U.T., the comparison is done on the basis of a simple Arithmetic Mean. "Arithmetic mean or average of a series is the simplest and perhaps the most widely used of all measures of averages. It is frequently referred to as 'Mean' and is obtained by the sum of the values of all observations in a series. (ΣX) by the number of items (N) constituting the series. Thus, Arithmetic mean of a set of number $x, x \ldots x$ is defined as Mean (X) = Sum of items/Number of items = $(\Sigma X)/N$" (Raj; 1990; p. 46).

Mean value indicates that the total mean value of the budget of all 7 SCLs put together comes to 76.5485 while the mean value of budget on Automation is a mere 1.3885 which clearly proves the hypothesis that the budget profiles for automation is very low in SCLs.

Hence, the hypothesis "the SCLs being the non-profit organisations hardly receive any attention of the State authorities in the matter of automation/computerisation of their information retrieval related activities and due to their low budget profile, the SCLs are at the threshold of the beginning of automation" is proved.

Hypothesis 6

Better Space for SCLs. For effective functioning of the SCLs, it is essential that they should be located in spacious buildings with adequate space for providing various services to the users and to stock the collection of the library for convenient retrieval by the users. Having this in mind, the hypothesis 6 is evolved as "The State Central Libraries are enjoying a better space structure in terms of their building and other physical facilities compared to any other public library system".

However, it is to be mentioned that since the survey covered only 27 State Central Libraries of India and also due to the fact that there are no authentic sources—primary or secondary—on the actual space availability of other categories of public libraries such as District Central Library, Branch Library, etc., the analysis has been limited to only the accommodation facility of SCLs and no other public library system is included for the reasons stated above.

For better analysis, the hypothesis is divided into two parts : For the first part, the total space of the SCLs is compared to the user population visiting the library on an average everyday. The second part compares the actual space available in the library with the average standard space stipulated for SCLs.

In this connection, RRRLF guidelines appear to be the only Indian standard available for verifying the accommodation requirement of SCLs. As per RRRLF guidelines, "The State Reference Libraries in States and Union Territories having a population of over 20 lakhs (I Category) will have a gross area of 50,000 sq. ft (4,645 sq.mt). The State Reference Library in States and Union Territories having a population of less than 20 lakhs (II Category) will have an area of 25,000 sq. ft (2,324 sq. ft)" (Kalia et. al; 1991; p. 67).

Based on this standard, the requirement of standard space for each SCL has been worked out. Wilcoxon Signed Ranks Test is applied for testing this hypothesis. The figures on actual space per user and standard space per user are compared for testing the first part of the hypothesis furnished in Table 7.6. Due to inadequacy of data, the test is applied on only 11 SCLs out of 27.

TABLE 7.6
Space per User in SCLs

Sl. No.	*Name of State/U.T.*	*User per Day*	*Actual Space (sq. mt.)*	*Standard Space (sq. mt.)*
1.	Andaman and Nicobar Islands	600	—	2,324
2.	Andhra Pradesh	5,126	—	4,645
3.	Arunachal Pradesh	378	100	2,324
4.	Assam	275	1,592	4,645
5.	Bihar	450	—	4,645

(Contd.)

6.	Chandigarh	1,667	—	2,324
7.	Delhi	6,263	—	4,645
8.	Goa	400	3,657	4,645
9.	Gujarat	1,785	24,384	4,645
10.	Haryana	1,667	1,526	4,645
11.	Himachala Pradesh	—	—	4,645
12.	Karnataka	1636	300	4,645
13.	Kerala	2,391	8,560	4,645
14.	Lakshadweep	95	—	2,324
15.	Madhya Pradesh	—	2,134	4,645
16.	Maharashtra	800	9,445	4,645
17.	Manipur	2,883	—	2,324
18.	Meghalaya	—	—	2,324
19.	Mizoram	250	114	2,324
20.	Nagaland	150	—	2,324
21.	Orissa	1,000	—	2,324
22.	Pondicherry	894	—	2,324
23.	Punjab	—	4,700	4,645
24.	Rajasthan	250	—	4,645
25.	Tamil Nadu	6,300	2,347	4,645
26.	Uttar Pradesh	—	5,354	4,645
27.	West Bengal	1,000	16,460	4,645
	Mean		5.59101	6.51212
	Std. Dev.		6.14385	6.65372

Mean Rank	Cases	
5.33	6	- Ranks (Actual space lesser than std space)
6.80	5	+ Ranks (Actual space greater than std space)
	Z=0.0889	

As per the analysis, the null hypothesis that there is no significant difference between the average standard space per user population and the actual space per user population is accepted at 5 per cent level of significance and it is concluded that there is no significant difference between the average standard space per user and the average actual space per user. This part of the hypothesis is proved.

The second part of the analysis is done between the standard space stipulated for each SCL and the actual space available in 14

SCLs. A comparative statement on the parameters used is furnished in Table 7.7.

The result of the analysis shows that the null hypothesis is accepted at 5 per cent level of significance and it is concluded that there is no significant difference between the average standard space per book and the average actual space per book. The above analysis has confirmed that there is no significant difference between the actual space and standard space.

Thus, the hypothesis—the SCLs are enjoying a better space structure in terms of their building and other physical facilities—is proved.

TABLE 7.7
Actual Space *vs* Standard Space

Sl. No.	*Name of State/U.T.*	*Actual Space (sq. mt.)*	*Std. Space (sq. mt.)*
1.	Andhaman and Nicobar Islands	—	2,324
2.	Andhra Pradesh	—	4,645
3.	Arunachal Pradesh	100	2,324
4.	Assam	1,592	4,645
5.	Bihar	—	4,645
6.	Chandigarh	—	2,324
7.	Delhi	—	4,645
8.	Goa	3,657	2,324
9.	Gujarat	24,384	4,645
10.	Haryana	1,526	2,324
11.	Himachal Pradesh	—	4,645
12.	Karnataka	300	4,645
13.	Kerala	8,560	4,645
14.	Lakshadweep	—	4,645
15.	Madhya Pradesh	2,134	4,645
16.	Maharashtra	9,445	4,645
17.	Manipur	—	2,324
18.	Meghalaya	—	2,324
19.	Mizoram	114	2,324
20.	Nagaland	—	2,324
21.	Orissa	—	4,645
22.	Pondicherry	—	2,324

(Contd.)

Sl. No.	Name of State/U.T.	Actual Space (sq. mt.)	Std. Space (sq. mt.)
23.	Punjab	4,700	4,645
24.	Rajashan	—	4,645
25.	Tamil Nadu	2,347	4,645
26.	Uttar Pradesh	5,354	4,645
27.	West Bengal	16,460	4,645
	Mean	.053514	.044223
	Std. Dev.	.084034	.036319

Mean Rank	Cases
8.57	7- Ranks (Actual space lesser than standard space)
6.43	7+ Ranks (Actual space greater than standard space)
	Z = 0.4708

Hypothesis 7

SCLs Rendering all Modern Services. The seventh and final hypothesis is evolved as "Owing to their vast resources and sound infrastructure, the SCLs are rendering almost all modern services to their clientele ranging from layman to intellect and from simple homelending to indexing and highly complex on-line services, but on a limited scale". For testing this hypothesis, various services offered by the SCLs of India are surveyed and the frequency of availing the services has been assessed from the Chief Librarians of SCLs. The kinds of services and the no. of SCLs offering these services are listed below in Table 7.8.

TABLE 7.8
Services Offered in SCLs

Sl. No.	Name of Services	No. of SCLs offering the Service
1.	Home Lending	23
2.	Lending within the Library Premises	25
3.	Reference Services	26
4.	Referral Service	21
5.	Current Awareness Services (CAS)	17
6.	Selective Dissemination of Information (SDI)	21

(Contd.)

Sl. No.	*Name of Services*	*No. of SCLs offering the Service*
7.	Bibliographic Service	15
8.	State Bibliography	08
9.	Inter Library Loan	17
10.	Online Searching	02
11.	Indexing and Abstracting	04
12.	Extension Services	17

$\chi_c^2 = 23.10 \qquad df = 10$

$\chi_t^2 = 18.31 \qquad \chi_c^2 > \chi_t^2$ – Significant

The table is tested by using χ^2 (Chi-square) test. As per the result, the calculated value of χ^2 at 5 per cent level of significance for 10 degrees of freedom is greater than the tabulated value. Thus, the null hypothesis is rejected. Hence, there is a significant difference in providing the modern services in SCLs.

By taking the term 'modern services' seriously, an analysis is done on the four specific modern services of (1) Current Awareness Service (2) Selective Dissemination of Information (3) Online searching and 4) Indexing and Abstracting Services. The results are as follows :

$\chi_c^2 = 8.23 \qquad df = 2$

$\chi_c^2 = 5.99 \qquad \chi_c^2 > \chi_t^2$ – Significant

The calculated value of χ^2 at 5 per cent level of significance for 2 degrees of freedom is greater than the tabulated value. Hence, there is a significant difference in providing the four modern services in SCLs of India.

Further, utilisation of modern services by the users of SCLs has also been studied. For this purpose, the Chief Librarians of SCLs have been requested to indicate the degree of utilisation of various services by marking as 'Regularly', 'Frequently', 'Rarely' and 'Not Used'. The rating of availing the services by the users, as reported by the Chief Librarians, is furnished in Table 68.

TABLE 7.9
Utilisation of Modern Services by Users in SCLs

Sl. No.	*Name of Service*	*No. of Libraries* Regularly	Frequently	Rarely	Not Used
1.	Home Lending	23	00	00	00
2.	Lending within the Library Premises	18	07	00	02
3.	Reference Services	17	08	01	01
4.	Referral Service	06	09	05	07
5.	Current Awareness Service	02	04	05	16
6.	Selective Dissemination of Information	01	01	04	21
7.	Bibliographic Service	00	03	11	13
8.	Inter Library Loan	00	04	13	10
9.	Online Searching	01	01	00	25
10.	Indexing and Abstracting	01	00	03	23

$\chi_c^2 > \chi_t^2$ – Significant

The analysis of the χ^2 (Chi-square) test for the category of users 'Regularly' using the various services in SCLs indicates that the calculated value of χ^2 at 5 per cent level of significance for 4 degrees of freedom is greater than the tabulated value.

Thus, the hypothesis *(the SCLs are rendering almost all modern services to their clientele)* became true.

Analysis of Data and Findings

Analysis of data involves a number of closely related operations that are performed with the purpose of summarising the collected data and organise them in such a manner that may yield answers to the research topic.

The enormous data collected for the present study is already analysed to the maximum extent in Chapter 3 and in the testing of hypotheses. However, certain basic data will be analysed in the succeeding paragraphs.

Utilisation of Reading Materials by Subjects

The State Central Libraries acquire reading materials on different subjects based on the needs of the users and the policies of the library authorities. It is necessary to analyse the subjects of interests of the users and the priority of the users with regard to different subject collections available in the library. This analysis will be helpful for modifying the collection development policy of the State Central Library.

In order to study the utilisation of reading materials by subject in different SCLs of India, the Chief Librarians of SCLs were requested to rate the intensity of usage of reading materials of different subjects by grading them as 'Regularly', 'Frequently', 'Rarely' and 'Not Used'. The ratings given by the librarians are tabulated in Table 7.10.

TABLE 7.10
Utilisation of Reading Materials by Subject

Sl. No.	*Subject*	*Regularly*	*Frequently*	*Rarely*	*Not Used*
1.	Philosophy	06	13	07	01
2.	Religion	08	13	06	00
3.	Social Sciences	17	08	02	00
4.	Languages	14	09	04	00
5.	Pure Sciences	12	10	05	00
6.	Applied Science & Technology	09	08	08	02
7.	Useful Arts	09	08	08	02
8.	Literature	26	01	00	00
9.	History, Geography and Travel	19	07	01	00
10.	Miscellaneous	08	13	06	00

$\chi_c^2 = 27.625$ $df = 9$

$\chi_t^2 = 16.919$ $\chi_c^2 > \chi_t^2$ – Significant

The utilisation of reading materials of different subjects is tested by χ^2 test. The test results reveal that the calculated value of χ^2 at 5 per cent level of significance of 9 degree of freedom (27.625) is greater than the tabulated value of χ^2 (16.919). Hence, there is significant difference which indicates that the usage of reading materials by subjects is not uniform in SCLs. The no. of libraries in which different subjects are 'Regularly' and 'Frequently' used as well as the no. of libraries in which books on different subjects are 'Rarely' used and 'Not Used' are graphically presented in Bar Chart 7.1. It is seen from

CHART 7.1
Utilisation of Subjects in SCLs

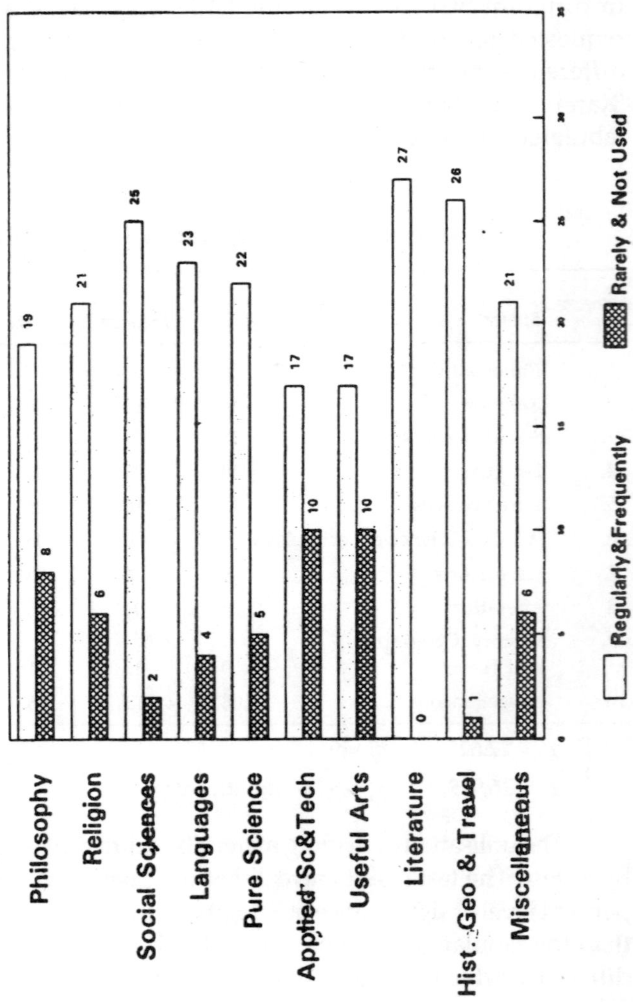

the chart that the reading materials on the subject of Literature is 'Regularly' and 'Frequently' used in all 27 SCLs (100%), followed by the subjects of History, Geography and Travel in 26 SCLs (96%), Social Sciences in 25 SCLs (93%) Languages in 23 SCLs (85%), Pure Sciences in 22 SCLs (81%), the subjects of Religion and Miscellaneous in 21 SCLs (78%) and Philosophy in 19 SCLs (70%). The subjects of Applied Sciences and Technology and Useful Arts are either 'Rarely' used or 'Not Used' in 10 SCLs (37%).

Utilisation of Reading Materials by Form. The SCLs acquire reading materials of different kinds, viz. books, magazines, newspapers, subject periodicals—current as well as back volumes—non-book materials, reference tools, children's literature, reports and reprints, patents/standards and other forms of reading materials. The utilisation of these materials in different SCLs and the frequency of utilisation of reading materials have been assessed from the Chief Librarians of SCLs who rated them as 'Regularly', 'Frequently', 'Rarely' and 'Not Used'. These ratings are tabulated in Table 7.11.

TABLE 7.11
Utilisation of Reading Materials by Form

Sl. No.	*Form*	*Frequency of Utilisation*			
		Regularly	*Frequently*	*Rarely*	*Not Used*
1.	Books	27	00	00	00
2.	Popular Magazines	25	02	00	00
3.	Newspapers	27	00	00	00
4.	Current Subject Periodicals	08	09	05	05
5.	Back Volumes of Subject periodicals	04	04	12	07
6.	Non-book Materials	04	04	10	09
7.	Reference Tools	14	11	01	01
8.	Children Literature	17	05	03	02
9.	Reports/Reprints	00	06	09	12
10.	Patents / Standards	01	01	05	20
11.	Other Forms	01	03	05	18

$\chi^2_c = 40.45$ $df = 7$

$\chi^2_t = 14.67$ $\chi^2_c > \chi^2_t$ – Significant difference

The column of utilisation of reading materials from 'Regularly' in various SCLs is tested by using χ^2 test. The result indicates that the calculated value of χ^2 at 5 per cent level of significance for 7 degree of freedom (40.75) is greater than the tabulated value of χ^2 (14.62). Hence $\chi^2_c > \chi^2 t$ which indicates that there is a significant difference in the utilisation of various forms of reading materials in SCLs. The utilisation of different forms in SCLs is assessed in Table 7.12.

TABLE 7.12
Regular and Rare Use of Reading Materials

Sl. No.	*Form*	*Reqularly and Frequently*	*% of use*	*Rarely and Not used*
1.	Books	27	(100%)	0
2.	Popular Magazines	27	(100%)	0
3.	Newspapers	27	(100%)	0
4.	Current Subject Periodicals	17	(63%)	10
5.	Back Volumes of Subject periodicals	08	(30%)	19
6.	Non-book Materials	08	(30%)	19
7.	Reference Tools	25	(93%)	02
8.	Children Literature	22	(81%)	05
9.	Reports/Reprints	06	(22%)	21
10.	Patents/Standards	02	(07%)	25
11.	Other Forms	04	(15%)	23

It is seen from the table that books, popular magazines and newspapers are 'Regularly' and 'Frequently' utilised by readers in all SCLs (100%) whereas the utilisation of Reference tools (93%), Children's Literature (81%), and Current Subject Periodicals (63%) are the next priority forms of reading materials used in SCLs. The less used forms of reading materials are in the order of Non-book materials (30%), Back volumes of subject periodicals (30%), Reports/Reprints (22%), Other forms (15%) and the least used being Patents/Standards (07%).

Findings

The study on the status of SCLs of India reveals the following findings:

1. At the collection front, 27 out of 30 SCLs in India possess a total book stock of 57,06,314 volumes; followed by 1,45,681 reference tools; 1,15,924 back volumes; 1,744 commission reports; 50,000 reprints; 1,060 patents and standards; 10,493 current journals and 413 titles of newspapers, thus achieving an average collection rate of 2,11,336 volumes per SCL.
2. The analysis on mode of annual additions of books reveals that, 99,597 books were added on purchase; 17,399 volumes were received as gifts, 225 volumes were collected on exchange basis; 55,089 titles were added on Delivery of Books Act, 1954 and Press and Registration of Books Act, 1867 thereby adding a total number of 1,77,898 volumes of books in a year in all SCLs put together with an average of 6,589 books per SCL every year. The percentage of annual growth of collection works out to 3.12 per cent of total collection.
3. Under the special collection category, a total of 1,71,201 books are available in SCLs of India forming only 3 per cent of total collection, having an average of 6,341 books in each SCL.
4. The survey on the stronger and weaker subjects reveal that the subjects of Social Sciences and Humanities are stronger in 8 SCLs and Literature is stronger in 7 SCLs while the subjects of Science and Technology are poorly represented in 10 out of 27 SCLs. The subject of Literature including fiction receives utmost attention in 16 SCLs whereas the subjects of Science and Technology are not the preferred subjects in 4 SCLs.
5. There are 9,863 items of various categories of non-book materials in SCLs of India making an average of 365 non-book materials for each SCL.
6. The manpower scenario of SCLs indicate that there are 1,387 staff members in 27 SCLs (an average of 51 staff per SCL) out of whom 32 per cent are professional, 20 per cent are semi-professional and 48 per cent are non-professional. The ratio of manpower versus collection is 1 : 5,600.
7. The average budget allotment for the last 5 years upto 1997 - 98 reveal that the budget of SCLs ranges from a mere Rs. 5,15,064 per year in Madhya Pradesh State to a maximum of Rs. 3,09,14,721 in Delhi U.T. The share of budget on different heads show that the staff salary takes the lion's share of 57 per cent, followed by 12 per cent for books and

periodicals, 6 per cent for office expenses, 4 per cent for furniture and maintenance while the remaining 21 per cent is consumed for other items.

8. The survey reports that only 7 SCLs have applied IT for their SCLs and the SCLs are providing the services of Circulation, Reference, Documentation, Bibliography, Photoduplication, Online Searching, E-mail and In-house operations of acquisitions, technical processing and serial control through Information Technology.
9. The SCLs are headed by the Director of Public Libraries only in 7 States whereas the Directors of Education/Art and Culture and the Secretaries at the Ministry level are the deciding authorities in the remaining SCLs.
10. Among the 27 States, only 15 States (56%) have a separate Library Committee for the SCLs.
11. Regarding the accommodation of SCLs, 21 SCLs (78%) are located in their own buildings, while 3 are situated in government buildings whereas 2 are still functioning in rented buildings. An average of 300 seats are available for the readers per SCL.
12. The year of construction of the buildings of SCL ranges from 1833 for Maharashtra State to 1995 in West Bengal State.
13. The survey on furniture items available in 27 SCLs of India reveals that there are 7,911 chairs, 2,261 tables/desks, 6,833 bookshelves/racks, 105 filing trays, 42 dictionary stands, 187 magazine display racks, 179 newspaper stands, 152 book trolleys, 1,567 almirahs, 659 catalogue cards, 80 steel cupboards, 2 xerox machines, 4 codexes and 2 sets of T.V., V.C.R. and Radio respectively.
14. Free services are provided to Members in 20 SCLs (74%) whereas 7 SCLs are levying a nominal fee. Orientation programmes are offered to Members in 14 SCLs.
15. Except 4 SCLs (15%), other apex public libraries do not have any connection or dependence on either National Library or any other categories of public libraries in India.
16. While the SCLs of Delhi, Maharashtra and Tamil Nadu acquire books as per the Delivery of Books Act, 1954, the SCLs of Andhra Pradesh, Goa, Gujarat, Karnataka, Maharashtra, Orissa and West Bengal States have added books under the Press and Registration of Books Act, 1867.

17. Only 19 SCLs (67%) have open access system, 2 SCLs having closed access while 6 SCLs serve the users with mixed access system.
18. The lending services are provided in 22 SCLs (81%) and 5 SCLs (19%) do not provide any home lending services.
19. Browne Charging System is practised in 17 SCLs (63%), DDC Scheme is adopted for classification in 24 SCLs (80%), AACR code is followed for cataloguing in 15 SCLs (55%) and Sear's List of Subject Headings is preferred in 18 SCLs.
20. On an average, 4 language divisions are available in SCLs of India. The SCL of Delhi has books in 16 languages followed by Maharashtra and Tamil Nadu (15 each). The languagewise analysis of collection shows that English books Constitute 37 per cent of the total stock, followed by 30 per cent in State language, 27 per cent in other languages and 6 per cent in Hindi languages.
21. Public Library Acts are passed in 10 out of 27 States (30%) of India, as on 1998.

Constraints and Deficiencies of SCLs

The constraints encountered by the State Central Libraries and the deficiencies in services, as observed in this study may be summarised, in brief, as follows :

1. The SCLs are facing the periennal problem of shortage of funds, except in a few cases.
2. While the situation of professional staff in SCLs is adequate, the staff members are not offered in-service training or deputed for training programmes.
3. The SCLs are far behind in the implementation of Information Technology.
4. The SCLs are offering mostly traditional library services. Modern services are offered in very few libraries on limited scale.
5. The SCLs do not appear to have any definite policy on collection development.
6. Most of the SCLs are controlled by non-professional administrators. The Department of Public Libraries have not yet been established in majority of the States/U.T.s to effectively advise and monitor the SCLs. It can be stated that most of the SCLs are supervised by the outsiders—those

who are engaged in non-library areas of vocation or profession.

7. Considerable number of SCLs do not have separate Library Committees to discuss the problems encountered by the SCLs and to take responsible decision for better maintenance of SCLs.
8. The SCLs are functioning in isolation. They are neither connected to other categories of public libraries within the State nor they are linked with other SCLs. They do not appear to have any hierarchical relation or dependance on National Library of India.
9. Majority of the SCLs have not been vested with authority or power to receive books under the Registration of Books Act, 1867.
10. One-third of the SCLs still follow Closed Access System by not allowing the users to physically browse through the stack room and to select the books required for them by feeling the books.
11. Special collection for the disadvantaged section of the public such as Braille, audit collection for the visually handicapped, Video collection for the hearing impaired and for other categories of such people have not been developed in SCLs with a definite policy.
12. The SCLs do not function as the apex public library of the State nor do they undertake any programmes or control/ supervision or guidance as the leader of public libraries of the State.
13. The SCLs do not have any policy of acquiring all the publications of the respective State government or the Central Government of India.
14. There is no evidence of State Central Libraries playing a major role in Inter State Loan or Intra State Loan of documents for the Members of SCLs or Members of any other service points of public libraries in the State, except a few stray cases.
15. It has not been clearly established whether the SCLs do perform their positive role in centralised acquisition, classification and cataloguing for the books acquired in the public library system of the States/U.Ts.

Suggestions

SCL as Reference or Lending Library

It is observed from the study that the State Central Library is functioning either as another home lending library, serving only the residents living in the capital city of the State—in 22 SCLs (81%) or as Reference Library—in 5 SCLs (19%).

Sinha Committee, constituted by the Govt. of India has categorically stated that "the State Central Library does not lend books for home under any circumstances whatsoever". At the same time, it strongly advocates the establishment of a State Lending Library. Regarding the functions of the State Lending Library, Sinha Committees further elaborates. "The State Lending Library will have two functions : as the home lending library for the city in which it is situated and as the library supplying the stocks of District libraries. We need not dilute here on the functions of the State Lending Library as the City Library except to say that, as far as possible, it should honour the tickets of all service points in the State " (Sinha ; 1959 ; p. 38).

On this much debated question whether the SCL should be a Reference Library or a Lending Library, the author arrives at the following suggestions:

1. At the apex level, every State/Union Territory should have uniformly one State Central Reference Library and one State Lending Library.
2. The State Central Reference Library should develop and maintain a sound 'Reference Collection'. Its collection should include all standard books of national and international importance. All books published in the State language should be collected and maintained for reference. All official publications of the respective State Government and the Central Government should be made available for reference and research.
3. At present, only 5 States—Assam, Karnataka, Orissa, Maharashtra and West Bengal—are maintaining State Central Reference Libraries. It is suggested that the remaining 22 States/Union Territories viz., Andaman and Nicobar Islands, Andhra Pradesh, Arunachal Pradesh, Bihar, Chandigarh, Delhi, Goa, Gujarat, Haryana, Himachal Pradesh, Kerala, Lakshadweep, Madhya Pradesh, Manipur, Meghalaya,

Mizoram, Nagaland, Pondicherry, Punjab, Rajasthan, Tamil Nadu and Uttar Pradesh should declare their State Central Libraries as State Central Reference Libraries while simultaneously establishing a strong State Lending Library.

4. State Lending Libraries, in terms of the recommendations of Sinha Committee, should be opened by the following 5 States—Assam, Karnataka, Orissa, Maharashtra and West Bengal—where the SCLs are functioning as State Central Reference Libraries without performing any home lending services.
5. In the State Central Libraries wherever lending services are provided, home lending facility should not be restricted to the residents of the capital city in which the SCL is situated. Any person residing in any part of the State/U.T. should be permitted to enroll as borrowing member of the State Central Library. The procedure of admission followed by National Library at Calcutta in allowing Membership to any citizen residing in any part of India should be emulated and adopted in SCLs so that the resources of SCLs can ensure optimal use.
6. Further, any person registered as Member of any public library in the State should be permitted to borrow books for home reading from the State Central Library. The SCL should honour the Borrower's Tickets of all service points of public libraries in the State/U.T. On the same analogy, the registered members of the SCL should be allowed to borrow books from any public library of the State.

Adoption of SCLs by Government of India

In Roads and Transport sector of India, all roads are categorised as National Highways, State Highways, District Roads and Rural Roads. In order to maintain efficient road services and uniform standards, the Government of India is sponsoring major roads and Inter-State roads in India designated as National Highways. At present, 97 National Highways for a total distance of 38,517 kilometres are funded by the Ministry of Surface Transport, Government of India by incurring an annual expenditure of Rs. 372 crores as on 1998 (Motor Transport; 1998; pp. 31-35).

Similarly, it is suggested that all State Central Libraries of India should be completely funded and supported by Government of India. The Ministry of Human Resources Development, Government of India should adopt State Central Libraries of all States/U.Ts and the entire expenditure incurred for the maintenance and development of SCLs should be borne by Ministry of H.R.D. Since the subject of 'Libraries' comes under the State subject, as per the Constitution of India, the direct administration and operational management of the SCLs can continue to be vested with State/U.T. governments. However, as has been done in the case of National Highways, the funding and monitoring can be done by Government of India.

Already this practice is partly adopted for the libraries designated to receive books and periodicals under the Delivery of Books Act, 1954. The same practice can be extended to all State Central Libraries. The implementation of this system can be effected through Raja Rammohun Roy Library Foundation which has already been implementing certain Schemes for the development of SCLs of India.

Free or Fee Based Library Service

This research project reveals that free services are provided only in 20 SCLs (26%) whereas 7 SCLs in the States of Arunachal Pradesh, Bihar, Meghalaya, Nagaland, Orissa, Tamil Nadu and Uttar Pradesh are levying annual/Life Membership charges for using the services and facilities of the apex public library of the respective State.

As per UNESCO Public Library Manifesto 1994 "The Public Library shall in principle be free of charge" (UNESCO; 1995; p. 66). In observance of the principles enunciated by UNESCO, the State Central Libraries, both reference and lending, should be declared as free public libraries. Membership charges—annual or life—should not be collected. However, caution deposits can be collected to ensure that the borrowers take care to return the books borrowed from the SCLs.

State Central Library Authority

It is suggested that a separate State Central Library Authority may be constituted through the provisions of Public Library Act of the State so as to enable the SCLs to take independent decisions and to function as the real apex public library as well as to play the role of the leader for all public libraries of the concerned State/U.T. The powers and duties of the said authority would be similar to the Local Library Authorities. The funds for State Central Library Authority may be released from the budget of the State or from State Library Fund. The jurisdiction of the State Central Library Authority shall be the whole State.

The State Central Library Authority should be empowered to establish Regional/Divisional Libraries in any part of the State. The State Central Library should function as the library for the whole State and every resident of the State should be entitled to enroll himself/herself as Member of the State Central Library.

"The Review Committee of Andhra Pradesh has also recommended that there should be a State Central Library Authority for the State Central Library and for its Regional Libraries" (Ekbote; 1987; p. 132). Justice Ebkote has elaborated on the composition of State Central Library Authority as follows:

1. Chairman-To be elected from the non-official members of the Authority at its first meeting.
2. The Secretary, Public Library Department; if it is separate, or the Secretary, Education Deparment.
3. The Secretary, Finance.
4. The Director of Public Libraries.
5. A senior librarian from Regional Libraries.
6. Two librarians from the Universities of the State—one from general universities and the other from the technological and professional universities.
7. President of the State Chamber of Commerce.
8. Two Chairmen of the Local Library Authorities.
9. Two Chairmen of Zilla Parishads.
10. Three experts with special knowledge or experience of public libraries.
11. The Mayor of the City Municipal Corporation.
12. The Chief Librarian of the State Central Library shall be the Member Secretary of the Authority.

In addition to these recommendations, it is suggested that a professional teacher having specialisation in Public Library System and Networking can also be co-opted as a Member of the proposed State Library Authority.

Networking

Library Networking facilitates sharing of resources of a group of libraries to provide speedy access to information resources located at different places through communication channels. It enables the library authorities to maximize the utilisation of existing resources (collections) of the libraries at lower operational costs and ensures optimum use of national resources.

Networking of SCLs Through 'PUBLIBNET'

"The Report of the Working Group of Planning Commission on Library and Informatics for the Ninth Five Year Plan 1997-2002 prepared under the Chairmanship of Shri B.P. Singh, Secretary, Department of Culture to modernize the libraries to take up the challenges of 21st Century scenario of information technology, networking and INTERNET has recommended as follows : It has been found that DELNET has emerged as an operational library network in India with 60 libraries in Delhi and 6 States as its members. It has developed on-line union catalogue of books and periodicals. It is recommended that DELNET be supported to create National database and develop on OCLC pattern" (Kaul; 1998; 263-64).

It is suggested that all State Central Libraries in India should be networked for which the required infrastructure should be developed. The Database to be created for SCLs should be standardized (using MARC format) while ensuring the compatibility of hardware and software. The network can be suitably named as 'PUBLIBNET'—Public Library Network—and be financially supported by Central agencies like Raja Rammohun Roy Library Foundation.

Considering the enormous potential and the urgent need for application of IT in public libraries, a model computerised network, exclusively meant for SCLs and other libraries in the Public Library System, named as 'PUBLIBNET' is proposed in Chart 15. Publibnet can be jointly organised by RRRLF, National Library of India, Delhi Public Library, NICNET and DELNET with direct linking of all SCLs of India, with an ultimate objective of reaching all the service points of public libraries in this country.

Expertise on library networking developed by agencies in India like DELNET may be utilised in this connection for consultancy on establishing an all India network of State Central Libraries. National Library of India at Calcutta, or Delhi Public Library', the State Central Library of Delhi U.T. - both maintained by the Government of India, may serve as the nodal agency for the

CHART 7.2
Public Library Network

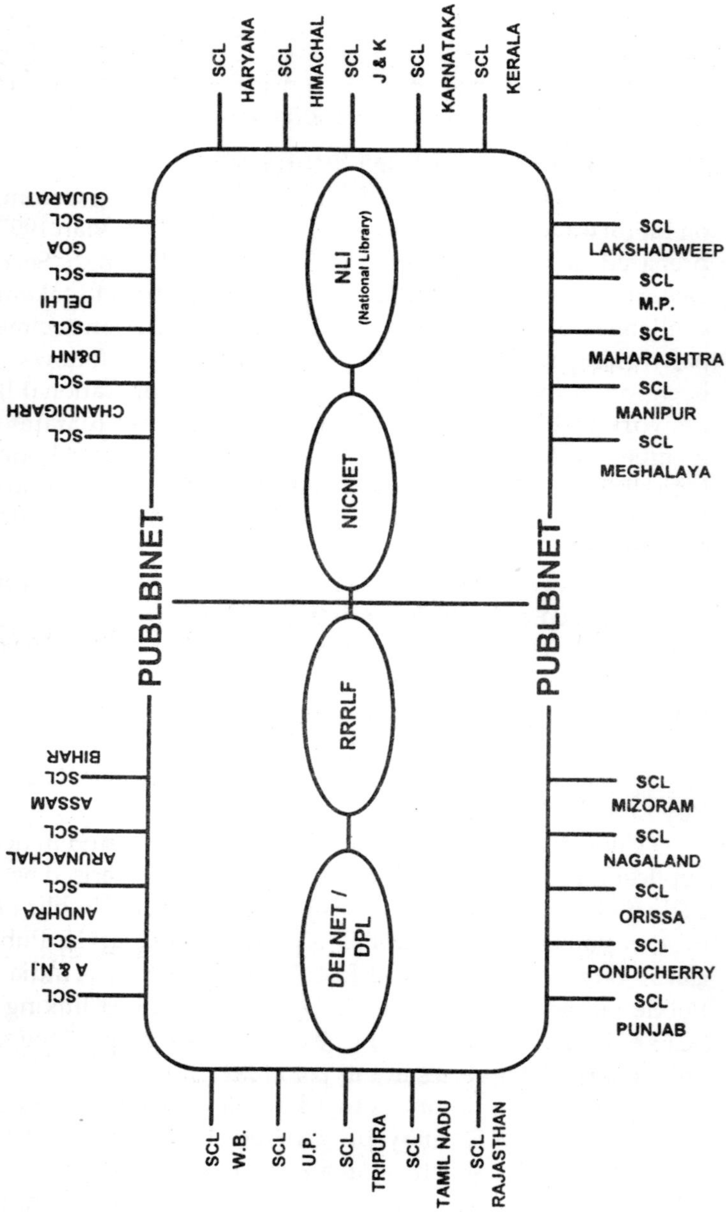

proposed 'PUBLIBNET' which shall link all State Central Libraries of India with 'National Library' at the top of the pyramid followed by SCLs, District Central Libraries leading to the lowest level of Village Libraries.

It is pertinent to mention, at this state, the following decisions of Raja Rammohun Roy Library Foundation, on the networking of public libraries and automation : "(1) To keep pace with the trend of modernisation, a suitable scheme is likely to be introduced to supply computers to State Central Libraries, to begin with, to facilitate the networking of public libraries. (2) Networking of public libraries upto State level is proposed to be undertaken in colloboration with DELNET" (RRRLF ; 1997 ; p. 2).

Networking with INFLIBNET

An initiative has already been taken by University Grants Commission to integrate all library systems and information networks into a national system—which is named as Information and Library Network or in brief as 'INFLIBNET'. It is a computer communication network of University and academic libraries, R&D institutions, autonomous bodies and bibliographical information centres to effect improvement in information transfer and access in which all institutions of higher learning and research covering all disciplines shall be participating in the network. It is suggested that all State Central Libraries may be linked with INFLIBNET so that the resources of SCLs can be accessed by institutions of higher learning and vice versa.

Review Committee on SCLs

It is suggested that a Review Committee on the working and functioning of the SCLs of India may be constituted by Government of India for studying the existing conditions of all State Central Libraries of India for evolving a uniform pattern for them. The Committee can devise the aims and objectives of the SCLs and suggest suitable measures and practical solutions for the SCLs to serve as the real apex libraries and as the leaders of all public libraries of the respective State/U.T.

The Review Committee set up by Government of India in 1969 under the Chairmanship of V.S. Jha can be taken as the model for the Review Committee suggested for this purpose to be constituted for SCLs by Government of India.

Suggestions of Librarians of SCLs

Further, the Chief Librarians of various State Central Libraries covered in the study were requested to offer suggestions for the improvement of their respective libraries and point out the areas of immediate attention. The suggestions of the Librarians of SCls are grouped under various headings as follows:

Administration

Andhra Pradesh	1.	State Central Library to be made as Reference Library.
Delhi	1.	State or Central Government should take over the administration of SCL.
	2.	Recruitment Rules to be changed.
	3.	Professional with MBA to be appointed.
Goa	1.	Due recognition to be given to public libraries.
Meghalaya	1.	Free hand for the Librarian in Administration.
	2.	Bureaucratic control should be removed.
Mizoram	1.	Autonomous administration.
Karnataka	1.	Publicity and public relations programmes should be launched.
	2.	List of new books to be sent to local newspapers periodically.
Tamil Nadu	1.	Librarian of State Central Library should be designated as the Registrar of books for the Press and Registration of Books Act, 1867.
	2.	Delegation of powers to Librarian for administration.

Automation

Bihar	1.	Automation should be introduced.

	2.	Modernisation through Information Technology.
Chandigarh	1.	Automation of information services.
	2.	Internet and E-mail will provide access to world databases.
Haryana	1.	Library should be computerised.
Kerala	1.	Computerisation to be done.
Orissa	1.	Automation
	2.	Internet
Punjab	1.	Automation
Tamil Nadu	1.	Modernisation of Library Activities
Building		
Andaman and Nicobar Islands	1.	Construction of new building with furniture and equipment.
Haryana	1.	Building to be extended
Collection Development		
Himachal Pradesh	1.	Books to be purchased as per the demand of the users.
Finance		
Bihar	1.	Adequate grant from State government and RRRLF is essential.
Haryana	1.	Budget should be enhanced.
Kerala	1.	More funds required.
Manipur	1.	More funds (10% of Education Budget) needed.
Mizoram	1.	More funds from the Government.

Uttar Pradesh	1.	More funds for (a) Old books maintenance (b) Modernisation and (c) Purchase of books and newspapers.
Manpower		
Delhi	1.	Adequate salary structure and time bound promotion to be provided for staff.
Haryana	1.	Additional staff needed.
Karnataka	1.	In-service training should be given for staff.
Kerala	1.	More staff required.
	2.	Training programme for professional staff.
Orissa	1.	Orientation programme for staff.
Uttar Pradesh	1.	More professional staff.
Public Library Act		
Delhi	1.	Legislation (Public Library Act) is required.
Manipur	1.	Public Library Act to be implemented.
	2.	Directorate of Public Libraries should be formed.
Mizoram	1.	Public Library Act to be implemented.
Resource Sharing and Networking		
Chandigarh	1.	Through networking resources can be shared.
Himachal Pradesh	1.	Modernisation and networking to be done.
Tamil Nadu	1.	Resource sharing with special libraries.
Services		
Andaman and Nicobar Islands	1.	Mobile library for every village.

Karnataka	1.	Orientation programmes for the users.
Orissa	1.	Compilation of State Bibliography
Punjab	1.	Mobile library service.
	2.	To visit the education institutions for motivating the teachers and students to join the library.
	3.	To inculcate the reading habits for better utilisation of the library.

Technical Processing

Andaman and Nicobar Islands	1.	Centralised cataloguing with networking to be done.

Out of the several suggestions brought forward by the Chief Librarians of State Central Libraries of India, the following 15 key suggestions are identified for analysis :

TABLE 7.13
Summary of Key Suggestions of SCLs

Sl. No.	*Key Suggestion of SCLs*	*No. of SLCs*	*Percentage*
1.	Automation/Computerisation/ Application of IT/Modernisation/ Use of Internet etc.	10	37%
2.	Resource sharing/Networking	3	11%
3.	User Orientation/Services	4	15%
4.	Compilation of State Bibliography	1	4%
5.	Mobile Library Service	2	7%
6.	Adequate Staff	3	11%
7.	Enactment of Public Library Law	3	11%
8.	Adequate Funds/Increase of Budget	6	22%
9.	Expansion of Building	2	7%
10.	In-service Training/Promotion of Staff	4	15%
11.	Technical Processing	1	4%
12.	To increase the bookstock	2	7%

(Contd.)

(Contd.)

Sl. No.	*Key Suggestion of SCLs*	*No. of SLCs*	*Percentage*
13.	Recruitment Policy	2	7%
14.	Less Bureaucratic Intervention/ Independent Administration/ Autonomous Status	5	19%
15.	Creation of separate directorate	1	4%

It stems from the above table of suggestions that, 10 SCLs (37%) have suggested for implementation of automation, IT, modernisation, etc., followed by 6 SCLs (22%) for adequate funds/ increase of budget; 5 SCLs (19%) for less bureaucratic intervention/ independent administration/autonomous status; 4 SCLs (15%) for user orientation/services and in-service training/promotion of staff; 3 SCLs (11%) for resource sharing/networking, adequate staff and enactment of public library law respectively; 2 SCLs (7%) for mobile library service, expansion of building, recruitment policy and to increase the book stock respectively and 1 SCL (4%) each for compilation of State Bibliography, technical processing and the creation of a separate directorate.

The suggestions of the Chief Librarians of State Central Libraries deserve special consideration and merit serious attention as they are borne out of direct supervision and personal experiences.

Areas for Further Study

1. Similar research on the status of the SCLs with emphasis on application of IT in SCLs either on regional basis—South, North, etc. or on the basis of the impact of Public Library Acts can be done.
2. Study on the remedial measures to be taken up on the improvements of SCLs shall be useful.
3. A survey of the user population of SCLs can be taken up as a separate study so as to determine their cross-sectional and cross-disciplinary interests.
4. The attitudes of the users in the selection of subjects in SCLs can be taken up for research.

5. The strengths and weaknesses of reference and research materials available in SCLs of India can be taken up and suggestions for enriching the reference collection can be offered in a separate study.
6. The Membership composition pattern of the users of SCLs, on the basis of occupation, education, area and age can be taken up for research and suggestions can be offered for collection development.
7. Assessment on the SCL as an apex library and the leader of the public libraries of the State can be taken up for detailed study.
8. The traditional and modern services offered by the SCLs can be analysed and the impact of such services of SCLs on the users of the library can be assessed.
9. The funds mobilisation and resource generation of the SCLs can be taken up as a separate study to assess whether the SCLs are able to mobilise enough funds for the mandatory services to be provided by the SCLs.
10. The linkage of SCLs with the Regional/Divisional Libraries, District Libraries, Branch libraries and other categories of libraries as well as the linkage with National library of India can be probed in depth.
11. The perennial question whether the SCL should be a free public library or fee based service library can be analysed in view of the present status and opinions of the users of the SCLs.
12. The role of SCL as a custodian of the collection of books received under Registration of Books Act, 1867/Delivery of Books Act, 1954 and the collection of books acquired/not acquired can be assessed.

In my opinion, the two vital areas to be taken up for further investigation in any study on SCLs are : (i) the assessment on the SCLs as an apex library fulfilling the role of a leader of all public libraries of the State and (ii) the linkage of SCLs with National Library, District Central Libraries and other Public Libraries in resource sharing and networking.

Conclusion

Public libraries are vital social institutions aimed at lifelong education of every citizen. The State Central Libraries are established as the apex public libraries in every State/U.T. in terms of the hierarchy of the public library system. The study undertaken on the status of State Central Libraries has thrown enormous light on the collection of books and other reading materials, budget provisions, subjects of interests to the users, manpower scenario, application of IT, administration, accommodation, technical status, acquisition by legislation, language divisions, impact of legislation, problems faced and the future prospects of SCLs.

On the whole, SCLs are having enormous potential resources of collection, manpower and services. However, the vital question is whether the SCLs fulfill their role as the apex public library and the role of a leader of public libraries in the respective States/U.Ts. D.R. Kalia, the veteran library professional in India with vast experience on public library system including SCLs, evaluates their performance in clear terms:

"The State Central Libraries have acted largely as public libraries to the city where they are located, whereas they were intended to be much more than that. They were required to establish linkages with all the libraries forming part of the State Public Library System; share their resources with them, through computerized network; compile state bibliography of books and journals published in the State and publications on the State published out of the State in any language; provide bibliographic and documentation services in the form of articles on the State and of State official documents; act as an exchange centre for the State and be a depository of less-used material deposited with them by other libraries in the State on trust. But none of these functions have yet been performed by any State Central Library. They are being rightly described as total failures as State Central Libraries. No service is generally offered by them to the potential users residing outside the State Capital" (Kalia; 1998; p. 36).

Though I do not wish to remark as critically as that of the senior professional Kalia, it is to be emphasized that SCLs have to go a long way in fulfilling their mandatory roles to justify their nomenclature as State Central Libraries.

The Library Authorities of SCLs as well the State and Central governments should take a serious note of the suggestions proposed in this research project and the Chief Librarians (Sections 7.8 and 7.9) and remedial measures may be taken to put the SCLs on the right track. The SCLs have greater role to play in leading the public libraries and in the development of the nation as a whole compared to what they are at present.

Bibliography

1. Batt, Chris. *Information Technology in Public Libraries,* 1998, Library Association Publishing; London, pp. 19-20.
2. Ekbote, Gopalrao. *Public Libraries System,* 1987, Ekbote Brothers; Hyderabad, p. 138.
3. Gupta, S.C. and Kapoor, V.K. Fundamentals of Mathematical Statistics. 1994, Sultan Chand; New Delhi, p. 1104
4. Kalia, D.R. *et. al.* Guidelines for Public Library Systems and Services. *Granthana Indian Journal of Library Studies,* Vol. 2; No. 1, Jan 1991, pp. 31-84.
5. Kalia, D.R. Public Libraries, *In* Jain, M.K. ed. 50 years Library and Information Services in India, 1998, Shipra Publication; Delhi pp. 19-36.
6. Kaul, H.K. From Printed Bibliographies to Online Databases : Role of Library Networks. *In* Jain, M.K. ed. *50 years Library and Information Services in India,* 1998, Shipra Publication. Delhi, pp. 263-64.
7. Moore, Nick. Measuring the Performance of Public Libraries : A Draft Manual, *Granthana: Indian Journal of Library Studies,* Vol. 3; No. 2. July 1992, p. 160-206.
8. Raj, H. *Theory and Practice in Social Research,* 1990, Surjeet Publications; Delhi, p. 46.
9. Raja Rammohun Roy Library Foundation. *RRRLF Newsletter,* XVII (2) April 1997, p. 2.
10. Siegel, Sidney and Castella, John, N. *Non Parametric Statistics for the Behavioral Sciences,* 1998. McGraw Hill Book Company, New York; p. 87.
11. Sinha, *Report of Advisory Committee for Libraries,* 1959, Government of India Press; New Delhi, p. 38.
12. UNESCO. Unesco Public Library Manifesto. *IFLA Journal* 21(1), 1995. p, 67.

Bibliography

1. Adhikari, A.K., Library Movement in Arunachal Pradesh. *In* Saha, Ramakrishna, *Ed. Library Movement in India*, 1989. Bengal Library Association, Calcutta, pp. 135-148.
2. American Library Association (A.L.A.). Committee on Post-war Planning. Post-war Standards for Public Libraries, 1942, A.L.A; Chicago, p. 7.
3. Asundi, A.Y., Library Scene in Karnataka, Nineteenth Century and Earlier. *In* Gupta, B.M., *Ed. Handbook of Libraries, Archieves and Information Centres in India*, Vol. 16.. Library Development in India, 1996; Segment Books; New Delhi, pp. 119-128.
4. Auvdaiappan, N., Role of State Central Library: Its Relation with District Central Libraries and National Depository Libraries. *In Proceedings of the National Seminar on Public library Movement*, Chennai, 1991. Tamil Nadu, Directorate of Public Libraries, Chennai, 1991, pp. 108-21.
5. Baba, Abdul Majid, *Library Movement in Jammu and Kashmir: Problems and Prospects*. Souvenir of All India Library Conference, 39th, Bangalore, 1994. Indian Library Association; Delhi, pp. 144-49.
6. Balekar, R.S., Role of State Central, Divisional and District Libraries in the National Development. *In* Kumar (R P) and others, ed. *Role of Libraries in National Development*. Papers of the 42nd All India Library Conference held at Calicut during Dec. 21-24, 1996. Indian Library Association; Delhi, pp. 119-24.
7. Barua, B.P., *Directory of Public Libraries*, 1986. Naya Prakash; Calcutta, p. 520.
8. Barua, B.P. Rural Library Services in India. *In* George, K.M., *Ed. Indian Libraries: Trends and Perspectives*, 1985. Orient Longman; Hyderabad, pp. 163-78.
9. Barua, Dilip Kumar. Libraries in Aparanta. *Herald of Library Science*. April-July 1977, Vol. 16. No. 23. p. 191.

10. Baskar, P., Use of fiction (English) in the Connemara (State Central) Public Library and the British Council, Madras: A Comparative Analysis MLIS Dissertation. (unpublished). May 1993. Dept. of Library Science ; University of Madras, Chennai.
11. Batt, Chris., *Information Technology in Public Libraries*, 1998. Library Association Publishing; London, pp. 19-20.
12. Bhattacharya, G., West Bengal. *In* Ranganathan, S.R. etc., *ed. Free Book Service for All: An International Survey*, 1968. Mysore Library Association, Mysore, p. 172.
13. Bills, Linda G. and Helgerson, Linda W. CD-ROM Public Access Catalogues: Database Selection and Maintenance. *Lib Hitech;* Vol. 16; No. 1; 1988; pp. 67-88. *In* Panda, K.C. and Karisiddappa, C.R., *Eds. New Dimensions in Information Science and Technology*, 1993, Parimal Pub., Delhi, pp. 89-90.
14. Bowers, Fredsor, Functions of Bibliography. *Library Trends.* u. 7. 1959, p. 495.
15. Buragohain, Alaka, Library Situation in the State of Assam: A Status Report. *In* Saha, Ramakrishna, *ed. Library Movement in India*, 1989. Bengal Library Association; Calcutta. p. 39.
16. Campbell, H.C., *Developing Public Library Systems and Services*, UNESCO, Paris, p. 186.
17. Carnousky, L., Measurement of Public Library Book Collection, 1953. *Library Trends*, u. 2 (1); p. 463.
18. Choudhry, Prabhir Roy, Public Library Development in West Bengal: A Review. *In* Saha, Ramakrishna, *Ed. Library Movement in India*, 1989. Bengal Library Association, Calcutta, pp. 135-148.
19. Cuadra, Charles A., *Ed. American Society of Information Science*, 1973, Washington, p. 222.
20. Danton, J.P., Education for Librarianship, 1949. UNESCO; Paris, p. 6.
21. Dasgupta, Kalpana, National Library : Programmes, Problems and Prospects. *In* Jain, M.K., *Ed. 50 Years Library and Information Services in India*, 1998. Shipra Publication, Delhi, p. 166.
22. Deshmuk, P.P., Manpower Needs for Agricultural Information Management in India, *In* Prashar, R.G., *Ed. Personnel Problems in Indian Libraries*, 1994. Madallion Press, New Delhi, p. 219.

23. Dilli, K.T., *Basics of Library and Information Science,* 1997, Vikas Publishing House, New Delhi, p. 133.
24. Dutta, Ajit Kumar, Andaman and Nicobar Islands: Marching towards modernised Public Library Movement in India. *In* SAHA (Ramakrishna), *ed. Library Movement in India,* 1989. Bengal Library Association; Calcutta, pp. 29-30.
25. Ekbote, Gopalrao, *Public Libraries System,* 1987, Ekbote Brothers, Hyderabad, p. 138.
26. Esperanza, M.A.C. The State Central Library, Patna. *In* Gupta, B.M. *Ed. Handbook of Libraries, Archives and Information Centres in India.* Vol. 16: Library Development in India, 1996. Segment Books, New Delhi, pp. 236-49, 258-70.
27. Ghosh, Malabika, Need for the Conservation Activities in State Central Library. *In Proceedings of the National Seminar on Public Library Movement,* Chennai, 1991. Tamil Nadu, Directorate of Public Libraries, Chennai, 1991, pp. 361-364.
28. Giridhari Singh, N., Development of Libraries in Manipur. *In* Saha, Ramakrishna, *Ed. Library Movement in India,* 1989, Bengal Library Association, Calcutta, p. 95.
29. Govinda Krishnan, U.B. Reading Pattern : Connemara (State Central) Public Library and District Central Library, Madras. MLIS. Dissertation. (unpublished). May 1980, Dept. of Library Science, University of Madras, Madras.
30. Gupta, S.C. and Kapoor, V.K., *Fundamentals of Mathematical Statistics,* 1994, Sultan Chand, New Delhi. p. 1104
31. Harrod, L.M., *Librarian's Glossary and Reference Book,* 1987, Gower Publishing, London, p. 636.
32. Housman, Edward M., Selective Dissemination of Information. *Annual Review of Information Science and Technology,* u. 8. p. 126.
33. Ijari, S.R., Library Movement in Karnataka; *In* Gupta, B.M., *ed. Handbook of Libraries, Archieves and Information centres in India.* Vol. 16. Library Development in India, 1996, Segment Books, New Delhi, pp. 174-208.
34. Ijari, S.R. and Khan, H.A., State Central Reference Library, Karnataka. *In* Gupta, B.M., *Ed. Handbook of Libraries, Archieves and Information Centres in India.* Vol. 16. Library Development in India, 1996. Segment Books, New Delhi, pp. 293-301.
35. Inamdar, N.B. Guidelines for Selection and Acquisition of

Materials for State Central Libraries - A Case Study of Andhra Pradesh. *Granthana: Indian Journal of Library Studies.* 1, 1; January 1990; pp. 40-54.

36. Inamdar, N.B., Development of Public Libraries in Andhra Pradesh. *Granthana: Indian Journal of Library Studies.* July 1992, Vol. III. No. 2. pp. 115-128.

37. Inamdar, N.B. and Shakira, A.W., Management of Libraries in the State of Hyderabad: An Overview. *In* Gupta, B.M., *Ed. Handbook of Libraries, Archieves and Information Centres in India,* Vol. 16. Library Development in India, 1996, Segment Books, New Delhi, p. 89.

38. India. Committee of National Policy on Library and Information System. National Policy on Library and Information System—A Presentation. *Granthana: Indian Journal of Library Studies.* 11th January 1990; pp. 62-72.

39. India. Ministry of Education and Youth Services. Report of the Advisory Committee for Libraries, 1959. Ministry of Education, New Delhi, p. 32.

40. India. Research, Reference and Training Division. India 1998: A Reference Annual,1998. Publication Division, New Delhi, p. 586.

41. Jain, V.K. and Hazarika, S., Dictionary of Computer, 1994. Academic (India) Publications, New Delhi, p. 245.

42. Janakraj, State Central Library, Haryana. *In* GUPTA (B M), ed. *Handbook of Libraries, Archives and Information Centres in India,* Vol. 16: Library Development in India, 1996, Segment Books, New Delhi, pp. 286-95.

43. Kalia, D.R., *et. al.* Guidelines for Public Library Systems and Services. *Granthana Indian Journal of Library Studies.* Vol. 2; No. 1. Jan 1991, pp. 31-84.

44. Kalia, D.R., Libraries in Fourth Five Year Plan. Proceedings of the All India Library Conference of the Indian Library Association, 15th, Mysore, 1965. Delhi; Indian Library Association. 1966, pp. 13-37.

45. Kalia, D.R., Public Libraries. *In* Jain, M.K., *Ed. 50 years Library and Information Services in India,* 1998, Shipra Publication; Delhi. pp. 19, 27-36.

46. Kalia, D.R., Report of the Sub-Group on Public Library System of the Working Group on Libraries and Informatics. 1988. Planning Commission. New Delhi.

47. Kalia, D.R., Scenario of Public Libraries in the 21st Century in the global and Indian context. Paper presented at the National Seminar on *'Public Library Scenario in 21st Century'* conducted by Raja Rammohun Roy Library Foundation during 22-23, May, 1997 at Calcutta. (unpublished).
48. Karisidappa and Kumbar, Library Development in India. In Gupta, B.M., *Ed. Handbook of Libraries, Archives and Information Centres in India,* Vol. 16. Library Development in India, 1966, Segment Books, New Delhi, p. 203.
49. Kaul, H.K., From Printed Bibliographies to Online Databases: Role of Library Networks. *In* Jain, M.K. *Ed. 50 Years Library and Information Services in India, 1998,* Shipra Publication; Delhi, pp. 263-64.
50. Kaula, P.N., Libraries in India. *Herald of Library Science.* Vol. 16. No. 2-3, Apr-June 1977, p. 165.
51. Kemp, D.A., Current Awareness Services, 1979. Clive Bingley, London, p. 12.
52. Kent, Allen and Lancour, Harold, *Ed. Encyclopaedia of Library and Information Science,* Vol. 24, 1978, Marcel Dekker, New York, p. 267.
53. Khanna, J.K., *Library and Society,* 1989, Esses Publication, Delhi, p. 236.
54. Khanna, S.N., Delhi Public Library—Past, Present and Future. *In* Gupta, B.M, *Ed. Handbook of Libraries, Archives and Information Centres in India.* Vol. 16 : Library Development in India, 1996. Segment Books, Delhi, p. 236-49.
55. Kumar, P.S.G., Modernisation vis-a-vis Library and Information Science Education in India. *In* Vashisth, C.P. , *Ed. Modernisation in Libraries,* 1988, Indian Library Association, Delhi, p. 158.
56. Magnanand, Growth of Public Libraries in Uttar Pradesh. *In* Sen, N.B., *Ed. Development of Libraries in New India, 1965,* New Book Society of India, New Delhi, pp. 47-61.
57. Mangla, P.B. National Policies on Libraries, Information Systems and Services in India : An Overview. *In* Neelameghan, A. and Prasad, K.N. *ed. Information Systems, Networks and Trends,* 1998, Ranganathan Centre for Information Studies, Bangalore, p. 5.
58. Manorama Year Book, 1999. Malayala Manorama; Kottayam, p. 457.

59. Martin, Susns., *Library Networks,* 1981, Knowledge and Industry Publication, New York, p. 1.
60. Merrifield, Bruce., Innovate, Automate or Evaporate, *Span,* 1986, Oct. p. 39.
61. Mookerjee, Subodh Kumar, and Sengupta, Benoyendra. *Library Organisation and Administration,* 1977. The Worldpress, Calcutta, p. 408.
62. Moore, Nick., Measuring the Performance of Public Libraries: A Draft Manual *Granthana:Indian Journal on Library Studies,* Vol. 3; No. 2. July 1992, pp. 160-206.
63. Murrison, W.J., *The Public Library,* 1988, Bingley, London, p. 23.
64. Nagaraj, M.N., Milestones in the Path of Library Service of India. Paper Presented during the National Seminar on *'Scenario of Public Libraries in 21st Century'* held at on May 22-24, 1997; Calcutta, p. 1-33 (unpublished).
65. Ohdedar, A.K. State Central Library, West Bengal. *In* Gupta, B.M., *ed. Handbook of Libraries, Archives and Information Centres in India.* Vol. 16 : Library Development in India, 1996, Segment Books, New Delhi, pp. 331.
66. Padhi, P. and Panda, K.C. Harekrushna Mahtab, State Library, Orissa: An Appraisal. *CLIS Observer.* 5(3-4); July/ Dec. 1988, pp. 13-24.
67. Philip, Sergeant W. The Ruler of Vadodra: An Account of the Life and Work of the Maharaja Gaekwad, 1928, J. Murray; London, p. 126.
68. Prashar, R.G. *Information and Its Communication,* 1993, A Medallion Press, Delhi, p. 65.
69. Prytherch, Ray, *Comp.* Harrod's Librarian's Glossary. Hants Gower; London, p. 61, 595.
70. Raj, H., *Theory and Practice in Social Research,* 1990, Surjeet Publications, Delhi, p. 46.
71. Raja Rammohun Roy Library Foundation. *RRRLF Newsletter.* XVII (2) April 1997, p. 2.
72. Raman Nair, Public Library Systems in Ancient South India. *In* Gupta, B.M., *Ed. Handbook of Libraries, Archieves and Information Centres in India.* Vol. 16. Library Development in India, 1996, Segment Books, New Delhi, p. 131.
73. Ramesh Babu, B. and Parameswaran, R. Attitude of the Public Library Staff Towards Automation of Public Libraries

in Chennai. Kannan, R. and Ramasamy, R., *Ed. Proceedings of the National Seminar on Library Movement in India After Independence-Problems and Prospects* held on 5-6, April 1999. Department of Public Libraries; Government of Tamil Nadu, Chennai, p. 117.

74. Ramola, K.C. and Arora, S., Computerisation of Central State Library at Chandigarh. *In Proceedings of the All India Conference of the Indian Library Association,* 39th, Bangalore, 1994. Indian Library Association; New Delhi, 1994, pp. 420-25.
75. Ranganathan, S.R., *Andhra Pradesh Seminar on the Organisation and Administration of Public Libraries,* 1962. Department of Public Libraries, Andhra Pradesh, Hyderabad, pp. 40-43.
76. Ranganathan, S.R., *Library Development Plan; Thirty Years Programme for India With Drafts of Library Bill for Union and Constituent States,* 1960, University of Delhi, Delhi, p. 274.
77. Ranganathan, S.R., *Library Manual: For Library Authorities, Librarians and Library Workers,* 1988, Sarada Ranganathan Endowment for Library Science, Bangalore, p. 414.
78. Ranganathan, S.R., Model Public Libraries Act. *In* Ranganathan, S.R. and Neelameghan, A., *Ed. Public Library System,* 1972. Sarada Ranganathan Endowment for Library Science; Bangalore, p. 57.
79. Rath, P.K., Public Library Development in India : A Bibliography. *CLIS Observer.* 5 93 and 4); July/Dec. 1988, p. 25-30.
80. Rath, P.K., Role of State Central Library and its Relation with District Central Library under the Public Library System. *In Proceedings of the National Seminar on Public Library Movement,* Chennai, 1991. Tamil Nadu, Directorate of Public Libraries, Chennai, 1991, pp. 122-30.
81. Richardson, E.C., Classification: Theoretical and Practical, 1930, H.W. Wilson, New York, p. 42.
82. Rodriques, Pia De Menezes, Goa State Central Library : Past, Present and Future Plans. *In* Gupta, B.M., *ed. Handbook of Libraries, Archives and Information Centres in India.* Vol. 16: Library Development in India, 1996. Segment Books, New Delhi, pp. 271-85.
83. Saxena, R.S., Uttar Pradesh. *In* Ranganathan, *Ed. Free Book Service for All: An International Survey,* 1968. Asia

Publishing House, Bombay, pp. 163-171.
84. Sayers, Berwick, W.C., *Ed. J.D. Brown's Manual of Library Economy,* 1949, Grafton; London, p. 226.
85. Seethapathy, R.K. Connemara (State Central) Public Library : Its Response to Social Changes. MLIS. Dissertation. (unpublished). May 1978. Dept. of Library Science; University of Madras, Madras.
86. Shah, P.R., The Genesis of Public Library Movement in Baroda and Sir Sayaji Rao Gaekwad-The Genius. *Souvenir of the Platinum Jubilee of Central Library-Baroda and All India Library Conference,* 31st, Baroda, 1-4 November 1988. Government of Gujarat; Baroda, pp. 10-13
87. Sharma, C.D., *Use of Libraries : Guide to Better Use of Libraries and Their Resources,* 1983, Printwell, Jaipur, p. 163.
88. Sharma, C.K., Modern Library Systems, 1990. Y.K. Publishers, Agra, p. 74.
89. Sharma, Narendra, Library Developments in Rajasthan, *In* Gupta, B.M., *ed. Handbook of Libraries, Archives and Information Centres in India.* Vol. 16. Library Development in India, 1996, Segment Books, New Delhi, pp. 226-227.
90. Sharma, O.P., Literature of the history of Library movement in India. *Herald of Library Science.* Vol. 6; No. 1. January 1968, p. 9.
91. Sharma, Pandey S.K., *Public Libraries in India,* 1985. Ess Publication, New Delhi, p. 1561.
92. Siegel, Sidney and Castella, John N., *Non Parametric Statistics for the Behavioral Sciences,* 1998, McGraw Hill Book Company, New York, p. 87.
93. Shera, J.H. *Sociological Foundation of Librarianship,* 1970, Asia Publishing House, Bombay, p. 60.
94. Singh Sukhdev. History of Library Movement in Punjab. *In* Gupta, B.M., *Ed. Handbook of Libraries, Archives and Information Centres in India.* Vol. 16. Library Development in India, 1996. Segment Books, New Delhi, p. 205.
95. Sinha, K.P., *Report of Advisory Committee for Libraries,* 1959. Government of India, Ministry of Education; New Delhi, p. 115.
96. Singh, Sohan, *History of Adult Education During British Period,* 1957. Indian Adult Education Association; Delhi, p. 80.

97. Sounderrajan, K. Romain Rolland Library, Pondichery. *In* Gupta, B.M., *Ed., Handbook of Libraries, Archives and Information Centres in India.* Vol. 16: Library Development in India, 1996, Segment Books, New Delhi, pp. 302-6.

98. Rao, Surya, G. and Babu Rao, C. Library Movement in India: A Historical Perspective. *In* Vashisth, C., *Ed. Library Movement and Library Development in India,* 1994, Indian Library Association, Delhi, pp. 23-31.

99. Swank, R.C. Inter Library Co-operation, Inter-Library Communications and Information Networks : Explanation and Definition. *In Proceedings of the Conference on Interlibrary Communications and Information Networks,* 1971. American Library Association, Chicago, p. 204.

100. Mohamed, Taher, Functions of the State Libraries : A Case Study of A.P. State Central Library, Hyderabad. *In* Gupta, B.M., *Ed. Handbook of Libraries, Archives and Information Centres in India.* Vol. 16: Library Development in India, 1996. Segment Books, New Delhi, pp. 236-49.

101. M.F., Tauber, Technical Services in Libraries, 1953. Columbia University Press, New York, p. 150.

102. Teague, S. John, Microform, Video and Electronic Media Librarianship, 1985, Butterworth; London, p. 96.

103. Thomas, V.K., *Public Libraries in India: Development and Finance,* 1997, Vikas Publishing House, New Delhi, pp. 3, 22-66.

104. Tomar, Surendra Singh, Public Library System in Madhya Pradesh, *Library Herald.* April-Sep. 1992. Vol. 31. No. 1-2. pp. 45-51.

105. Trehan, G.L, *Modern Public Library: Movement and Services in India,* 1982, Library Literature House; Chandigarh, p. 6.

106. Unesco. Unesco Public Library Manifesto 1994. *IFLA Journal* 21(1), 1995, p. 67.

107. Unesco. Unesco Public Library Manifesto 1994. *UNISIST Newsletter.* 23(1), 1995; Paris, p. 10.

108. Venkatachallappa, M., Bihar. *In* Ranganathan, S.R. *et. al., Free Book Service for All: An International Survey,* 1968. Mysore Library Association, Mysore, p. 69.

109. Venkatappaiah, Velaga, Andhra Pradesh. *In* Ranganathan, S.R., *et al., Free Book Service for all: An International Survey,*

1968. Mysore Library Association, Mysore, p. 52.

110. Venkatappaiah, Velaga, Connemara (State Central) Public Library, Madras. *In* Gupta, B.M., *Ed. Handbook of Libraries, Archives and Information Centres in India.* Vol. 16: Library Development in India, 1996. Segment Books; New Delhi, p. 326.

111. Venkatappaiah, Velaga, Public Library Movement Before Independence in Andhra Pradesh. *In* Gupta, B.M., *Ed. Handbook of Libraries, Archives and Information Centres in India.* Vol. 16. Library Development in India, 1996, Segment Books, New Delhi, pp. 138-45.

112. Venkateswara Rao, L., Opening of School and College Libraries to Public. *In* Vashisth, C.P. *et.al., New Horizons in Library and Information Science,* 1974, T.R. Publications, Madras, p. 371.

113. Viswanathan, C.G., *Public Library Operations and Services : A Short Manual,* 1985. Print House (India), Lucknow. p. 59.

114. Wadikar, A.L., Library Service in Madhya Pradesh. *In* SAHA (Ramakrishna), *ed. Library Movement in India,* 1989. Bengal Library Association, Calcutta, p. 84.

115. Yenawine, Warfue S., *Introduction-Current Trends in Circulation Services,* 1957, University of Illinois Press, Illinois, p. 3. Services.

116. Young, P.V. and Schmid, C.F., *Scientific Social Surveys and Research,* 1994. Prentice Hall Publishing House, New Delhi, pp. 16, 103.

Index